There's been a **major correction** in the
an **ASPRIN** or a **poison pill**? Consult a
booth moll? Erect a **chinese wall**? Say **R**
and ride the **Elliott wave**?

What does all this *really* mean?

And what about these terms? —
● Aussie Mac ● bracket creep ● cash cow ● caps and collars
● DATES ● dirty float ● eurokiwi ● FANMAC
● FASTBAC ● Fibonacci numbers ● gensaki ● golden circle
● GRUF ● hurt money ● naked warrant ● triple witching
hour ● scrubber ● virgin bond ● wood duck ● zaiteku
● ZEBRAS

THE LANGUAGE OF MONEY II
presents more than 1600 entries which explain the words and
phrases most commonly used today in

● finance
● commerce
● money markets
● foreign exchange markets
● share trading
● economics
● accounting
● commercial law

These terms have been explained clearly and succinctly, in
language that is easily understood by all, and each entry has been
checked by a panel of experts.

THE LANGUAGE OF MONEY

EDNA CAREW

Sydney
ALLEN & UNWIN
Wellington London Boston

First published in 1985
Third impression 1987
This edition published 1988
Allen & Unwin Australia Pty Ltd
An Unwin Hyman company
8 Napier Street, North Sydney,
NSW 2060 Australia

Allen & Unwin New Zealand Limited
60 Cambridge Terrace, Wellington, New Zealand

Unwin Hyman Limited
15–17 Broadwick St, London WIV IFP, England

Allen & Unwin Inc.
8 Winchester Place, Winchester Mass 01890 USA

National Library of Australia
Cataloguing-in-Publication entry:
Carew, Edna, 1949–
The language of money (revised edition)
ISBN 0 04 3030084
1. Money—Dictionaries. I. Title.
332.4′03

Produced in Malaysia by
SRM Production Services Sdn Bhd

Preface

The glossary in *Fast Money* sowed the seeds of *The Language of Money*. The work that has emerged goes further than a dictionary, though it stops well short of an encyclopaedia. *The Language of Money* spans many areas—it is not a lexicon specifically of finance or economics, or accounting or foreign exchange. It is a collection of commonly used words and phrases from a variety of fields connected with money and is designed for those who read about and work with money.

In the pursuit of the true meaning of these terms I have tapped the knowledge of a range of experts, who have accumulated years of experience in finance and economics, money market and foreign exchange, banking and merchant banking, accounting, law and securities markets. Some are involved in industry, others in academia; they all made a generous contribution to the definitions included in this book.

I particularly thank Dr Tom Valentine for his careful examination of the text; his helpful comments and guidance were patiently given and gratefully received.

I would also like to note my appreciation of the special help given by Peter Jonson, Graeme Thompson and others in the research department of the Reserve Bank, who read the initial draft and responded with constructive comments which contributed much to the moulding of the finished product.

Jeff West and Bruce Donald also have my particular thanks for coping with the whole manuscript; so has David Clark (University of New South Wales) for his contribution to the economics content and particularly his colourful instruction on economic history.

Many others generously shared their knowledge and gave detailed help in specific areas: Victor Argy, Nat Brancatisano, Marc Bleasel, Jo Coffey, Peter Davidson, Tony Dreise, Michael Eyers, Stuart Grieve, Peter Groenewegen, A. W. Hooke, Louise Jackson, Peter Marshman, Elizabeth McCloy, Willa McDonald, Graham Partington, John Phillips, Peter Purtell, David Rutledge, John Snelson, Jill Tam.

And I thank these people for their willingness in responding helpfully and enthusiastically to requests for information. Percy Allan, Richard Allan, Rob Barry, Warren Bird, Bob Biven, Ray Block, John Brady, Kerry Bryan, Will Buttrose, Brian Cassidy, Andre Cohen, Michelene Collopy, Derek Condell, John Craig, Satyajit Das, Mary Donnelly, Dianne Everett, Masabumi Furuichi, Brian Gatfield, Peter Gilbert,

PREFACE

George Gleeson, Joan Glennie, John Godfrey, Lincoln Gould, Phil Gray, Eddie Grieve, Paul Harris, Bruce Hogan, John Hunt, Ian Huntley, Will Jephcott, Richard Lambert, Paul Lindholm, Joan Linklater, Rodney Maddock (for *A Child's Guide to Rational Expectations*, by Rodney Maddock and Michael Carter), Greg Maughan, Annette McCarthy, Malcolm McIntosh, John McMurtrie, Peter McWilliam, John Murray, Graham Newell, Sheila Norbury, Janet O'Connor, John O'Connor, Ian Parkin, Les Pegg, Maria Pethard, Paul Pinnock, Stuart Piper, Warwick Poulden, Max Powditch, Clive Powell, Anne Rankin, Graeme Richardson, Chris Roberts, Paul Robertson, Rob Roder, Rabbi David Rogut, Bruce Rolph, Trevor Rowe, Ray Schoer, Leigh Scott-Kemmis, Phil Sibree, Graeme Simpson, Ross Smyth-Kirk, Vernon Spencer, Rob Stewart, John Stroud, Richard Stubley, Peter Swan, Shuichi Takahashi, Chris Talbot, Gwennie Trimble, Peter Trout, Chris Trumbull, David Watson, Lindsay White, Raymond Yeow.

I thank Hoffers for his cheerful help and fortitude in the face of yet another project, and Venetia Nelson for her labours with the structure of this expanding work.

Edna Carew
Sydney 1987

How to use this book

The Language of Money is a dictionary dedicated to the idea of plain speaking. For an equally plain understanding, its structure has been kept as simple as possible. A few points, however, need to be explained.

ENTRIES are listed alphabetically. The only exception to this is a number of economists, who are grouped together under the headword **economists**. Each name also occurs in the general alphabetical sequence, for example you will find the entry '**Keynes, John Maynard** see **economists**'.

ABBREVIATIONS. Financial jargon uses a great many acronyms and abbreviations. Both the full and the abbreviated forms are listed in alphabetical sequence, but the definition will be found under the full form. For example, at the headword **AMBA** you will simply find '**AMBA** *abbrev.* **Australian Merchant Bankers Association**'. At the end of the entry **Australian Merchant Bankers Association** you will find '*Abbrev.*: **AMBA**'. All abbreviations and acronyms have been treated this way for the sake of consistency, even those which are usually referred to in their shortened form, such as **CEDEL**.

OTHER INFORMATION. At the end of the entries, as well as an abbreviation, you may also find variant forms and cross-references. The entry for non-bank financial institutions is an example of all three kinds of information:

> **non-bank financial institution** a term that has been around for years but which arrived in popular use recently, after the Campbell Report was released in 1981 . . . Also **non-bank financial intermediary**. *Abbrev.*: **NBFI**. See **Campbell Report**.

CROSS-REFERENCING is thorough. Financial terminology is a finely tuned language in which shades of meaning can be crucial to a full understanding. It may be helpful to read cross-referenced entries in conjunction; sometimes the further reference will provide additional information. Corresponding terms, such as **long term** and **short term**, are also cross-referenced to each other.

Another kind of cross-referencing picks out words or expressions used in definitions but not deserving their own definition. Thus, should you come across the expressions **jawboning** and **window guidance** you will find them under the alphabetical listing in the dictionary, but they will simply be cross-referenced to **moral suasion**, of which they are variant terms.

As well as this, the cross-referencing makes sure that words used in any definition, if not immediately apparent as ordinary English, appear in the dictionary. Thus the words **onsell** and **onlend** are given entries.

NOUN OR VERB? Several entries have a use both as noun and verb, or as other parts of speech. This book places less emphasis on grammatical distinctions than a conventional dictionary, but where a word has more than one use examples of different uses are given, for example **discount** and **rollover**.

AUSTRALIAN USAGE is given preference. Where UK or US usage lends a different meaning to a term, I have attempted to explain this.

COMMERCIAL USAGE is also given preference. The language of money has adopted many common words and ascribed particular meanings to them. For example, in this book **subscriber** means a person who agrees to buy securities; **security** has more to do with shares and bonds than with locks and alarms.

The Language of Money attempts to cover an area of terminology that is still alive and growing. Financial markets are changing rapidly and linguistic inventiveness of the type that gave us **bears**, **bulls** and **butterfly spreads** continues. Any gaps in this text are evidence of the pace of innovation.

Definitions are of course hazardous things, but one feels impelled at least to attempt one.

EDWARD I. SYKES
The Law of Securities

A

AAA the top credit rating accorded by ratings agencies such as the US's Moody's Investor Services and Standard & Poors, and Australia's Australian Ratings Pty Ltd. Securities issued by companies, banks and countries are rated from AAA downwards, for example AA+, then AA and so on. There is also *Triple A*, the regional banking and financial magazine.

ABA *abbrev.* **Australian Bankers' Association**.

abnormal items an accounting term to describe events that arise in the normal course of a company's business but which have been unusually large during the reporting period.

above par security such as a bond, debenture or share which is selling at a price higher than its face value is said to be above par. For example, if a bond has a face value of $100 and its market price is quoted at $103 then it is well above par. In the case of securities carrying coupons—such as Commonwealth bonds—these are above par if their market yield is below their coupon rate. See **coupon, face value, par, premium**.

above the line all items in the profit and loss statement that are included in determining the operating profit or loss after income tax, i.e., normal revenue and expenditure items. See **below the line**.

ABS *abbrev.* **Australian Bureau of Statistics**.

accelerator theory This explains business investment in terms of a mechanical, rather than a proportionate, adjustment to past changes in demand. When the economy is improving, business is supposed to overinvest, a process that ultimately causes the economy to hit the 'ceiling'. Then the process is reversed until the economy hits the 'floor'. The theory was fashionable in the 1960s but has since been discredited.

acceptance the acknowledgement of, and agreement to abide by, the terms of a contract.

acceptance fee a commission generally charged by a bank or merchant bank for the drawing of bills of exchange under a line of credit. It is an additional expense for the borrower.

accepting house one of a very select group of UK merchant banks. The name derives from the merchant banks' main function of 'accepting' bills of exchange, thereby facilitating the lending of money. Originally accepting houses bought these bills of exchange to finance trade; their activities have now extended into other areas of finance, such as taking deposits, making loans and arranging clients' investments. UK accepting houses with a solid pedigree are well-known names such as Baring Brothers, Hambros, Hill Samuel, Kleinwort Benson, Samuel Montagu, Morgan Grenfell, Rothschild, J. Henry Schroder Wagg and S. G. Warburg. These companies have merchant banking interests in Australia, where companies carrying out the role of accepting houses have come to be known as merchant banks. See **Australian Merchant Bankers Association, merchant banks**.

acceptor   the party to whom a bill of exchange is addressed and who accepts the primary liability to pay on due date the face value of a bill of exchange, drawn on them, to the holder of the bill. See **bill of exchange**.

accommodation bill (of exchange)   the type of bill of exchange now most commonly used in Australian financial markets. The accommodation bill grew out of the trade-related bills of exchange, which had been widely used since the last century in financing world trade. At present, accommodation bills are a means of providing finance (lending) without necessarily having an underlying trade transaction, whereas trade bills are based on specific transactions. Accommodation parties are defined under the *Bills of Exchange Act* 1909–1973 thus: 'An accommodation party to a bill is a person who has signed a bill as drawer/acceptor/endorser, without receiving value therefor, and for the purpose of lending his name to some other person.' The idea behind the accommodation bill is to lend the weight of the stronger party's name (through accepting/drawing/endorsing the bills) to another party whose name is less marketable. See **bill of exchange, trade bill**.

accountancy   the profession that specialises in the organised classification, recording and analysing of all transactions and events in terms of money affecting a business or individual. Its practitioners are called accountants. See **accounting**.

accounting   As distinct from the profession of accountancy, accounting is the application of the process of analysing and recording, in money terms, the financial transactions of a business or individual. Accounting also includes the presentation and interpretation of the results of those transactions, which will assess performance over a given period, as well as the projection in monetary terms of future activities. Accounting also provides the economic information necessary for decision-making.

accounting period   Companies prepare reports of their financial transactions over specific periods of time, referred to as accounting periods. These are usually for one year, though interim reports are often drawn up for use by internal management at monthly or quarterly intervals.

accounting standards descriptions of acceptable standards of accounting practice. They are issued by the Australian Accounting Research Foundation, an organisation sponsored by the Australian Society of Accountants and the Institute of Chartered Accountants in Australia. See **Accounting Standards Review Board, Australian Accounting Research Foundation, Australian Society of Accountants, Institute of Chartered Accountants in Australia.**

Accounting Standards Review Board an organisation formed in 1984, which has the role of approving all accounting standards before they become law.

accounts payable the amounts of money owed by a business or individual to creditors, usually for goods bought or services rendered.

accounts receivable money owed by a debtor (outside party) to a business or individual, usually for goods sold or services rendered.

across the board in general or as a whole. The phrase, in general business usage, means 'most'. 'Interest rates rose across the board' indicates a broad range of rises on most maturities and instruments.

accrual basis of accounting the method of adjusting accounts to allow for accrued expenses and accrued revenue. There are two systems:

- **partial accrual**, where accounts are based on cash and credit trans-actions;
- **full accrual**, where end-of-period adjustments are made for accrued expenses and accrued revenue.

accrued expenses expenses incurred but not yet paid.

accrued interest interest accounted for but not yet due for payment; a receivable not yet due. See **receivables**.

accrued revenue income earned but not yet received.

accumulated profits see **unappropriated profits**.

acid test see **current ratio, liquid ratio**.

ACTU *abbrev.* **Australian Council of Trade Unions.**

ACU *abbrev.* **Asian currency unit.**

ADB *abbrev.* **Asian Development Bank.**

ADF *abbrev.* **approved deposit fund.**

ad valorem Latin for 'according to value'. This phrase is used when describing stamp duty or tax which is levied as a percentage of the value of the item that is dutiable or taxable and not at a flat rate. See **excise, purchase tax, sales tax**.

adjustable rate mortgage   see **variable rate mortgage**. *Abbrev.*: **ARM**.

ADR   *abbrev.* **American depository receipt.**

advance   any extension of credit. Bankers talk of advances when the rest of us mean loans. An advance from a banker in this context could be in the form of a drawing under an overdraft facility, a fully drawn advance or term loan, a line of credit with a bill option, a bill facility or a personal loan.

AFC   *abbrev.* **Australian Finance Conference.**

AFCUL   *abbrev.* **Australian Federation of Credit Unions Ltd.**

affidavit   a voluntary statement of facts sworn (or affirmed) before a witness of a category described under the Oaths Act, of example a solicitor. The affidavit, which gives details of the person swearing it (the deponent), may be admitted as evidence in a court of law, unlike a statutory declaration, which is not sworn.

agenda   a list of activities or items for discussion at a meeting.

aggregate demand   the total demand for goods and services produced in a country. Usually this is identified with gross domestic product minus imports, plus exports. Expenditure on imports is included in consumption and investment. See **gross domestic product**.

aggregate supply   what is produced in a country for domestic consumption, plus its imports.

AIDB   *abbrev.* **Association of International Bond Dealers.**

AIDC   *abbrev.* **Australian Industry Development Corporation.**

air-pocket stock (share)   A US term used to describe a share that has fallen abruptly, usually following the release of bad news about the company or the industry in which it is involved. The share price plummets — as does a plane in an air-pocket.

algorithm   At its simplest an algorithm is a formula, or a recipe; it is the formal sequence of the necessary steps to be gone through to execute a task. An ancient form of the word is 'algorism', which means the process of doing arithmetic using Arabic numerals. An eighteenth-century German mathematical dictionary defines 'algorithmus' as follows: 'Under this designation are combined the notions of the four types of arithmetic calculations, namely addition, multiplication, subtraction and division.' A process must have certain characteristics before it can be said to be an algorithm, for example each step of the algorithm must be precisely defined, it must be possible to carry out the prescribed action, the algorithm must end (it cannot go on indefinitely), and it always produces the correct answer to the task set. Financial markets have borrowed the term *algorithm* from the jargon of computer science.

alligator spread   a US commodity traders' expression for the situation where the commission is so large that it 'eats' the client (chews up the client's cash).

allonge   the additional strip of paper attached to a bill of exchange to provide extra space for endorsement signatures when the back of the bill is already filled. See **chain of title**.

all ordinaries index   A stock exchange measure, this is an index of the market prices of more than 250 Australian companies listed on the Sydney and Melbourne stock exchanges. The market value of these companies totals almost 90 per cent of the value of all listed shares. The all ordinaries index is calculated continuously each day and is published daily. See **Dow Jones index**, **Financial Times index**, **Nikkei Dow Jones index**.

all ordinaries share price riskless indexed notes   these notes securitise the price movement in Australian domestic share prices, as represented by the all ordinaries index, over the term of the notes. Designed by Bankers Trust Australia. *Abbrev.*: **ASPRIN**.

AGM   *abbrev.* **annual general meeting**.

AMBA   *abbrev.* **Australian Merchant Bankers Association**.

American depository receipt   a piece of paper representing shares owned by a US citizen, in an overseas company. The receipt is held by a US bank. The shareowner is entitled to dividends paid by the foreign company which issued the shares. The receipts are tradeable and are a convenient way for non-US companies to issue equity in the US. *Abbrev.*: **ADR**.

American option   an option that is tradeable and can be exercised at any time up to the date it is due to expire. The options traded on the Sydney Futures Exchange are an example of an American option. See **European option**.

American Stock Exchange   Located in Manhattan, New York, this exchange ranks in the top half-dozen US exchanges in terms of trading volume. It is estimated to have begun in business in the 1849 gold rush, and was known as the Curb Exchange until 1921, because trading took place outdoors (at the curb). The American Stock Exchange trades small and medium-sized companies' shares, whereas the New York Stock Exchange carries the big name, mature companies. *Abbrev.*: **AMEX**.

AMEX *abbrev.* **American Stock Exchange**.

amortisation an accounting term used to describe the writing down of the book value of an asset over time or the systematic repayment of a debt. Amortisation of a debt is the gradual reduction in value of the debt through the payment of regular instalments until the total amount has been discharged, as in a mortgage. A loan which is not amortised would involve the borrower paying only interest during the life of the loan and then repaying the principal in full. Accountants use the term 'amortisation' to describe a phenomenon the rest of us would call 'depreciation'. Amortisation is synonymous with depreciation but is usually applied to intangible assets such as patents or capitalised oil exploration expenses. See **depreciation**.

Annie Mae a mortgage-backed pass-through security issued by the AusNat Mortgage Pool Agency Ltd. The certificates are directly backed by pools of commercial and residential first mortgage loans, which have been advanced by lenders such as banks, building societies, mortgage bankers and other financial institutions. The securities are issued at par for maturities up to five years. See **AusNat Mortgage Pool Agency Ltd, pass-through security**.

annual general meeting meetings in which the directors and shareholders of a company get together once a year. The AGM is open to all shareholders but usually only a small proportion of them attend. AGMs can be exciting if a shareholder with a gripe or controversial query arrives to air his or her views. Otherwise—and for the most part— AGMs are fairly routine affairs at which the company chairman announces the results for the year, finds reassuring reasons why they might not be as satisfactory as the board would like or are more satisfactory than they appear to be, and makes guarded forecasts about the coming year. Journalists, stockbrokers and other professional outsiders are often the most interested parties at an AGM. *abbrev.*: **AGM**.

annuity a form of life assurance which operates in the opposite way to the traditional pattern and which is normally used to provide retirement income. The person who takes out an annuity (the annuitant) pays the life office a lump sum and in return receives a series of payments. Effectively, each time the life office makes a payment, the annuitant is getting back a portion of the money originally outlaid, plus interest. The amount received back from the life office would depend on the interest rate, the mortality rate (life offices calculate how long a policyholder might reasonably be expected to live) and the pattern of payments. The basic form is a **life annuity** by which payments continue until the death of the annuitant; a lucky person would live to get his or her money's worth, or more, from the annuity; an unlucky one might depart this life having received only one month's payment.

A more advisable form of annuity is the life annuity with guaranteed period or term-certain annuity. These provide for payments to go to the annuitant's beneficiaries should he or she die before the stipulated period is up. The **life annuity with guaranteed period** provides for payments to continue until the death of the policyholder, even if he or she lives beyond the period of the guarantee. With a **term-certain annuity**, the payments cease at the end of the agreed term, so that the policyholder could survive the term of the annuity and have no more payments due. Annuities can be arranged on a joint basis, so that if one life expires the payments continue for the other, either in full or at a reduced rate. Annuities can be inflation-linked and can be taken out on a deferred basis, for example the first payment delayed till age 65. See **indexed bonds**.

anomaly   in ordinary use a deviation, a departure from the accepted norm. Traders talk of anomalies in the yield curve when they mean imperfections in the curve—a departure from the conventional shape. Money can be made by astute traders who spot anomalies in the yield curve and take advantage of them. Anomalies can also emerge between markets, between securities, such as bills and bonds, and between time zones. See **arbitrage**, **window open**, **yield curve**.

applied economics   This uses economic theory to analyse real-world problems and often highlights the gap between theory and practice.

appreciation   the increase in the value of an asset or the increase in the value of a currency against other currencies.

approved deposit fund   a type of fund launched in the second half of 1984 in response to changes to taxation treatment of lump-sum superannuation payments. These changes applied from 30 June 1983 and raised the tax levied on benefits paid to employees on retirement or resignation. The federal government was conscious of the abrupt change and was keen to encourage the build-up of funds for retirement, and so ruled that payments placed in approved deposit funds would be accorded favourable taxation treatment. The approved deposit funds have been established by several banks, merchant banks and life offices. *Abbrev.*: **ADF**.

arbitrage   to take advantage of different rates, prices or conditions between different markets or maturities. Arbitragers—sometimes called 'arbitrageurs'—make the most of inconsistencies between prices in different markets, for example if a good sells for a lower price in one market than in another, an arbitrager would buy it at the lower price and sell it at the higher. There is little risk involved.

ARDB   *abbrev.* **Australian Resources Development Bank**.

ARM   *abbrev.* **adjustable rate mortgage**.

arrears   money owed but not yet paid.

Article 65 (of Japan's Securities Exchange Law)   Enacted after World War II, this is Japan's version of the US Glass Steagall Act, which bans Japanese commercial banks from underwriting, dealing, broking and distributing securities other than government, local government and government-guaranteed bonds and debentures.

articles of association   the document which sets out the rules by which a company operates. The articles deal with a company's internal rules, whereas the memorandum of association spells out external activities. The articles are subject to the memorandum. See **memorandum of association.**

ASB   *abbrev.* **Australian Savings Bond (Aussie Bond).**

Asian currency unit   The department of a Singapore bank which is licensed by the Monetary Authority of Singapore to deal in external currencies but restricted in what it can do in the Singapore domestic currency market. *Abbrev.*: **ACU.** See Monetary Authority of Singapore.

Asian Development Bank   Founded in 1966 as a regional version of the World Bank, the Asian Development Bank is headquartered in Manila (Philippines) and provides economic and technical assistance to the developing member countries (DMCs) in the Asian Region. *Abbrev.*: **ADB.**

Asian dollar market   See **eurocurrency.**

ASPRETTE   a short-dated, capital-guaranteed all ordinaries share price index linked certificate of deposit; it is the short-term (less than one year) version of ASPRIN. See **ASPRIN.**

ASPRIN   *abbrev.* **all ordinaries share price riskless indexed notes.**

asset backing   what's behind your shares. To find out their net asset backing divide the estimated value of the company (use total assets less liabilities) by the number of shares on issue. Get the figures from the company's latest annual report. A company can have a poor earnings-per-share rate but still have solid asset backing. See **earnings per share.**

assets   put simply, what you as an individual or company own. Assets can be in the form of money, such as cash at the bank or bills owed to you, or can be fixed, such as property, or they can be intangible (your good reputation). Assets are generally classified as current or fixed, and tangible or intangible. Net assets are what is left after liabilities have been deducted from total assets. For accounting purposes, assets are things with future economic benefits, for example providing future cost savings or generating future revenue.

asset stripping   the profitable process of buying a company listed on the stock exchange (or an unlisted company) and selling off most of its assets. The profit comes from buying the company cheaply because for some reason its market price is below the value of its assets.

associate company   a company of which between 20 and 50 per cent is owned by another.

Association Cambiste Internationale   an international society of foreign exchange dealers with its headquarters in Paris.

Association of International Bond Dealers   a professional association, established in 1969, with more than 350 member institutions; its headquarters are in Zurich, Switzerland. It recommends rules and regulations for dealing, collates and publishes quotes and yields for the eurobond market. *Abbrev.*: **AIDB**. See **eurobonds, euromarkets**.

assurance   the term commonly used in connection with life policies, which do not depend on a possibility, as does insurance, but on a certainty—either death or reaching a certain age. Since the *Life Insurance Act* 1945 and the recent preference for the word 'insurance', the two have become interchangeable in the context of life policies. See **insurance**.

ASX   *abbrev.* **Australian Stock Exchange Ltd.**

at best order   A futures trader may execute an at best order at a price that he or she believes to be the best price that can be achieved during the day's trading. It is a type of order with discretion, giving the trader ultimate discretion. See **order with discretion**.

at call   Funds placed 'at call' can be withdrawn on demand or without notice. In the short-term money market, funds can be placed at 11am call or 24-hour notice of call, as against being fixed for a specified period of time. See **11am call money, 24-hour call money**.

ATM   *abbrev.* **automatic teller machine.**

at market   see **market order**

at par   see **par value.**

ATS   *abbrev.* **Automated Trading System.**

at the money   a term used in option trading to describe an exercise (or strike) price that is at or about current market levels. See **in the money, out of the money**.

audit   a periodic, independent examination or verification of the assets and liabilities and financial transactions of a company to determine the reliability of its accounting records. An audit entails a systematic examination of the activities and status of a business based principally on investigation and analysis of its systems, controls and records. An audit is carried out by an auditor (a type of accountant) who is professionally qualified to judge the accuracy of a company's accounts and form an independent opinion. The audit aims to ensure the honesty, integrity, consistency, accuracy and reliability of the management of a company on the shareholders' behalf, although it cannot guarantee the competence of the management.

AusNat Mortgage Pool Agency Ltd   a corporate issuer of mortgage-backed securities known as Annie Maes. The agency is a wholly owned subsidiary of the merchant bank Security Pacific Australia Ltd and provides facilities for lending institutions which originate mortgage loans to securitise these loans and trade the resulting instruments in the market. See **Annie Mae.**

Aussie Mac   a mortgage-backed certificate issued by the National Mortgage Market Corporation, partly owned by the Victorian Government. Aussie Macs were first issued in April 1985. They are similar to a promissory note and are sold at a discount from face value. See **National Mortgage Market Corporation.**

Austraclear   Australia's answer to CEDEL and Euroclear; a computerised cash and securities settlement system for the money market. See **CEDEL, Euroclear.**

Australian Accounting Research Foundation   an organisation established in 1966, jointly sponsored and funded by the Australian Society of Accountants and the Institute of Chartered Accountants in Australia, which issues auditing and accounting standards. See **accounting standards, Accounting Standards Review Board,**

Australian Associated Stock Exchanges   the six major stock exchanges of Australia which joined in 1937 to coordinate operations (although each exchange remains autonomous), protect the interests of the investing public and to consider uniform regulations.

Australian Association of Permanent Building Societies   an industry association established at national level to promote Australia-wide development of permanent building societies. The association was formed in 1964 and is based in Canberra.

Australian Bankers' Association   industry mouthpiece for the banks, it also undertakes extensive research on banking matters. *Abbrev.:* **ABA.**

Australian Bureau of Statistics   the government's numbers machine. It can provide information about demography, debts, defence, details about finance and forestry, the manufacturing and minerals industry and answer any of your queries about what adds up to Australia. *Abbrev.:* **ABS.**

Australian Conciliation and Arbitration Commission Established under the *Conciliation and Arbitration Act* 1904, the commission stands at the centre of the various arbitration systems in Australia. Its constitutional function is to prevent and settle interstate industrial disputes. In the course of its evolution the commission's activities have developed into three practical directions:

- the establishment and maintenance of codes governing wages and conditions in various industries and areas of employment;
- the setting of national wage levels and standard industrial conditions;
- the settlement of disputes on individual industrial issues.

Among the many amendments to the Act, perhaps the most significant was that made in 1956 following the Boilermakers' Case, when the High Court ruled that the arbitral and judicial functions should not be vested in the same tribunal, which was then the Commonwealth Court of Conciliation and Arbitration, as it had existed since 1907. The 1956 amendment set the present structure of tribunals in which the Industrial Court (now the Federal Court in its Industrial Division) exercises the judicial powers and the Australian Conciliation and Arbitration Commission has arbitral and dispute settlement powers. The commission settles disputes and makes continuing orders and awards arising from these disputes. The court interprets and enforces those orders and awards. The court also has extensive powers concerning the registration of organisations of employees and employers, the enforcement of their rules, and inquiries into elections of officers etc.

A third arm of the system is the administrative and registration division. This consists of the Industrial Registrar, his deputies and registry staff in all States, who register organisations of employees and employers, control many of their operations and carry out the day-to-day administrative tasks necessary for the proper functioning of the commission. The Australian Conciliation and Arbitration Commission consists of presidential members and commissioners, divided by the president into panels, each of which deals with groups of industries. The president must have legal qualifications. Deputy presidents may have legal qualifications or equivalent qualifications in economics or subjects related to industrial relations, or extensive experience at a high level in industry, commerce, industrial relations or government service. Commissioners need no specific qualifications, but those appointed usually have extensive practical experience in industrial relations. The single member is concerned with the day-to-day processes of making awards or settling industrial disputes.

Australian Council of Trade Unions Formed in 1927 with headquarters in Melbourne, the ACTU is the central trade union body organising union activity in Australia. State counterparts are the Labor

Councils which operate as the ACTU's State branches. The ACTU Congress, which meets every two years, is the policy-making body and its decisions are binding on affiliated trade unions. The Trades and Labor Councils deal with unions at State level. Unions cannot affiliate with the ACTU unless they are affiliated with a State body. *Abbrev.*: **ACTU.**

Australian Federation of Credit Unions Ltd This organisation was formed in 1966 as a trade association to represent the interests of the credit union industry to government and to carry out research. Its head office is at 500 George Street, Sydney. *Abbrev.*: **AFCUL.**

Australian Finance Conference the industry body of finance companies, formed in 1958 as a national association of non-retailer finance companies. It is concerned with the maintenance of ethical standards of borrowing and lending; it represents the finance company industry in discussions with the government and other authorities on matters relevant to the industry and its users. Its address is 388 George Street, Sydney. *Abbrev.*: **AFC.**

Australian Industry Development Corporation This was established in 1971 and is owned by the Commonwealth. It borrows mainly overseas and lends in Australia to provide development funds for Australian industry, especially mining and manufacturing. *Abbrev.*: **AIDC.**

Australian Merchant Bankers Association This was formed in 1979 by an amalgamation of the Accepting Houses Association and the Issuing Houses of Australia. It is the industry mouthpiece of the merchant banks. *Abbrev.*: **AMBA.**

Australian Ratings Pty Ltd Australia's corporate credit rating agency, established in 1981 and based in Melbourne.

Australian Resources Development Bank This organisation began operations in 1968 and like the AIDC was founded to help Australian entities raise funds to enable them to participate in projects with offshore enterprises and therefore raise the level of Australian ownership in the development of Australian resources. *Abbrev.*: **ARDB.**

Australian Savings Bond (Aussie Bond) These were introduced in January 1976 to replace the Special Bonds. The minimum investment is $100 and the maximum, at the time of writing, is $200 000 per application. Aussie Bonds are available from banks, including the Reserve Bank, stockbrokers and post offices and are cashable on 30 days' notice after an initial holding period. The Aussie Bond rate is set by the federal government and not by the market, as is the case with Commonwealth (Treasury) bonds. *Abbrev.*: **ASB.**

Australian Society of Accountants Established in 1952, the society is the largest professional accounting association in Australia. Membership totals almost 52 000. The society holds courses and seminars as part of its educative role for the profession. Together with the Institute of Chartered Accountants in Australia, the society sponsors and funds the Australian Accounting Research Foundation, which issues the accounting standards. See **accounting standards, Accounting Standards Review Board, Australian Accounting Research Foundation, Institute of Chartered Accountants in Australia.**

Australian Stock Exchange Limited   the national organisation that came into being on 1 April 1987, replacing Australia's previous State-based exchanges. The birth of the Australian Stock Exchange is regarded as the first stage in the development of electronically traded share markets. *Abbrev.*: **ASX.**

authorised capital   the amount of equity capital, measured at par value, that a company is allowed to raise by issuing shares as set out in its memorandum of association. By issuing shares at a premium, a company can raise an amount of cash that is considerably more than its authorised capital. A company's authorised capital might be $10 million and its paid-up capital $5 million. A company may increase its authorised capital at a general meeting (of shareholders) provided it is so authorised by its articles of association. See **issued capital, paid-up capital.**

authorised dealer (in the short-term money market)   one of the nine (at the time of writing) authorised dealers which constitute the 'official' short-term money market in Australia. The authorised dealers have a special relationship with the Reserve Bank which includes a lender-of-last-resort facility as a backstop for that market. They began life in their present form in 1959 and were established primarily to stimulate trading in government securities and to provide safe investment opportunities for ultra-short-term cash surpluses. The nine authorised dealer companies in early 1985 are: All States Discount; AMP Discount Corporation; AUC Discount; Capel Court Securities; Colonial Mutual Discount Company; First Federation Discount Company; National Discount Company; Trans City Discount; Short Term Acceptances.

Automated Trading System   a computerised trading system that links all major centres in a country. *Abbrev.*: **ATS.**

automatic teller machine   These have blossomed in recent years with the march of electronic banking. Instead of entering a bank, building society or credit union and talking with a human teller, the customer communicates with his or her account by feeding a plastic card into the mouth of an automatic teller machine located outside. Using different codings, the card activates a computer response so that the machine not only accepts deposits and delivers cash withdrawals but also can transfer funds between accounts and provide account balances. *Abbrev*.: **ATM**.

award rate   the minimum wage rate established by bodies such as the Conciliation and Arbitration Commission and generally expressed as an amount paid per hour.

B

B/A   see **banker's acceptance**.

back bond   the security created when a debt warrant is converted. Also **virgin bond**.

backdoor listing   the process by which listing of an enterprise is achieved through the acquisition of an already listed company structure and the injection into that structure of new activities. Often companies using this method do meet listing requirements but find acquisition and listing through the 'back door' quicker and cheaper.

back-to-back   a term referring to offsetting loans, often made in one currency in one country against a loan in another currency in another country. Essentially any back-to-back deal involves two parties matching assets and liabilities in opposite directions. In the futures market, back-to-back describes an equal number of bought and sold contracts held by one trader in one month. See **parallel loans**.

back-to-back credit   a credit opened by a bank on the strength of another credit. The term derives from the custom of British finance houses acting as middlemen between foreign buyers and foreign sellers.

backwardation   This describes a futures market situation where prices are higher in the nearer delivery months than in the distant months. For example, if at the time of writing (November 1984) the share price index futures for a delivery in March stood at 745.00 and for a June delivery at 740.00 then the backwardation for three months to March would be five points. The opposite of backwardation is contango. Also **inverted market**. See **contango**.

bad debt   a debt whose recovery is so unlikely that the amount owed is written off as a loss. Companies make provision in their balance sheets for bad and doubtful debts. Companies whose sole business is lending money are particularly vulnerable to bad debts. The only certain way to avoid bad debts is never to lend money, give credit or sell any goods and services.

BAD tax   see **bank accounts debit tax**.

balance date   the date at the end of an accounting period, by which all ledger accounts must be in balance. Most Australian companies balance at 30 June.

balance of payments   This is the record of a country's financial transactions with the rest of the world, often used as one measure of a country's economic health, though not necesarily an accurate barometer. (In some cases, for example Australia, it is necessary to import capital so the country has to run a deficit on the capital account.) The balance of payments is made up of two accounts, the current and capital accounts. The current account includes trade transactions, imports and exports of goods (visibles) and invisibles such as tourism and dividend and interest payments. The capital account is made up of borrowings and loans by government and corporations, investment and short-term capital flows. See **exchange rate**.

balance sheet   a detailed statement, based on the balance sheet equation, summarising the assets and liabilities of a business, giving a picture of its wealth at the time. Balance sheets tend to be several months out of date (three months on average) when they are published and so cannot be used as a reliable guide to the company's future performance; rather they are a snapshot of the company's position at a specific date.

balance sheet equation   Assets equal liabilities plus owners' equity. It is the equation on which all accounting reports are based. Rearranging the equation, the difference between assets and liabilities represents the owners' claims on the business. Owners' equity equals assets minus liabilities. The change in owners' equity from period to period (after adjustment for capital transactions and dividends) represents the owners' income or profit from the business.

balloon payment   The term generally refers to one big final payment at the end of a loan arrangement which wipes out the borrower's debt.

bank   from the Italian *banca* meaning 'bench', the table at which a dealer in money worked. A bank is now a financial institution which offers cheque accounts, makes loans and provides other financial services to customers, making its profits mainly from the difference between interest paid on deposits and charged for loans plus fees for accepting bills and other services. In Australia, banks are financial institutions authorised under the *Banking Act* or under State legislation. Other relevant legislation for banks is the *Banks (Shareholdings) Act* and the *Reserve Bank Act*. The *Reserve Bank Act* gives the Reserve Bank of Australia (the central bank) a wide range of powers over the banking sector.

bank-accepted bill of exchange   a bill of exchange on which a bank's name appears as the acceptor—i.e. the bank has the primary liability to pay the amount of money due on the bill's maturity date to the holder of the bill. See **bank bill of exchange, bill of exchange**.

16

bank accounts debit tax   a federally levied tax on debits (withdrawals) from bank accounts where a cheque is used. It was introduced in April 1983. *Abbrev.*: **BAD tax**.

bank bill of exchange   a bill of exchange on which the name of a bank appears, either as acceptor or endorser. Where the bank is the acceptor, the bill ranks as a bank-accepted bill; where the bank has endorsed the bill on the back, either through buying the bill in the market or for a fee to raise the bill's status, it ranks as a bank-endorsed bill of exchange. See **bill of exchange**.

bankcard   the Australian trading banks' joint credit card, introduced in 1974 for domestic use. At the time of writing (November 1984) it is the dominant plastic card in use in Australia, but it faces increased competition with the introduction of major international cards. See **credit card**.

bank cheque   a cheque on which the drawer is a bank drawing on itself; no individual or company name appears. In the short-term money market the term bank cheque refers to funds which the banks lend to the unofficial market; these are 'uncleared' funds as against the funds in the banks' exchange settlement accounts with the Reserve Bank of Australia which are 'cleared' funds and can be deposited with the official short-term money market. See **clearing**, **exchange settlement accounts**.

banker's acceptance   the US version of a bank-accepted bill of exchange, commonly referred to as B/A. It is a negotiable money market instrument, based on an underlying trade transaction. A B/A is created by a bank's customer drawing a bill of exchange on the bank, which the bank accepts (i.e. agrees to pay the holder the face value on maturity). Two names, the customer's and the bank's, appear on the bill. The bank charges a fee for its acceptance of the paper and the B/A is discounted at the prevailing market rate.

Bank for International Settlements   a body organised as a commercial bank, with publicly held shares and 80 per cent held by central banks; shareholders have no say in the running of the bank. The bank is immune from government interference and taxes, under an international treaty. It was established in 1930, originally to facilitate the payments to countries still owed World War I reparations by Germany. Since then it has evolved into a central bank for many of the world's central banks. Countries regularly represented at the BIS meetings are those belonging to the IMF's Group of Ten. Other countries represented from time to time include the remaining members of the European Economic Community, some Eastern European countries and other countries such as Saudi Arabia, as required. The BIS takes deposits and makes loans and plays a role in international finance, especially when speculative transactions are involved. Directors of the BIS hold a monthly meeting

BANK LINE

at the bank's head office in Basle, Switzerland. Its board includes representatives of the central banks of the UK, France, West Germany, Belgium, Italy, Switzerland, the Netherlands and Sweden. *Abbrev.*: **BIS**. See **Group of Ten, International Monetary Fund**.

bank line   a flexible line of credit, granted to a customer by a bank, allowing the customer to borrow up to a specified amount during a specified period. See **line of credit**.

Bank of England   the UK central bank, founded in 1694 and known affectionately as the Old Lady of Threadneedle Street, because of its location in that street in London.

bank paper   see **paper**.

bankruptcy   a term applied to individuals only: a person goes bankrupt; companies are wound up. A debtor may be declared bankrupt by the Federal Court (either at his or her instigation or that of creditors), which will place his or her estate in the hands of the official receiver, who will distribute the estate according to the provisions of the Bankruptcy Act. An individual can have assets and still be made bankrupt if the assets cannot rapidly be converted into cash to meet debts as they fall due.
   The word 'bankrupt' comes from the Italian *banca rotta* meaning 'broken bench'. See **bank**.

bargain basement   Money market transactions thus described are deals that take place above or below the market level (depending on whether it is the standpoint of a lender or borrower). They are attractive deals.

barter   the age-old custom of exchanging goods or services of equivalent value, instead of using money (which involves a sale). Barter has come to be used in modern trade finance; it is particularly useful for a country whose so-called 'soft' currency leaves it unattractive as a trading partner, or for a country which has limited access to 'hard' currencies such as the $US or sterling. See **countertrade**.

base metal   a commercial metal, such as lead, zinc or copper. The term was coined to distinguish these metals from the superior precious metals of gold and silver.

base rate   Financial institutions often publish their base rate, which is a guide for their lending rates. Loans are generally written at a margin above the published base rate, with the margin varying according to the borrower's credit ranking.

basis   This can have various meanings in futures trading but the most common interpretation is that basis is the difference between the cash market price and the futures market price. Hence **basis trading** involves taking a view on the price differences between the cash market and the futures market.

basis point   one-hundredth of 1 per cent: 100 basis points = 1 per cent; 10 basis points = 0.1 per cent; a bill yield that moves from 10.20 per cent to 10.30 per cent has risen by 10 basis points.

basis swap   a swap that is carried out between two floating rates set against two different reference rates. The interest payments exchanged are calculated from two different floating rate indices, usually in $US, such indices being the commercial paper or US prime rate, LIBOR, certificate of deposit rate or US Treasury bill.

basket   in economic jargon, a mixture. A basket of currencies is a mixture of different currencies, combined to produce a single unit of value which can be used as an index. A basket of commodities goes into the calculation of the consumer price index which is used to measure Australia's inflation rate. See **ECU**, **CPI**, **trade-weighted index**.

basket of currencies   see **currency basket**.

Basle Concordat   Formulated in 1975 and revised in 1983, this agreement by the Basle Supervisors' Committee sets out the principles governing the supervision of banks' foreign establishments by parent and host authorities. The concordat deals exclusively with the responsibilities of central banks in their role as monitors of the prudential conduct and soundness of banks' foreign branches and subsidiaries. Responsibility is allocated between the parent bank and the host authority so that no foreign banking operation escapes the supervisory net.

bear   someone who believes prices are heading down (interest rates are heading up). A 'bear' market is one in which there is a sustained fall in prices and which does not look like recovering quickly. The Sydney Stock Exchange terminology leaflet explains bear as one who 'claws prices down'. The 1984 annual report of the Sydney Stock Exchange provides some colourful background to the term: 'London of the late seventeenth and early eighteenth century is the period responsible for the zoological terms that have become part of today's stock market jargon... bears attack by clawing the prices down—the sellers undercutting each other with lower offers to produce a falling market—a "bear" market... The term "bearskin jobber" was often used for those jobbers who "sold short" (sold stock they did not own) in anticipation of purchasing when the price had fallen.' The report says the essayist Joseph Addison, writing in a 1709 edition of the London *Tatler*, likened short-selling to 'selling the bear's skin before one has caught the bear'—hence the UK term 'uncovered bear' which indicates someone selling short. Bear is the opposite of bull. See **bull**.

bearer   Used in 'bearer security' or 'pay to the bearer', this means the person carrying the document (cash cheque, promissory note or bond). In the case of bearer securities the owner is not registered with the issuer but physically holds the documents. Bearer securities are payable to the holder on maturity and transferable by delivery. Losing them is like losing currency notes. Purchases of bearer securities have been popular as a method of avoiding tax; bearer securities issued overseas are exempted from interest withholding tax.

bear spread   an options market technique used in the US that aims to take advantage of a fall in price of a commodity or share. A trader would buy and sell options of the same class, for example buy and sell call options on the same commodity or share, with the objective of benefiting from a fall in the price of the underlying commodity or share. A bear (or bull) spread can refer to a futures market position, as well as to an options technique, but is more commonly used with options. See **bull spread, option spread**.

bed and breakfast deals   a UK term for stocks purchased and held overnight only.

beggar-my-neighbour   trading practices based on agreements which benefit some countries (those in the agreement) at the expense of others (those not in the agreement). Protectionism and tariffs are policies which benefit one country at the expense of another. The General Agreement on Tariffs and Trade was aimed partly at mitigating the effects of such practices. See **General Agreement on Tariffs and Trade, Tariff**.

Belgian dentist   generic term for the European retail buyer of eurobonds. The mythical figure describes the high-income professional such as a dentist, doctor or lawyer who is keen to minimise tax and maximise the return on investments. He or she is an enthusiastic buyer of euro-$A and eurokiwis because of the high interest rates offered and also because the relative weakness of the domestic currencies of the low countries encourages diversification into assets in a different currency. The buying enthusiasm was tempered at times by a flood of issues and, in the Australian case, by a sharp fall in the value of the currency. The buyers tend to favour known names, such as German banks and prime corporate issuers.

bells and whistles   special add-on attractions that dress up an otherwise conventional investment or instrument to give it novelty. Bells and whistles can range from a cheque account with an interest-bearing sweep (retail product) to the more exotic capital market bonds and warrants. They are often used to improve the credit of securitised assets. The new twists are limited only by the imagination of the inventors—typically the Wall Street wunderkinder. See **rocket scientist**.

bellwether   a barometer. Financial markets commentators talk of a particular bond being the 'bellwether' of the market, meaning that the movements in its price are an indication of the mood or health of the market in general.

below par   a bond or share is below par when it trades for less than its face value. See **above par**.

below the line   all items in the profit and loss statement that are below the 'operating profit or loss after income tax line', for example extraordinary items. See **above the line**.

benchmark rate   a rate used as a yardstick for measuring or setting other market interest rates, for example, the banks' prime lending rate, which banks use to price loans, or the Commonwealth bond rate which is widely used as a base from which other securities such as semi-government stock and corporate debentures are priced. See **prime rate**.

beneficial owner   the person who is entitled to enjoy the benefit of (who is the real owner of) property or goods of which the legal title may be vested in a trustee.

Bentham, Jeremy   see **economists**.

best efforts basis   a general commercial agreement to try hard without promising a particular degree of success. Selling an issue of shares or other securities this way does not involve a full underwriting commitment as to price or amount. The sellers agree to market the securities to the fullest extent possible at the best price available.

beta factor   in share and futures trading, an estimate of the historical volatility (sharp movement) of a commodity's price against a related composite index, for example movements in the gold price against the precious metals index. If gold were to rise by 6 per cent and the index by 5 per cent then gold's beta factor would be 1.2, being the ratio of 6:5.

bid and ask   buy and sell prices. Traders also speak of a **bid price**, the price offered; the **asking price** is the price requested. These usually indicate the top price a purchaser will pay and the lowest price a seller will accept.

bid rate   an alternative expression (used in share and bond markets and foreign exchange) for buying price.

Big Bang   the term used to describe the freeing up of the UK stockmarket which took place on 27 October 1986, when stockbroking firms were allowed to incorporate, foreign companies could buy into British broking firms, and the previous system of jobbers and brokers was dismantled. Automated share trading was also introduced on that date. See **May Day**.

Big Board a US expression for the New York Stock Exchange. Companies listed on the Big Board are larger and longer established than those on other, smaller exchanges. See **main board, second board**.

big figure, the a term used in foreign exchange markets, and in US bond and futures markets to indicate the figure on the left-hand side of the decimal point. If the $A were quoted at 89.10 US cents, then the figure 89 would be the 'big figure'. When rates fluctuate wildly, traders talk of 'even the big figure jumping'. See **figure, the**.

Big Four the four largest UK banks (clearing banks): Barclays, Lloyds, Midland and National Westminster.

big ticket (items) items such as aeroplanes and machinery whose cost can run into millions of dollars. See **leveraged leasing, project finance**.

bill line a line of credit from a bank or merchant bank, funded by discounting bills of exchange.

bill of exchange A form of postdated cheque, a bill of exchange is a negotiable instrument, usually sold at a discount. The person holding it has proof of debt. A bill is an unconditional order in writing, addressed by the drawer to the drawee, requiring the drawee to pay a sum of money on demand or at a specified future time to the payee (who might be the drawer or another party) or to the bearer. If the drawee accepts the bill, by writing on it and signing it, he becomes the acceptor and therefore primarily liable to pay the bill when it becomes due. If the acceptor fails to pay, the drawer or an endorser must compensate the holder. (Every endorser of a bill of exchange is in the nature of a new drawer and is liable to every succeeding holder should the acceptor and drawer default on payment.)

The formal definition of a bill of exchange under the *Bills of Exchange Act* 1909-1973 is: 'An unconditional order in writing, addressed by one person to another, signed by the person giving it, requiring the person to whom it is addressed to pay on demand, or at a fixed and determinable future time, a sum certain in money to the order of a specified person, or to bearer.'

Bills of exchange date from the fourth century BC and became popular in the eighteenth and nineteenth centuries as a means of financing expanding world trade. They are widely used in the money market, issued by companies borrowing funds and traded through a range of holders until they mature, at which point the holder receives face value from the acceptor. Bills of exchange can be bank-accepted or bank-endorsed, or can rank as commercial bills, in which case no bank name appears on the bill. Parties to a bill of exchange include the following:

- **acceptor**   the party to whom a bill of exchange is addressed and who accepts a bill of exchange drawn on him. Until the bill is signed and accepted, this party is called the drawee. The acceptor agrees to pay the person presenting the bill on the due date the face value of the bill. The acceptor of the bill has a direct liability through that bill; he is primarily liable to pay out the funds on the due date. But if the acceptor fails to pay, the drawer has to compensate the holder of the bill or any endorser who has paid out.
- **drawee**   A bill of exchange is addressed to the drawee, who is required to pay the stipulated sum of money (the face value of the bill) at a specified future date to the payee named on the bill or to bearer. Once the drawee accepts the bill, by writing on it and accepting it, he becomes the acceptor and is primarily liable to pay out when the bill matures.
- **drawer**   the party who issues the bill, who makes the order for the bill to be accepted and paid. The drawer signs the bill as its maker and has a contingent liability on the bill until it matures as, in the event of default by the acceptor, the drawer is obliged to pay out the face value of the bill on its due date to the holder.
- **endorser**   (sometimes written *indorser*) the party signing on the reverse side of the bill as confirmation of purchase and title to the bill. The list of endorsers' signatures on the back of the bill establishes the chain of ownership of the bill.
- **payee**   the person to whom the face value of a bill of exchange is to be paid (as with a cheque). The payee appears as the first endorser on the reverse side of the bill and this endorsement starts the chain of ownership of the bill. The picture becomes complicated when it is remembered that the payee on a bill of exchange can also be the drawer or another party.

See **bank bill of exchange, bank-accepted bill of exchange, trade bill.**

bill of lading   a receipt issued by a shipping company for goods transported. The bill serves as a record of the contract, setting out terms and conditions.

bill of sale   in the US, a document giving evidence of a sale, but in the UK and Australia, a security, a document assigning rights to goods or property, or mortgaging goods. State laws require registration of such bills in most circumstances.

bill option   a line of credit which includes the option of using bills of exchange rather than cash, so that the loan can be liquidated by selling the bills.

bill strip   a technique that creates a synthetic longer-dated bill of exchange by setting end-to-end a physical bill and a series of futures contracts. This can be done to achieve a higher yield than would be available from either the physical bill or the futures market alone, or it can be used as means of locking in a term rate for, say, one year.

BIS *abbrev.* **Bank for International Settlements.**

black   When you are 'in the black' you have money in the bank or you are making a profit. In bank statements, debits (what you owe the bank) used to be written in red ink, credits (what is owed to you) in black ink. See **red**.

Black Friday   an expression used to describe a day that sees a sharp drop in financial market prices. It takes the name from a Friday in September 1869 when an attempt in the US to corner the gold market triggered a panic and then a depression.

black knight   the opposite of a white knight, a black knight is someone who makes a takeover offer that is unfavourable and/or unfriendly to a company's management. See **white knight**.

black market   buying or selling prohibited or controlled goods or currencies through illegal or unlicensed traders, often taking a risk for profit or getting around a government regulation, such as price control. If your transaction in the black market falls through, you cannot bring an action in a court of law.

Black-Scholes option pricing model   This device was developed in the early 1980s by two US economists, Fischer Black and Myron Scholes, to help assess the value of option contracts. The model was instrumental in influencing the US Commodity Futures Trading Commission to allow options to be traded again (they had been banned since 1933) as it showed the potential of options for limiting risk. It has become the basic option-pricing formula.

black tax   see **withholding tax**.

blue-chip   the highest-valued gambling chips are blue, and this mark of top quality has flowed from the casino to the stock markets, where 'blue-chip' stocks are those of the highest market value. Blue chips are not infallible, though, or invulnerable to losses. In the UK Rolls Royce was revered as a blue-chip stock right up to its collapse in 1971.

board meeting   formal meetings of company directors (board members), held usually once a month, ostensibly to examine business performance and management of the company and to discuss plans for the future. As with most meetings, board meetings are time-consuming and demand a degree of preparation frequently out of proportion with the progress they achieve. See **agenda, director, board room**.

board order   see **market-if-touched order**.

board room   A space usually reserved for regular meetings of company directors. It is often discreetly but comfortably furnished to allow bored board room occupants to snooze unobtrusively. Board rooms have large, highly polished tables and are often equipped with cocktail bars disguised by wood-grain panelling or suede wallpaper. People trying to telephone an executive may be told he or she is unavailable—'in the board room'. That is presumably what prompted a well-known Sydney hotel to name one of its bars exactly that: The Board Room.

bond   a statment of debt, similar to an IOU. A bond is a piece of paper issued by borrowers such as governments, State authorities, companies or any person or entity who issues the bond in return for cash from lenders and investors. Interest is paid by the borrower to the lender or investor throughout the life of the bond. Borrowers seeking funds from the public through bond issues usually announce the details of these issues in the financial press and increasingly through radio and television advertising as well. Details of bond issues to the public are spelled out in each issue's prospectus; prospectuses are available from stockbrokers, banks and, in the case of Commonwealth securities, also from the Reserve Bank. Attempts to define a bond include 'A coupon security offering more than one interest payment' but the emergence of zero coupon bonds has complicated the picture. Bonds are generally medium- to long-term fixed-interest securities. Two types of government bonds are available in Australia: Australian Savings Bonds and Commonwealth (Treasury) bonds. The latter are sold by periodic tender, mostly to large-scale investors who set the price levels. Australian Savings Bonds (Aussie Bonds) are aimed at the household or small investor and are constantly available. See **Australian Savings Bond, Commonwealth bond, fixed interest, tender, zero coupon bonds**.

bond market   the market where bonds are bought and sold. Unlike share trading, most bond trading takes place over the telephone rather than on the floor of the Stock Exchange. Bond trading which takes place on the exchange floor is referred to as 'on 'change'; the transactions executed over the telephone are 'off 'change' dealings. Bonds are traded among short-term money market dealers, banks and life assurance companies as well as between stockbrokers acting on clients' behalf.

bond tender   A tender is a form of auction. Commonwealth bonds have been sold through a tender system in Australia since July 1982. See **tender**.

bonus issue   shares in a company which are issued free to existing shareholders. They are sometimes called a 'scrip' issue. A company might make a bonus or scrip issue as an alternative to increasing its dividend payout. New shares are issued to existing shareholders in proportion to their holdings, for example one bonus share for every five shares held. See **entitlement issue, rights issue**.

book   Money market and foreign exchange dealers talk of their 'book' when referring to total purchases and sales. It is a record of how much they have bought and sold, borrowed and lent.

book value   the value of an asset as stated in a company's financial records. Accountants distinguish between **book value** and **net book value**. **Book value** is the original (historical) purchase price of an asset, possibly revalued. It is not necessarily the price that asset would fetch if sold in the market, nor what it would cost to replace. **Net book value** is the book value of an asset less the total depreciation which has been charged against the asset over the years. Confusingly, accountants would say that book value has nothing to do with the market value of an asset.

boom   onomatopoetically, the reverberating sound of confidence; in effect, a buoyant phase in the trade cycle, characterised by rapid growth and an increase in economic activity—something more than just an upturn in the trade cycle. Booms can be speculative, such as the minerals boom of the early 1970s. See **resources boom**.

booth moll   futures market slang for the clerk standing at the phone booth on the trading floor, passing orders to and from the **floor trader**.

bottomish   jargon to describe a market that has fallen to a level that indicates an imminent reversal of the downward trend. Opposite of toppy. See **toppy**.

bottom line   the final result. Financiers are just as fond of talking about the 'bottom line' as of the 'final analysis', meaning the final or real cost or result. The term comes from the profit and loss statement layout in which the bottom line shows the extent of the profit (or loss) made after all income and expenses have been taken into account.

bottom-of-the-harbour   This describes a tax scheme where shareholders in a company which has earned profits in the current year sell the shares in the company to a tax promoter (someone selling tax-avoidance schemes) for full value less a discount, thus effectively avoiding payment of tax on the profits. The tax promoter often onsells the company to 'straw' people who 'dump' the books and records at the 'bottom-of-the-harbour'. Such schemes were often wrongly called Wet Slutzkins. See **Slutzkin**.

bounce   A cheque 'bounces' when a bank dishonours it (declines to pay out the amount for which the cheque was written) because there are not enough funds in the account or because of some other technical reason. The cheque is returned to the customer, politely endorsed 'refer to drawer'. The cheque therefore 'bounces' back to the person who wrote it.

bourse   French for 'stock exchange' the word has become widely used as an effete alternative for the share market. *Bourse* is French for 'purse' hence 'purser', 'bursar'.

boutique in the financial world, a small, specialised bank or broking firm that concentrates on a narrow range of products that appeal to a correspondingly narrow group of clients. The opposite of the financial supermarket. Also **niche**. See **financial supermarket**.

bracket creep This occurs as companies compensate employees for rising inflation by giving them pay increases, which in turn push the tax-paying employees into higher income tax brackets (the pattern depends on the existence of a progressive system of tax, in which marginal tax rates rise with increasing income). The government collects a greater proportion of the tax base.

break-even analysis the study of the relationship between fixed costs, variable costs and revenue to determine the point at which total costs equal total revenue (that is, no profits and no losses) so that any revenue beyond that point will be profit.

break-forward a foreign exchange contract that can be unwound at a predetermined date. The contract is similar to forward and option contracts in that it allows the buyer to hedge or protect against adverse currency movements by locking in a fixed rate. Unlike options, though, break-forwards do not require a premium to be paid when the contract is made, as all costs are included in the fixed rate. Break-forwards are marketed by the Midland Bank, and by the Hambros Bank as a forward with optional exit. See **forward with optional exit**.

Bretton Woods the New Hampshire (USA) location of the 1-22 July 1944 international conference which led to the establishment of:
- a new international monetary system;
- the International Monetary Fund (IMF);
- the International Bank for Reconstruction and Development (World Bank).

Representatives of 44 nations met to work out proposals for a new international monetary system. The outcome was a modified version of the gold standard. Under the new system, most currencies were tied to the $US (some, for example the Australian currency, were tied to sterling) and the $US was in turn tied to gold. The objectives of the Bretton Woods conference were to establish an international monetary system with stable exchange rates, to eliminate exchange controls and to bring about the convertibility of all currencies. Exchange rate fluctuations were to be held within a narrow band around parity and no change in parity was to take place without IMF approval. The $US held a key role in this system; when that currency ceased to be convertible in 1971, following consistently large US balance of payments deficits, its fall brought the Bretton Woods system down with it. New exchange rate parities were set up under the Smithsonian Agreement but the fixed exchange rate system was on the way out and in early 1973 most of the major countries floated their currencies. See **fixed parity, float, gold standard, International Monetary Fund, Smithsonian Agreement, World Bank**.

bridging finance   short-term funding from a bank, finance company or other source, pending arrangements by the borrower for longer-term, cheaper loans. Bridging finance is often used when buying and selling houses, to 'bridge' the gap between receipt of funds from the sale of one house and the need to pay out for another. Bridging finance is generally considered a last resort because its convenience is usually rivalled, if not outweighed, by its cost.

Brigden Report   the report of a committee chaired by J. B. Brigden, set up in 1927 to examine the pros and cons of Australia's protection policy. The report appeared in 1929 and found that, on balance, Australia's protection policies had been beneficial but warned against further extension of tariffs. It also concluded that protection had supported wages above levels that would otherwise have been obtainable and thus had encouraged immigration. The report attracted international attention for the 'Australian case for protection' because of its arguments in support of tariffs for an economy such as Australia's and for its efforts to measure the excess cost of protection. The report was one occasion when Australian economists have contributed something of note to the 'dismal science'. Soon after the release of the report, and despite its recommendations, tariff levels were dramatically raised by the Scullin Labor government. See **free trade, Premiers' Plan**.

broad money   the widest measure used by the Reserve Bank when calculating Australia's money supply growth. It is M3 plus the borrowings by non-bank financial institutions, including cash management trusts. See **money supply**.

broker   someone who buys and sells on behalf of others (his clients). In the world of financial middlemen there are sharebrokers, money brokers, fixed-interest brokers and futures brokers. By definition brokers do not usually take positions, or deal directly, themselves.

brokerage   what the brokers charge; their commission for buying and selling on the instructions of their clients. Brokerage is usually calculated as a percentage of the amount invested or scaled according to the number of securities traded.

bucket shop   trading operation on the fringe of conventional business practice. Once anyone selling at a discount was said to be running a bucket shop, but the term is now applied commonly in the UK to travel agents selling cheap airline tickets. Those recognised as bucket shops are not members of the National Association of British Travel Agents but they receive an allocation of tickets and sell them at a discount.

budget   Everyone, from householders to governments, tries to allocate funds to the best advantage. A budget is a plan in monetary terms for income and expenditure over a future period which is supposed to be used to achieve the stated objectives, whether that means buying aircraft carriers or paying kindergarten fees. The Australian government announces ('brings down', as the jargon goes) an annual budget in August, showing expected revenue and expenditure, forecasting how much it expects to borrow and outlining any changes in the way it will raise revenue (mainly taxation). Sometimes a government will bring down a mid-year 'mini-budget' to change a previously decided course. Companies draw up budgets, with each department having control and responsibility over its spending. The word 'budget' originally meant 'a bag containing papers'.

budget cycle   The cyclical sensitivity of the budget—a deficit arises in economic downturns—means that the monetary authorities do not have complete control of fiscal policy. See **fiscal policy**.

buffer stock   what is kept on hand for a rainy day or unexpected demand. It can also refer to parcels of stock which have been deliberately stored, to be sold later to influence prices.

building societies   Cooperatively owned organisations established chiefly to lend funds for housing. Australian building societies date from the 1840s and are modelled on the UK institutions which originated in the self-help movements of the late eighteenth century. The US equivalent is the Savings and Loan Association. Building societies in the past 30 years have become increasingly important in the Australian financial system. Each society, operating under State controls, has a board of directors elected by the members. The societies raise funds from individuals and corporations and use these funds to lend to home buyers (preference is usually given to members). The societies have to compete for funds with other financial institutions such as banks and credit unions, and more recently with the cash management trusts. In Australia, there are three categories of building societies.

- **Permanent Building Societies** are dominant. They raise their funds through issued share capital, members' deposits and borrowings from financial institutions. Permanent building societies have carved a significant niche in the financial system, offering flexible services and sophisticated technology, and often longer trading hours than banks. Permanent building societies tend to make larger housing loans than the savings banks, although their interest rates are usually higher.
- **Terminating Building Societies** are now called Cooperative Housing Societies in some States. In New South Wales, legislation was passed in 1981 to change the status of these societies from terminating (being wound up as loans were repaid) to being

continuing organisations. Originally terminating building societies operated by pooling members' funds; loans were allocated to members by ballot. Modern cooperatives raise funds from institutional sources and from government and semi-government authorities, applying that money to housing finance.

Starr Bowkett Societies are a special type of terminating society. They pool members' contributions and lend the funds out through a ballot process as loans on the security of real estate. The Starr Bowkett system had its origins in England in the 1840s and owes its existence to Dr Thomas Edward Bowkett and Mr Richard Benjamin Starr. The first Australian Starr Bowkett society was formed in Sydney in 1868 and terminated in 1882. Starr Bowkett societies were banned in England about 90 years ago as being too uncertain for home buyers, who like to plan their borrowings. True Starr Bowketts continue in Australia, operating on the basis of paying no interest on members' deposits and charging no interest on loans. They are still run as terminating societies, often with a number of societies grouped under a management body.

bull   someone who is optimistic about the market and interest rates, who sees share prices rising and interest rates falling—and whose activity reinforces those trends; the opposite of a bear. A bull market is characterised by sustained and enthusiastic buying. The Sydney Stock Exchange terminology guide explains that bulls 'attack by tossing the prices into the air with their horns—the buyers bidding in competition with each other to produce a rising market—"bull" market'. The Sydney Stock Exchange's 1984 annual report concedes that the origins of 'bull' are less distinct than those of 'bear' but comes up with an early eighteenth-century reference to the term 'bull' in the poetry of Alexander Pope. Pope alludes to Greek mythology and the passion of the god Zeus for Europa; Zeus turns himself into a bull and carries her off to Crete. This happy legend crops up in some lines written to celebrate the (short-lived) bullish attitude to the South Sea Company of the early eighteenth century.

> Come fill the South Sea Goblet full;
> The Gods shall of our Stock take care;
> Europa, pleas'd accepts the Bull,
> And Jove with Joy puts off the Bear.

See **bear, South Sea Bubble**.

bulldog bonds   sterling-denominated bonds issued in the UK by foreign borrowers; the UK equivalent of Samurai and Yankee bonds. See **Samurai bonds, Yankee bonds**.

bullet loan   a Euromarket term denoting a single-repayment loan with no amortisation, that is, a loan which is not paid off in instalments.

bullion   gold or silver of specified weight.

bull spread   As with a bear spread, this technique involves the purchase and sale of the same class of options, though it can be used with conventional futures contracts. A bull spread would be the purchase and sale of call or put options on the same share or commodity that is designed to benefit from a rise in market prices. See **bear spread, option spread**.

Bundesbank (Deutsche)   the central bank of West Germany.

burn-out   what overstressed traders and executives suffer: exhaustion, usually associated with a serious feeling of disenchantment for the work they do — for the occupation that earns them high salaries but at the price of considerable personal stress. The term can also refer to a tax shelter that is no longer effective; what began as a shelter has begun to produce income on which tax has to be paid. See **corporate menopause**.

business confidence   a fragile but desirable quality which every government hopes to promote and foster.

business cycle   Economic activity never stays at exactly the same level and the fluctuations between boom times and bad times are known as the business (or trade) cycle. The term also implies that the fluctuation is fairly regular. Business cycles can be politically inspired, for example ahead of an election when a government initiates an expansionary policy.

butterfly spread   a futures market term to describe a spread or straddle position in three delivery months in the pattern of one-two-one; for example, the trader's position would be an agreement to sell one futures contract maturing in March, to buy two futures contracts maturing in June and to sell one futures contract maturing in September. It is a sophisticated trading strategy for managing risk; it has been popular in the US and is expected to be used more frequently in Australia.

buy-back   an agreement that the seller will repurchase securities within a specified time, at a predetermined price. These are known as 'repos' in the money market. See **repurchase agreements**.

buyers' market   a market where supply outstrips demand. Prices fall, so that buyers are able to set their preferred terms and conditions and get away with it.

buyers over   a futures market term to describe what occurs when a trade has taken place at a given price and buyers remain unsatisfied in the market. See **sellers over**.

C

---

cable   foreign exchange traders' jargon for the $US/sterling exchange rate quote.

CAC   *abbrev.* **Corporate Affairs Commission.**

calendar spread   see **option spread.**

call   When a company makes a 'call' on shares it asks the holders of partly paid shares to contribute more money. A 'call' in futures trading refers to a 'margin call'. Funds can be placed on the money market 'at call', which means they have not been lodged for a fixed term. See **11 am call money, margin call, 24-hour call money.**

call option   see **options.**

cambist   someone who deals in foreign currencies. The word can also refer to a handbook of currency tables. It comes from the Italian word *cambio*, 'a money exchange'.

Cambridge School   a branch of economic thinking influenced by economists at the University of Cambridge, England, since the late nineteenth century. Alfred Marshall was an early influence on the Cambridge School; he held the Chair of Political Economy until 1908. The School's theories have continued in various guises since then. After World War II, the Cambridge School rejected the ideas of the neo-classical school, and instead further developed the ideas of J. M. Keynes, while retaining some influence of the early classical period. Joan Robinson was a leading figure in the post-World War II era, when the Cambridge School emphasised the macroeconomic approach as opposed to the microeconomic approach of the neo-classical school. The theories of the Cambridge School have progressed through many stages and produced a number of splinter groups, including the New Cambridge School, which has very distinctive ideas about economic policies and the role of the exchange rate. Cambridge School thinkers have been an important influence, and are particularly so in the UK; they are prone to frequent changes in ideas, which has led their critics to label them a bunch of eccentric economists. See **classical economics, neo-classical economics** and **Keynes, John Maynard, Marshall, Alfred** and **Robinson, Joan** in **economists.**

Campbell Report   the result of the Australian Financial System Inquiry, conducted by a committee chaired by Mr (later Sir) Keith Campbell (1928–83), who was chairman and chief general manager of

32

Hooker Corporation Ltd. The Campbell Committee, as it was known, was established in 1979 to examine the Australian financial system and to recommend changes. It was the first inquiry of this nature since the 1935-37 Royal Commission into Money and Banking; it covered a wider range of issues than the royal commission, reflecting the increased complexities of the financial system.

The terms of reference of the committee were to inquire into and report on the structure and operations of the Australian financial system, including the following institutions:

- banks and non-banks, including their role in foreign exchange;
- the short-term money market, both official and unofficial;
- specialist development financial institutions including the Australian Resources Development Bank, the Australian Industry Development Corporation, Commonwealth Development Bank and Primary Industry Bank of Australia;
- the Reserve Bank of Australia.

The committee was to inquire into and report on regulation and control of the system, and make recommendations for the improvement in its structure and operations, regulation and control. It was also to make recommendations on existing legislation concerning the financial system, including the *Reserve Bank Act*, the *Banking Act* and the *Financial Corporations Act*.

The Interim Report of the Campbell Committee was tabled on 28 August 1980. It examined the existing structure and operations of the financial system, identified the issues which had emerged from submissions and from deliberations of the Campbell Committee. The final report was tabled on 17 November 1981. In the intervening years since it had been established, the committee had listened to and read an enormous mass of evidence, through public hearings and written submissions.

Recent changes which flowed from the committee's findings include:

- a tender system for selling Treasury Notes and Treasury Bonds;
- gradual relaxation of bank interest rate and maturity controls and an end to quantitative bank lending guidelines;
- greater flexibility for semi-government borrowers and the establishment of central borrowing authorities;
- increased flexibility for authorised money market dealers;
- more flexible asset structure for savings banks;
- freer foreign exchange market, the float of the $A and lifting of most exchange controls;
- deregulation of the stock market and the incorporation of broking firms;
- the establishment of management and investment companies.

The Campbell Committee had been created by a Liberal–Country Party Coalition government under Prime Minister Malcolm Fraser. That government lost office in March 1983; the Hawke Labor government, on gaining office, established the Martin Group to examine some of the findings of the Campbell Committee in the light of Labor's economic and social objectives. See **Martin Committee (Review Group)**.

Members of the Campbell Committee, other than the chairman, were: Alan Coates, general manager, AMP Society; Keith Halkerston, financial adviser; R.G. (Dick) McCrossin, general manager, Australian Resources Development Bank Ltd; Jim Mallyon, chief manager, Reserve Bank of Australia; Fred Argy, first assistant secretary, Department of Treasury.

CAP *abbrev.* **common agricultural policy**.

cap   the maximum rate a borrower pays for funds. A 'cap' is a ceiling set on interest rates, offering a form of protection or insurance in that a borrower cannot pay more than the rate agreed under the cap. A cap can be customised, i.e. written by a financial institution for an individual client, or it can be in the form of a 'stripped' cap, one which is separated from a capital market transaction. Also **interest rate condom**. See **collar**.

capital   the value of your investment in your house or business, represented by total assets less total liabilities. The basic funds and assets used by people, governments and businesses to sustain and equip their income-earning activity. That is the economic definition of capital; the accounting concept of capital refers to authorised capital, the owner's initial contribution to a business. See **authorised capital**.

capital asset pricing model   a model that shows the relationship between expected risk and expected return on an investment, based on the accepted theory that the higher the risk associated with an investment, the higher the expected return. The model shows that the return on an asset incorporates the risk-free return plus a premium that increases with the extent of risk involved. Since a sensible portfolio is one that covers a mix of investments rather than a concentration in one area, as diversification spreads the risk, the capital asset pricing model is useful as it shows the contribution made by each investment to the overall risk of a portfolio.

capital base   the issued capital of a company, that is the money contributed by the shareholders who first acquired shares in the company, plus reserves and retained profits.

capital employed   the money used by a business to fund its operations--that is, to buy stock, pay wages, install new equipment.

capital expenditure   payment made, or to be made, for the acquisition of a long-term asset, such as land, house or machinery. In accounting, this would be recorded in the long-term asset account.

capital flight   what happens when investors panic and send their money out of the country in large quantities. Political upheaval domestically or a severe economic downturn often pushes people to send their money overseas as a protective measure. The process becomes self-fulfilling as word spreads that money is fleeing the country and a trickle turns to a flood as investors seek alternative, often temporary but, they hope, safer havens for their money.

capital gain   the result of selling a capital asset at a higher price than it cost you. Whether an investor makes a capital gain or not depends on the purchase price of an asset compared to its selling price, the effect of depreciation on its value, and whether inflation has bitten into the investor's profit margin. Capital gain has different meanings for the tax department, the economist and the accountant. See **capital gains tax**.

capital gains tax   A general definition of a capital gains tax is 'a tax on income (gain) arising from changes in the market value of assets'. Capital gains tax does not raise huge revenue for governments; rather its support stems from the notion of introducing equity into the tax system by differentiating between tax on income and tax on capital gains. Usually in countries where a capital gains tax has been imposed, it does not apply to the profit made on the sale of your own house. The Australian tax law purports to tax income but there is some uncertainty whether particular profit is income or capital gain.

Although there is no capital gains tax as such in Australia, there are certain provisions in the *Tax Act* that approximate imposing a capital gains tax. The most obvious examples are Section 26AAA which taxes profits from the sale of property sold within twelve months of purchase date, and Section 26(a) which renders liable to tax profits from the resale of an asset acquired for resale at a profit or from a profit-making undertaking or scheme. At present 'taxable income' does not include capital gains accrued or capital gains realised if the asset sold has been held for more than twelve months. It does not necessarily follow, though, that selling an asset held for more than twelve months will escape tax.

A professional sharetrader (as against the individual dabbling in shares) is liable for tax on all profits, regardless of time span, although he or she benefits by being able to claim tax deductions for trading losses and expenses such as brokerage. The decision on whether a taxpayer is liable for tax rests with the Commissioner for Taxation and the courts; much depends on the taxpayer's intentions, the type of investments made and the frequency with which he or she traded.

capital-guaranteed bonds   see **insurance bonds**.

capital-intensive   a term referring to industries which make heavy use of assets and machinery and few employees, such as farming, as opposed to labour-intensive operations such as clothing manufacture. The tide of technology is changing previously labour-intensive industries such as banking or car assembly into highly computerised capital-intensive operations.

capitalised expenditure   expenses carried forward in the balance sheet as assets to be matched against future revenue.

capitalism   a form of economic and social organisation under which the means of production, distribution and exchange remain predominantly under private (not State) ownership and resources are allocated according to relative prices.

capital markets   securities markets, generally for medium- to long-term investments and fundraising, as against the money markets which focus on the short term (one to three years).

captive market   a market where purchasers are obliged, either through legislation or lack of alternatives, to buy a particular item, range of products or type of securities. Examples of captive markets for government securities (at the time of writing, November 1984), are the banks and authorised dealers, who have to hold a certain proportion of their assets in public sector securities. See **30/20 Regulation**.

CARDs   *abbrev.* **certificates of amortising revolving debts.**

CARPS   *abbrev.* **controlled adjustable rate preferred stock.**

CARs   *abbrev.* **certificate for automobile receivables.**

career-limiting move   an ill-thought-out strategy, such as a one-sided arbitrage. *Abbrev.*: **CLM.**

cartel   a number of businesses or organisations which have grouped together and agreed, often implicitly, to influence the price or supply of goods. Generally this is considered a pejorative term, implying underhand manipulation of markets by powerful interests for their own benefit. Most capitalist governments legislate to control cartels and monopolies. See **monopoly**.

cash and carry   a futures market practice which involves the purchase of a physical commodity against the forward sale of that commodity on the futures market, for example the purchase of $1 million of bank bills of exchange against two bank bill futures contracts. The physical commodity is delivered to fulfil (or close out) the futures contract. Cash and carry is useful when the distant futures months are trading at a premium over the physical spot price. For example, if March gold futures is at a premium to (i.e. is at a higher price than) the spot gold price, a trader would buy the physical gold, sell March futures and deliver the physical gold to satisfy the March futures position—and would have earned a good return on the futures in the meantime. See **close out, futures.**

cash and conversion loan   a loan, usually a government or semi-government issue, which offers existing subscribers the opportunity to reinvest their money for a further term in a new but similar issue, and at the same time seeks subscriptions from new investors. The borrower is trying to attract new money and roll over the old. Cash and conversion loans were a standard method of selling government securities before the introduction of the tap system, which in July 1982 was replaced by the present tender system. See **rollover, tender.**

cash base   the cash base of the financial system is the sum of currency in circulation and the deposits of the banks with the Reserve Bank. It is the narrowest money measure. It is called Little Mo in the UK. Also **money** or **monetary base.**

cash-box company   a company with significant amounts of cash and a well-known name running it and its investments. The company is able to raise cash not because of its asset base, but because of the reputation of its management, who, investors believe, can maximise returns on funds.

cash cow   a company that generates a constant flow of cash, usually in a mature industry, for example a brewery (unless the world were to turn its back on beer).

cash flow   the net amount of money received by an individual or business in a given period. If cash flows are budgeted correctly, enough funds should be available to meet cash payments as they occur. Cash flow should not be confused with profits and losses; many companies have gone out of business while making profits, simply because they ran out of cash.

cash flow accounting   non-accrual accounting. This is the basis of accounting for government departments, not for organisations seeking to account for profit.

cash management trust   a type of unit trust first introduced to the Australian market in December 1980 by the merchant bank Hill Samuel Australia Ltd. A number of merchant banks, broking firms and building societies launched cash trusts subsequently. The Australian Bank Ltd, the first new bank on the Australian scene for 40 years, opened a cash management trust in 1981, operating a sweep mechanism which uses surplus balances in customers' cheque accounts. Cash management trusts took off in the US in the 1970s as money market mutual funds and prospered there, as they did in Australia, because of their coincidence with soaring interest rates and the steeply inverse yield curve. The trusts were a response to the prevailing controls on interest rates offered by traditional borrowers of household dollars, such as trading and savings banks. The trusts operate by pooling investors' money into high-yielding money market instruments which normally are available only to professional investors with hundreds of thousands of dollars at their disposal. Investors can buy into cash trusts with as little as $2000. In the heady days of 1982 they were earning yields as high as 19 per cent on 24-hour call money. Cash trusts operate with a trust deed, a trustee overseeing activities and a management company responsible for investment strategy. See **money market mutual funds, sweep.**

cash ratio   Similar to liquidity ratio, this is the amount of cash and easily marketable securities held by a company as a proportion of its current liabilities.

CATS   *abbrev.* 1. **computer-assisted trading system**; 2. **certificate of accrual on treasury securities.**

caveat emptor   Latin for 'let the buyer beware'. In common law, if someone is sold defective goods he or she has no redress: the buyer has a responsibility to examine the goods closely or read the fine print carefully. The principle has been modified, almost reversed, by consumer protection legislation and warranty provisions.

CBA   *abbrev.* **central borrowing authority.**

CBT   *abbrev.* **Chicago Board of Trade.**

CCA   *abbrev.* **current cost accounting.**

CD   *abbrev.* **certificate of deposit.**

CEDA   *abbrev.* **Committee for the Economic Development of Australia.**

CEDEL   *abbrev.* **Centrale de Livraison de Valeurs Mobilieres.**

ceiling price   the highest a buyer will bid, from the same metaphor as floor price. See **floor price.**

central bank   All developed countries have a central bank which, as agent for the government, oversees the monetary system, controls the issue of currency notes, acts as banker to the government and the banking system and makes available lender-of-last-resort loans to approved money market dealers and to banks. Through its open market operations, a central bank can influence interest and exchange rates. In Australia, the central bank is the Reserve Bank of Australia; in the UK it is the Bank of England and in the US, the Federal Reserve system. See **central bank intervention, open market operations, Reserve Bank of Australia.**

central bank intervention   action taken by a central bank to influence monetary conditions. Intervention can be by direct controls, for example interest rate ceilings, quantitative lending controls, exchange controls in foreign exchange, or through open market operations and informal chats. The open market operations could involve purchases or sales by the central bank in foreign exchange or domestic financial markets. Generally, central banks these days have decided that markets are best left to set exchange and interest rates, so that their intervention tends to be restricted to 'smoothing' operations, merely ironing out the more volatile fluctuations in, say, exchange rates. See **moral suasion**.

central borrowing authority a group of semi-government authorities which band together to streamline their borrowings rather than approach the market individually. Australian semi-government authorities grouped into CBAs State by State in 1983 (the move had been recommended in the Campbell Report as being more efficient). In New South Wales all semi-government authorities are grouped under the CBA umbrella of the NSW Treasury Corporation; in others major borrowers such as electricity commissions remain independent. The change to centralised borrowings is based on the principle that big borrowers have more clout in competing for funds. It is also more economical for one large borrower to make approaches on behalf of several smaller entities than to have the small borrowers raising funds on their own, bearing the expenses of advertising and printing prospectuses and having to queue for market timeslots. *Abbrev.*: **CBA**.

Centrale de Livraison de Valeurs Mobilieres a computerised system for the delivery, settlement and safe custody of eurobonds and other securities. It was founded in 1970 by a group of international financial institutions and operates from Luxembourg. *Abbrev.*: **CEDEL**.

CEO *abbrev.* **chief executive officer.**

CER *abbrev.* **closer economic relations.**

certificate of deposit a negotiable bearer security issued by a bank or company as proof of debt. A CD is repayable at a fixed date. The paper trades at a discount from face value and bank CDs trade at rates similar to equivalent maturing bank-accepted bills of exchange. Federal government regulation used to restrict the minimum period for which a bank could raise funds through the issue of CDs; the minimum period was reduced from 30 days to fourteen days in March 1982 and completely freed of maturity controls on 1 August 1984. *Abbrev.*: **CD**.

certificates for automobile receivables Created by Salomon Brothers, these are pass-through securities issued by a trust against a pool of car loans. The certificates are bought and traded by institutions. *Abbrev.*: **CARs**.

certificates of accrual on treasury securities Created and sold by

Salomon Brothers, these zero-coupon securities are receipts written against US Treasury Bonds sold at a deep discount from face value, paying no interest during the life of the bonds and full face value on maturity. They are listed on the New York Stock Exchange and actively traded. *Abbrev.*: **CATS**. See **deep discount bonds, DINGOS, TIGR**.

certificates of amortising revolving debts   Created by the investment bank Salomon Brothers, these are pass-through securities issued by a trust that has acquired credit-card receivables. *Abbrev.*: **CARDs**.

certificates on government receipts   Banque Paribas' equivalent of Merrill Lynch's TIGRs and Salomon Brothers' CATS, these are securities representing future principal/coupon payments to be made on specified issues of US Treasury Bonds. *Abbrev.*: **COUGARs**.

certified practising accountant   a new membership level within the Australian Society of Accountants. It was announced in August 1983 and indicates a member of the society who has completed a minimum number of additional hours of study, above the society's entry requirements, and intends to continue to keep up to date on accounting developments. *Abbrev.*: **CPA**. See **Australian Society of Accountants**.

CFTC   *abbrev.* **Commodity Futures Trading Commission (US)**.

chain of title   the list or chain of ownership of a security or property throughout its life. On the back of a bill of exchange, it is shown by the list of endorsers who have bought and sold the bill (and who have a contingent liability through the bill until it matures). The chain of title to real estate is recorded in the series of conveyances between the various owners.

chalkie   one of a breed that will become extinct when electronic trading finally takes over the stock exchange. Chalkies mark the prices at which the listed stocks trade, with a piece of chalk on a board. Also **board boy**.

charge   a form of security, giving a creditor such as a bank, finance company or individual lender the right to receive payment from a specific fund or from the proceeds of the sale of a specific item of property or asset of a business, should a borrower default. If your bank has a charge over, say, your car, it may have the power to sell that car and recover its debt from the proceeds if you default on a repayment of a debt to the bank or on performance of any other obligation.

All charges are either fixed or floating charges. With a **fixed charge**, a lender or creditor has a charge over and claim to a particular asset of the borrower (debtor) as security for a debt. With a **floating charge** the creditor's charge or claim is not lodged over one particular asset of the borrower (debtor) but fixes on a specific asset or assets if the borrower defaults. This process of fixing on an asset or group of assets is called crystallisation of the charge. A floating charge leaves the debtor free to sell, buy and vary the assets subject to the charge until he or she defaults, at which time the floating charge crystallises and the lender can deal with any of the assets then existing. See **prior charge**.

chartists   in today's language, cartographers of the economy, interest rates, exchange rates and stock and commodity prices. (The word has nothing to do with the nineteenth-century economic and social reform movement, Chartism.) Chartists today rely on graphs and inhabit the opposite camp from the 'gut-feel' traders or the 'fundamentalists' who rely on economic theory. Chartists draw their maps carefully but sometimes are surprised by the peaks and valleys the real world can produce. See **fundamentalism**.

cheque   an unconditional order in writing to a bank by its customer, requesting the bank to pay a specific sum to a specified person— although a cheque made out to 'cash' or 'bearer' can be exchanged for cash by whoever hands it to the bank. A cheque becomes 'stale' if not negotiated within twelve months of being issued and may be rejected by a bank. (This period is to be extended to fifteen months under the proposed Cheques Act). See **cheque account, Cheques Bill**.

cheque account   a bank account which offers the depositor the facility of writing cheques which will be honoured by the bank if sufficient funds are in the depositor's account to cover the amount for which the cheque was written. Cheques were the first stage in the cashless society; plastic cards and electronic banking are further stages. Traders often demand identification from people paying by cheque, as cheques have been known to 'bounce'. Some banks, under certain conditions, pay interest on funds lodged in cheque accounts. These accounts are also known as current accounts. See **bank, bounce, current account, drawer**.

Cheques Bill   this legislation (still to become an Act at the time of writing, November 1984) has been devised to allow the law of cheques to develop separately from the law on bills of exchange (historically the two have been intertwined but the volume of cheques justifies separate legislation). The aims of the proposed Act are to speed up the processing of cheques, to provide a response to technological changes in the banking industry (though it will not regulate electronic funds transfer systems). Under the proposed Act, cheques will not become 'stale' until fifteen months after they have been issued; at present they become 'stale' after twelve months. See **cheque**.

Chicago Board of Trade   the largest commodity exchange in the world. The Chicago Board of Trade was established in 1848 and accounts for 51 per cent of the turnover in futures contracts in the US and the bulk of the world's grain futures trading. The CBT offers contracts in a variety of commodities, ranging from soyabeans to long-term US government bonds. *Abbrev.*: **CBT**.

Chicago Mercantile Exchange the second largest commodity exchange in the world. The Mercantile Exchange began life in the nineteenth century as the Chicago Butter and Egg Board, but the name was changed in 1919. Contracts are available in a wide range of commodities, such as live hogs, frozen pork bellies and frozen skinned hams. Through its division known as the International Monetary Market, the Chicago Mercantile Exchange trades currencies and financial instruments. *Abbrev.*: **CME**. See **International Monetary Market**.

Chicago School so-called after the University of Chicago, which has become associated with notable free-market economists such as Milton Friedman. Many of them would support the idea that inflation can be controlled by controlling the money supply, though disciples of the Chicago School are not necessarily all monetarists. They are sceptical of the benefits of regulation and government interference in the economy. See **libertarianism, Friedman Milton, quantity theory of money**.

chief executive officer a new title favoured by heads of companies. The chief executive officer might be the managing director or even the chairman of the board; he or she is the person responsible for running the company according to board policies. *Abbrev.*: **CEO**.

Chinese walls in financial institutions, the ethical dividing wall between different divisions of a bank or investment bank to avoid conflict of interest. The origin is from the walls built around Chinese courtyards which were staggered so that there was no straight line of entry. In Chinese mythology evil spirits could travel only in straight lines, so the Chinese wall protected the occupier from any unwelcome intrusion. A 'Chinese wall' is said to exist between the corporate advisory area and the broking division, to separate those giving corporate advice on takeovers from those advising clients about buying shares. The walls are thrown up to prevent the leaks of inside information which could influence the advice given to clients and could allow staff to take advantage of facts that are not yet known to the general public. Recent Wall Street and City of London scandals have made something of a mockery of the notion of Chinese walls, with well-placed executives of respectable firms trading illegally on inside information for their own benefit.

CHIPS *abbrev.* **clearing house interbank payments system**.

churning This term indicates a massive amount of trading, often for trading's sake or to push up prices. This is good for the brokers involved as clients have to pay the commission costs regardless of the level of profit, or loss, made on the trades.

CIF *abbrev.* **cost, insurance, freight**. Also **cif**.

claim   a right, evidence of something due, title to something such as an asset or sum of money. In law, a claim is an assertion (by a claimant) that he or she has a right to some legal remedy. The word now has a number of derived meanings similar to 'title' or 'security'.

class   Put and call options based on the same underlying contracts or shares are termed as being in the same class, for example options on the December 1987 bank bill contract.

classical economics   The foundations of classical economic theory were laid by economists in the late eighteenth century, led by Adam Smith. Their ideas were further developed by Malthus, Ricardo and Mill (and by neo-classical economists in the US) and are at present enjoying a revival in macroeconomics and in a quite different manner among 'post-Keynesians' at Cambridge and elsewhere. Classical economics focuses mainly on the long-term dynamics of growth and development. The key contribution to this line of thought was the idea of a physical surplus of output over inputs. This made distribution the central theme: who gets what and why. Most thinkers believed in the 'invisible hand', in minimum government interference. Their theory of value stressed the supply side—the cost of production—rather than the role of consumers' demand. Classical economics also provided important foundations for Marxian economics. It is easy to play a game by arguing that none of the so-called classical economists were really classicals, according to any textbook definition. See **Cambridge School, Keynes, John Maynard** in **economists, neo-classical economics**.

clean float   see **float**.

clear   To 'clear' a cheque means to process a cheque through the clearing system so that the person in whose favour the cheque was drawn (the payee) receives value for the cheque. See **clearing, clearing bank, clearing house**.

clearing   in banking, the mutual exchange of debits and credits by banks. Clearing houses in capital cities and major regional centres operate during the day and well after the close of banking, sorting and clearing the day's cheques drawn on the various banks. 'Cleared' funds are those cheques which have been processed through the clearing house. Today's cleared funds are tomorrow's exchange settlement money. In futures, clearing services on contracts are provided by a clearing house, which in Sydney is the International Commodities Clearing House. See **clearing house, exchange settlement account, International Commodities Clearing House, uncleared funds**.

clearing bank   Usually a bank which is a direct member of the clearing house, i.e. clears its own paper and sometimes also paper on behalf of other banks. In Australia, the major trading banks, the Reserve Bank of Australia, the Australian Bank, Banque Nationale de Paris, Bank of

New Zealand and the various State banks are clearing house members.

clearing house   in Australian banking, the institution in each capital city through which banks in the State exchange cheques drawn on them; in futures trading, the central body guaranteeing all futures contracts. Floor members of the Sydney Futures Exchange are members of the clearing house, which has a separate identity from the Futures Exchange. The clearing house maintains a continuous record of futures market trading. Clearing house services are provided for the Sydney Futures Exchange by the International Commodities Clearing House. See **International Commodities Clearing House**.

clearing house interbank payments system   New York's electronic system for making payments between banks which are members of the system, associate member banks and account holders of those banks. It is the formal name for the US equivalent of the Australian banks' clearing system. *Abbrev.*: **CHIPS**.

CLM   *abbrev.* **career-limiting move**.

closed economy   a theoretical concept describing a country which does not trade with the rest of the world.

closed shop   a business or industry in which employees must be members of particular trade unions; employers can hire only union members. Closed shops are promoted by unions to protect employment opportunities for their members and to guard against dilution of working conditions.

close out   in futures and foreign exchange trading, to liquidate a position or fulfil an obligation by taking an equal and opposite position. For example, a trader who has contracted to buy a futures contract would close out, or get out that contract, by taking out a contract to sell.

Closer Economic Relations   the agreement signed in December 1982, between Australia and New Zealand, under which the two countries are to become a full free-trade area. *Abbrev.*: **CER**.

CME   *abbrev.* **Chicago Mercantile Exchange**.

CMO   *abbrev.* **collaterised mortgage obligation**.

codicil   a document made subsequent to a will or deed, changing certain conditions or terms contained in the original.

cofinancing   the term used to describe cooperation in lending between lending agencies such as the World Bank or the Asian Development Bank and commercial lenders such as trading or development banks. The lending agencies cannot always provide sufficient funds to meet the needs of developing economies and funds are supplemented by loans from additional sources.

collar   A collar sets a ceiling and a floor on rates, that is it provides for a maximum and a minimum interest rate. The maximum, or ceiling, works like a cap; the minimum sets a floor so that if the market rate falls below a stipulated level the buyer of the collar reimburses the seller for the difference between the market and the agreed rate. Collars are cheaper than caps because the seller has the chance to benefit if interest rates fall below the minimum agreed to under the collar. See **cap, floor**.

collateral   property or assets made available by a borrower as security against a loan. In Australia, the word means additional security, perhaps an asset of someone other than the debtor. A comedian once boasted of an uncle who was so untrustworthy that when he paid cash the family had to put up collateral. More commonly, you might pledge your boat as additional security against a mortgage on a holiday home. In the US, 'collateral' is simply an alternative word for 'security'.

collateralised mortgage obligation   mortgage-backed securities issued in the US since 1983. The mortgage cash flows are segmented into categories with short-, medium- and long-tern mortgage collateralised bonds, ranging from five to 30 years. *Abrev.*: **CMO**.

collectables   investments of a genteel sort, such as paintings, artefacts, coins and antiques which are expected to increase in value.

collusion   conspiratorial agreement between parties, usually to the disadvantage of others.

COLTS   *abbrev.* **continuously offered long-term securities**.

combination   a futures market strategy that involves buying and selling the same number of put and call options, though not at the same strike price. It is similar to a spread. Also called a strangle. See **spread**.

Comecon   *abbrev.* **Council for Mutual Economic Assistance**.

Comex   *abbrev.* **Commodity Exchange of New York**.

commercial bill   a non-bank bill of exchange (loan) generated by merchant banks and companies. The bill is evidence of the borrower's debt and commitment to repay at the due date. These bills are covered by the *Bills of Exchange Act* 1909–1973, as are bank bills, but they are called 'commercial' to indicate they are issued by non-bank institutions. See **bill of exchange, paper**.

commercial paper   the technical term used in the US to describe domestic short-term promissory notes issued as evidence of debt. The issuer/seller/borrower raises the funds for a fairly short period (one to six months) though most likely under a term facility with periodic rollovers. Funds raised this way are usually used for working capital and liquidity. In Australia promissory notes, commercial bills and non-bank certificates of deposit are types of commercial paper. See **euro-commercial paper**.

commitment fee   a charge made by a bank or merchant bank when loan facilities are established for a borrower.

Committee for Economic Development of Australia   an independent organisation which provides an open forum for discussion and exchange of ideas on the Australian economy. It was established in 1960 by a group of businessmen and academics, led by Sir Douglas Copland. The organisation now has more than 500 members throughout Australia, representing a cross-section of the business and academic communities, and has links with similar organisations overseas. The aims of the committee concentrate on starting objective research into issues concerning national economic development and fostering public debate and understanding of economic policy. *Abbrev.*: **CEDA**.

Committee of Economic Inquiry   see **Vernon Report**.

commodity   any physical item produced for trade. In futures trading, commodities usually fall into a number of categories, such as wool, grain, other agricultural products and precious metals such as gold and silver.

Commodity Exchange of New York   the third largest commodity exchange in the world, founded in 1933. It is mainly a metals exchange, best known for gold and silver futures trading. *Abbrev.*: **Comex**.

Commodity Futures Trading Commission (US)   a federal agency formed in 1975 to regulate commodity trading in the US. *Abbrev.*: **CFTC**.

common agricultural policy   An agreement adopted by the European Economic Community to maintain agricultural prices and therefore farmers' income. *Abbrev.*: **CAP**.

Commonwealth bond   a security issued by the commonwealth government, as borrower, in return for cash from the general public and companies, who invest their funds with the government for a given period (the life of the bond) in return for interest paid by the government. Commonwealth bonds are sold through periodic tenders. Australian Savings Bonds are a type of Commonwealth bond. Also **Treasury Bond**. See **Australian Savings Bond, bond, tender**.

communism   Ideally, a socioeconomic system in which the means of production, distribution and exchange are under common ownership. In practice, political and economic control remain in the hands of a ruling ideological elite, usually the Communist Party. Neither of the major communist governments—the Soviet Union and the People's Republic of China—claims to have achieved pure communism, which would require the abolition of wages and money. Many would argue, including people living in non-capitalist economies, that such a goal is a will-o'-the-wisp. Certainly, Marx did not provide a blueprint of how such an economy could be organised and run; to him it was more an ideal than simply something that would follow a revolution.

Companies Act   an Act of Commonwealth Parliament which provides for the incorporation of companies, regulates the raising of funds through share or debenture issues, or trusts, sets out the framework in which companies may lawfully operate and lays down ground rules for the protection of investors, creditors and shareholders. The *Commonwealth Act* is strictly applicable only in the ACT, but through legislation in the States, the provisions of the *Companies Act* apply as law in the States, where they are known as the Companies Code. The 1981 *Companies Act* replaced previous legislation; the law relating to companies had been made more or less uniform throughout Australian in the *Uniform Companies Act* passed by the States in 1961-62. See **Companies Code, Corporate Affairs Commission, National Companies and Securities Commission**.

Companies Code   This refers to the laws regulating companies at State level. The code derives from the provisions of the *Companies Act*, which are applied to the States by State legislation. The Companies Code is effectively the State version of the *Companies Act*. The Act and codes are administered by the National Companies and Securities Commission; in the States and the ACT they are largely administered by the Corporate Affairs Commissions or offices under delegation. See **Companies Act, Corporate Affairs Commission, National Companies and Securities Commission**.

company   Any two people can form a private company for lawful reasons. The formation of a public company requires five people. Companies can be in a variety of forms:

* a **company limited by shares** is the most common type, in which the shareholders' liabilities are limited to the amount of the unpaid shares;
* a **company limited by guarantee** is generally used for clubs in which members' liability is limited by the company's memorandum of association to an amount that has to be contributed should the company be wound up;
* a **company limited by shares and by guarantee** imposes a double liability on the shareholders, as they must contribute the value of the unpaid shares as well as whatever amount is specified in the memorandum of association should the company fold;
* an **unlimited company** is an incorporated partnership in which the members are not limited in their liabilities;

- a **no-liability company** is one in which shareholders are not bound to pay calls on their shares. This construction is restricted to mining companies. See **no liability**.
- a **proprietary limited company (private company)** is limited to no more than 50 members and operates with restricted right of transfer of shares. A proprietary limited (Pty Ltd or P/L) company can neither invite the general public to subscribe for its shares nor take deposits from the public.

company doctor   a colloquialism for a management expert or consultant engaged to diagnose the problems of an ailing company and treat them by prescribing policy changes and corporate reorganisation. It also means a medical practitioner employed in some businesses to dispense aspirin, sticking plaster and sick-leave authorisations.

company tax   a tax levied on the income of companies, separately from the income of its shareholders. Company tax has been levied since the 1976/77 financial year at a flat rate of 46 cents in the dollar. It has been collected in quarterly instalments since 1978/79.

company town   a one-industry town in which the main employer controls secondary activity and infrastructure such as housing, power and water supply, roads and other services. The industry may also own or subsidise small businesses in the town.

compound interest   interest paid on accumulated interest as well as on the capital invested. For example, $100 invested for one year at 10 per cent per annum would yield $10 in its first year and at the end of the second year would pay 10 per cent on $110 (being the original $100 plus the $10 earned in the first year). The second year's interest would thus be $11, which would be added to $110 when calculating the third year's interest entitlement. Under simple interest, 10 per cent would be earned each year on the capital invested, i.e. the original $100 would yield $10 for each year it was invested. See **flat rate of interest, simple interest**.

Comptroller of the Currency   a US federal office established in 1863 to monitor the regulation of commercial banks.

computer-assisted trading system   the trading system used in the US, Canada and Europe, similar to the Australian Stock Exchange's automated trading system. *Abbrev.*: **CATS**. See **stock exchange automated trading system**.

Conciliation and Arbitration Commission   see **Australian Conciliation and Arbitration Commission**.

confirming house   a financial institution which acts as an intermediary between overseas traders and local importers and exporters. A confirming house is mainly engaged in financing the movement of goods into the country by offering short-term credit to importers and guaranteeing, or confirming, payment to the suppliers.

conglomerate   a merging of a number of businesses into one large, multi-purpose organisation which (ideally) operates more efficiently.

consolidated accounts   financial statements representing the combined position of a group of companies, i.e. parent and subsidiary companies. Also **group accounts**.

consolidated profit   the profit of a group of companies, parent and subsidiaries.

consortium   *plural* **consortia**   a group of organisations, sharing the same goals, which combine their resources and risks. Consortium banking was popular in the late 1970s, when a number of major banks would combine to form a merchant banking or financing offshoot. Many of Australia's merchant banks were formed as consortia with European, Asian and US banks joining forces with Australian banks.

consumer credit   loans made available to individuals, generally through hire purchase (now called consumer credit), personal loans or credit cards.

consumer demand   the demand or desire of individuals to buy goods and services. Consumer spending constitutes the realisation (usually only partial) of such demands. Economists suggest that consumer demand depends on such factors as income, wealth, interest rates, expectations about prices and confidence generally about the future.

consumer price index   a measurement, taken four times a year (in the December, March, June and September quarters), of movements in the prices of a fixed list of goods and services. About 80 000 prices are regularly collected for each quarter's result. The CPI is used as a guide in adjusting award wages and other costs that are linked to the inflation rate. The CPI was established in 1960, replacing the previous Retail Price Indices. *Abbrev.*: **CPI**. See **Index**.

contango   a futures market expression to describe a situation in which the spot (immediate) prices are lower than those for transactions in the forward (future) months. See the opposite, **backwardation**.

contingent liability   a potential expense which may or may not eventuate, depending on how future events turn out, but which should be provided for in properly kept accounts or budgets. Examples of a company's contingent liabilities might include damages from a pending law suit against the company; guarantees given to secure another company's borrowings; or having the company's name on the back of a bill of exchange as endorser, when the bill has yet to mature.

continuously offered long-term securities   a debt instrument first issued by the World Bank in 1986. These are fixed-rate securities with maturities between three and 30 years and are the World Bank's version of medium-term note. *Abbrev.*: **COLTS**.

contract   a legally enforceable agreement between individuals or entities. In real estate, an exchange of contracts accompanied by payment of the deposit is a binding commitment to buy and sell. An employment contract guarantees remuneration, conditions and length of service. In futures markets, a contract is the unit of a commodity traded on the futures exchange, for example a bank bill futures contract is $A500 000 face value of bank bills of exchange. The contract is a bilateral agreement between buyer and seller, defined in the information brochures of the Sydney Futures Exchange as a 'standardised agreement to buy or sell commodities or securities at a date in the future, at a price agreed on today'. See **futures**, **hedge market**.

contract note   confirmation sent from broker to client detailing the purchase or sale of shares carried out on the client's behalf.

contractual savings   see **forced savings**.

contributing shares   shares on which only part of the capital amount and any premium due has been paid. The outstanding amounts are payable at a time chosen by the company issuing the shares. Also **partly paid shares**.

controlled adjustable rate preferred stock   a US term to describe a preferred stock (preference share) whose dividend is adjusted from time to time to bring it into line with the current rate on US Treasuries, plus a premium. *Abbrev.*: **CARPS**.

controlling interest   a stake of sufficient size to allow the holder to control the company, though this would also depend on the spread of existing shareholders. A controlling interest can represent less than 50 per cent of the company's capital, depending on the spread of share holdings, but is generally thought of as being 50 per cent or more.

convention   a residential gathering of people with similar interests, ostensibly to discuss matters of mutual professional importance, and often associated with travel, expense accounts and country motels with good golf courses.

convertible currency   a currency that is readily exchanged for another, or for gold. Major currencies such as the $US, sterling and the deutschmark are easily converted. Minor, less stable, currencies may be under strict exchange control by their countries' governments and therefore difficult or impossible to buy and sell; they are unattractive investments, not in demand, usually associated with countries with a high inflation rate and high interest rates. See **hard currency**, **soft currency**.

convertible note a fixed-interest security issued to a lender by a company in return for cash. It differs from a debenture in that it offers the investor the option of converting the loan at a later date into equity (shares) in the issuing (borrowing) company.

convertible redeemable preference shares a relatively new and still rare stock exchange animal. These shares have a specific date at which they are redeemable (i.e. exchanged for cash by the issuing company). They are broadly similar to convertible notes, in that they may be converted to ordinary shares, though the holders of convertible redeemable preference shares rank after noteholders should the issuing company be wound up. See **convertible notes, redeemable preference shares.**

cooperative once described as an organisation of individuals who had combined for mutual benefit, such as bulk buying or selling. The term has taken on a more formal definition in the commercial world, and cooperative societies are governed by legislation and regulation. See **building societies, credit union, friendly society.**

Copland, Douglas see **economists.**

cornering the market buying so much of a commodity or share that a degree of control over its price is achieved.

corporate an adjective—as in 'corporate client'—that has become popularly used as a noun, for example 'corporates' to indicate clients or customers who are companies as against private individuals. The dictionary defines corporate as 'belonging to a united body'. The word comes from the Latin *corpus* meaning 'body'.

Corporate Affairs Commission The Corporate Affairs Commission (or equivalent office) in each State or Territory is responsible for the regulation of the cooperative companies and securities legislation in that State or Territory, as delegate of the National Companies and Securities Commission. CACs first emerged in the early 1970s; they operate as State government agencies, monitoring the activities of the stock exchange, the securities industry and a range of financial institutions; they incorporate companies and administer the provisions of the Companies Code. The CACs supervise companies and trusts which raise funds from the public and ensure that they observe the provisions of the legislation. In New South Wales, the CAC's activities include the supervision of the futures market under the *Futures Market Act* 1979, and the administration of the *Business Names Act* 1979. The CACs also aim to provide relevant information to the public, and detect and prosecute offences against legislation which falls within their field of responsiblity. National policy formation rests with the National Companies and Securities Commission, and the CACs function as its delegate in the States or Territories. *Abbrev.*: **CAC**. See **Companies Act, Companies Code, National Companies and Securities Commission.**

corporate menopause   general disenchantment with corporate life. See **burn-out.**

corporate raider   a takeover merchant; someone who trades in companies rather than in the products of the companies, making a profit on undervalued shares or assets which may be bought at a relatively low price but fetch more when sold later.

corporate strategy   a high-sounding label for thinking up ways for a company to conduct its business and make more money.

corporation   an association of individuals recognised under law as collectively having an existence and rights and obligations separate from each of them individually. As a whole, the individuals form a legal entity—the corporation. See **incorporated, incorporation.**

correction   a movement that reverses a previous trend in prices, usually taking them lower after a period of sustained increase. Corrections occur in the prices of shares, bonds, commodities and futures contracts. When world stock markets crashed in October 1987, after what had been an unusually prolonged rise, some analysts and commentators sought a euphemism such as 'a major correction' as an alternative to more colourful descriptions such as 'the bottom's fallen out of the market'. See **technical correction.**

correspondent bank   a bank which acts as point of contact for another in a country or State where the latter does not have a branch or agency. Each party maintains accounts with the other, in nostro and vostro (ours and yours) accounts. See **nostro account, vostro account.**

corset   a set of restrictions placed on UK banks in 1973 to control the growth of some forms of interest-bearing sterling and foreign currency deposits. The corset was resented by the banks because it steered business towards other financial institutions. When the corset was removed in 1981 the UK money supply waistline expanded alarmingly.

cost-benefit analysis   evaluation of the pros and cons of a course of action. Is it worth spending or doing X to gain or achieve Y? It is impossible, of course, to put a dollar value on all costs and benefits.

cost-cutting   trying to improve business performance by using cheaper methods of production, for example retrenching some workers. It may require shedding of less productive activities, such as counting paperclips. It can be instructive to assess and evaluate which products or services in your operation are generating cash.

cost, insurance, freight   the full cost of imports, not merely the price of goods once landed. The term is used to describe the charge where the purchaser (importer) pays the supplier a single price for delivered goods. *Abbrev.*: **CIF, cif**. See **free on board**.

cost-plus pricing   working out a price ticket for a manufactured item which takes account of the fixed and variable expenses of production and puts a bit of profit on top.

cost-push inflation   see **inflation**.

COUGARs   *abbrev.* **certificates on government receipts**.

Council for Mutual Economic Assistance   a non-voluntary association of communist countries which trade with each other, often by exchanging commodities instead of buying and selling. Comecon countries include East European communist countries, Vietnam and Cuba. The Soviet Union has presided since the council was set up in 1949. *Abbrev.*: **Comecon**.

counterparty risk   the credit and performance risk in any financial transaction, such as a foreign exchange contract or a swap. It is the risk that the party on the other side of the transaction might not meet its obligations.

countersignature   an additional signature on a document to guarantee its authenticity. As a precaution against error or fraud, it shows that the document has been scrutinised by another person.

countertrade   a generic term used to describe any form of international trade that has an element of reciprocity. The US Department of Commerce has defined a countertrade transaction as 'one in which a seller provides a buyer with deliveries and contractually agrees to purchase goods from the buyer equal to an agreed percentage of the original sales contract value'. Countertrade involves a bilateral agreement between two countries, one a seller, one a buyer, to exchange a specific amount of goods with no exchange of money. **See barter**.

coupon   the voucher attached to bonds, exchangeable for cash when the interest payments are due (usually half-yearly). The voucher represents the annual rate of interest promised to the bondholder. A 16 per cent coupon entitles the holder to receive $16 a year for each $100 invested, for the life of the bond, paid in two half-yearly instalments.

cover note   a temporary document. In insurance, a cover note is issued to an applicant, usually for a month, to cover the risk until an official insurance policy document can be prepared and delivered, and the appropriate premium paid to the insurance company.

CPA   *abbrev.* **certified practising accountant**.

Crawford Report   the report of the committee chaired by Sir John

Crawford, set up to investigate the possibilities of long-term structural readjustment of the Australian economy. The 1973 report called for a long-term commitment to the reduction of tariff levels. In the same year a 25 per cent across-the-board tariff cut was implemented which was. criticised by many commentators as being too unselective in its impact. The Industries Assistance Commission was asked to prepare yet another report and, more than a decade later, the debate still continues.

crawling peg   see **exchange rate**.

credit   the power to buy without money on condition that you pay later. Those who use credit benefit from the immediate possession of the things they desire; those who give credit benefit usually by charging interest on the deferred payments. Credit means 'money' in terms like 'credit squeeze'. In accounting, if your bank account is 'in credit' you have cash in the account; credit is the opposite of debit. See **credit squeeze, debit, double-entry bookkeeping, hire purchase**.

credit card   Also known as plastic money, this is an increasingly popular facility enabling people to buy goods and services without having to handle cash. Bills for the amounts spent are presented periodically (usually monthly) by the credit card company for payment in full or on extended, interest-bearing terms, with a minimum payment required monthly. See **debit card**.

credit foncier   a type of loan, structured with regular (usually monthly) repayments which incorporate principal and interest. Most mortgages operate this way. The term derives from the French *foncier*, meaning 'of the land', and the French institution called Credit Foncier de France dates back to 1852, when it was established to provide house and land purchasers with low-cost mortgage finance. See **amortisation, mortgage**.

credit limit   the maximum debt a customer is allowed to run up under a borrowing facility such as a line of credit, overdraft or credit card. Borrowers and lenders in money and foreign exchange markets operate under credit limits which set ceilings on activities between individual companies.

credit rating   a measurement of the creditworthiness of an individual or business. The rating is based on the opinions of banks and other financial institutions, plus investigations of financial stability and credit history. The computer age has seen the development of 'banks' of such information which can provide instant references. See **Australian Ratings Pty Ltd, Dun and Bradstreet, Moody's Investor Services, Standard & Poor's**.

credit reference bureau   one of the information 'banks' which compile records of the credit performance of individuals and businesses, and provide the information to potential lenders. See **credit rating**.

credit squeeze   the outcome of government monetary policy to restrict the expansion of credit; a credit squeeze makes it tougher and more expensive to borrow money. Credit squeezes are intended to reduce aggregate demand by making credit (money) scarce and dear. Australia had severe credit squeezes in 1961 and 1974. Trading banks were asked to reduce lending, savings banks made less money available for housing and interest rates rose sharply.

creditor   someone to whom money is owed. A secured creditor is someone who holds a security over an asset of the person or company owing him or her money and usually can realise (sell) the asset to recover the debt without having to bankrupt the debtor or (in the case of a company) put it into liquidation. See **debtor**.

creditors' scheme   see **scheme of arrangement**.

credit union   A cooperative, a credit union is one of a number of varieties of non-bank financial institutions which accept deposits from, and provide loans to, their customers (members). Credit unions evolved on the basis of a common bond among members, through employment or community interests; they offer funds for housing and provide consumer finance loans for purchases of items such as cars or boats. Credit unions have been a rapidly growing sector of Australia's financial markets; they made inroads into EFT (electronic funds transfer) years ahead of the banks and have traditionally promoted an image of flexible hours and service to customers through financial packages aimed at maximising convenience in money management. See **building societies, friendly society**.

crossed cheque   a cheque across which have been drawn two parallel, diagonal lines with the words 'not negotiable' written between them. A crossed cheque must be paid into a bank account and cannot be cashed over the counter.

cross-currency swap   a swap that involves the exchange of obligations for both the principal sums and the interest streams. (Interest rate swaps involve no exchange of principal, only of interest streams.)

cross-elasticity (of demand)   the impact on the demand for, say, cream if the price of milk rises. It helps determine whether goods are (economically speaking) in the same market or not.

crossing   the situation where a broker acts on both sides of the transaction, as agent for the buyer and the seller of the same line of shares or futures contracts. Also **crossed trade, marriage**.

cross-rates   These are calculated by using the rates of two currencies against a third currency (usually the $US) to arrive at the relationship of the two currencies to each other. For example, if one $US were equal to 1.6 deutschmarks and one $US were equal to 132 yen, then one deutschmark would be equal to 79.51 yen. A typical cross-rates table would read as follows.

	$US	deutschmark	yen
$US	1	1.6620	132.00
deutschmark	0.6020	1	79.51
yen '000	7.5672	12.5766	1

rates as at November 1987

cross-subsidisation   funding the loss or low return from one line of goods or services by raising the price of another. For example a bank or other lending institution might charge a less than economic rate on certain loans or services and compensate by charging a more than economic rate on other loans or services. The practice occurs less frequently in today's deregulated financial markets. See **unbundled**.

crowding out   This is said to occur when a government, to finance a budget deficit, borrows much of the available cash, forcing interest rates higher and squeezing out private sector borrowers. Its effect would then depend on the demand for funds and the readiness of the private sector to compete for cash. Keynesians deny that the concept exists. See **deficit spending**.

cum dividend   a label for shares, which when sold, carry an entitlement for the purchaser to receive a dividend due on an appointed day. When the seller picks up the dividend before selling, or retains the right to the dividend, the shares are 'ex-dividend'. 'Cum' is Latin for 'with'.

cum interest   Similarly, this describes securities traded with the right to the next interest payment.

cum rights   Shares which are quoted 'cum rights' are those whose price includes the right to a new issue. See **ex-rights**.

cumulative (shares)   usually   preferred   shares   whose   holders accumulate or accrue dividend entitlements in years when the dividend is not paid by the company that issued the shares.

currency basket   a combination of different currencies to produce a single index or unit of value, such as the European currency unit. The composition and weighting of a basket depend on the purposes for which it was established. The $A was pegged to a basket of currencies until it was floated in December 1983. The basket was compiled of the currencies of Australia's major trading partners, weighted according to their significance in trade flows. Also **basket of currencies**. See **basket**, **European currency unit**.

currency cocktail   a borrowing made up of a variety of currencies, to minimise exchange rate risk.

currency swap   see **swaps**.

current account   a running account with a person or business. In banking, a current account (from which balances are withdrawable on demand) is the same as a cheque account. In external trade, the current account is a record of a country's receipts and payments for imports and exports, traded services (such as shipping, banking and tourism) and remittances from abroad. See **balance of payments, cheque account**.

current cost accounting   an alternative method to historical cost accounting; a system of valuing assets based on their replacement cost rather than their cost when purchased or produced. Charges to the profit and loss account, for inventories sold and depreciation, are based on the value of assets to the business at the date they are used. Balance sheet values of non-monetary assets are stated at their value to the business at balance sheet date. Adjustments are required to depreciation, cost of sales, working capital and gearing, and are reflected in the balance sheet as a current cost reserve. The current cost accounting method is used in the UK but as yet is not used by most companies in Australia. The Standard Accounting Practice One issued in 1983 strongly recommended that all businesses in Australia report current cost information as supplementary details. *Abbrev.* **CCA**: See **accounting standard, historical cost accounting, inflation accounting**.

current liabilities   accounting language for financial obligations which must be met within the normal operating cycle for a business. Generally it is assumed that the operating cycle is no longer than twelve months—and is defined as such in the Companies Code.

current ratio   a measure of liquidity. It measures the proportion of current assets available to offset current liabilities. The current ratio is calculated by dividing current assets by current liabilities. Also **working capital ratio**. See **liquid ratio**.

customs (duty)   federal government duty levied on imports to Australia. Customs and excise were significant sources of tax revenue in the early twentieth century but have since declined in importance. They are classified broadly as indirect taxes. The federal government in Australia took control of customs and excise at Federation (1901). See **excise**.

cyclical deficit   see **deficit**.

D

daily adjustable tax-exempt securities   a type of US municipal bond, designed by the investment bank Salomon Brothers, on which interest is calculated daily and distributed monthly, based on an index of 30-day tax-exempt commercial paper. *Abbrev.*: **DATES**.

daisy chain   a form of rigging the market. A group of traders would actively buy, giving an impression of active and healthy demand, which would attract genuine investors. Once the unwary have been drawn in, the riggers sell, making a gain and leaving the investors with no genuine buyers, and a collapsed market. See **rigged market**.

data   This has two meanings:
- the set of relevant facts;
- numerical facts (statistics).

In the latter sense it has been used for some time; now it has come to mean what you know about anything, a piece of information. It has become common jargon since the popularisation of mathematics and particularly since the advent of computerspeak. Before the microchip people simply knew facts; now they compile data, talk grandly of a 'data base'. Sources of economic data are the monthly *Reserve Bank Bulletin*, the daily *Australian Financial Review*, the regular Treasury round-up. Those eager to be overwhelmed by data can subscribe to the Australian Bureau of Statistics.

DATES   *abbrev.* **daily adjustable tax exempt securities**.

dawn raid   a swift and unexpected assault on the share market, usually buying a large parcel of a company's shares at above-market prices. The speed of the raid leaves the small shareholders little time to take advantage of the higher prices and sell their shares. Also **premium raid**.

daylight overdraft   a facility which allows you to spend more than you have in your bank account during the day, provided that the account is in credit at the end of the day. The authorised money market dealers in Australia have 'daylight' overdraft facilities with the Reserve Bank so that their trading runs smoothly; they are able to draw cheques to pay for securities or make repayments before recalled deposits have reached their Reserve Bank accounts.

days of grace   a reasonable number of days allowed after a debt or other arrangement falls due to give the benefit of the doubt to late payers. Insurance policies usually stipulate a 'days of grace' period so that late payment of premiums will not necessarily invalidate the insurance contract.

daytrading   buying into and selling out of the market within one day for profit (though it could involve a loss); avoiding holding an overnight position. Similar to jobbing in Australian futures trading. Also **daylight trading, jobbing the market**. See **jobber**.

DCM   *abbrev.* Don't come Monday. Fired.

dealership   a small group of banks or investment banks which sells securities such as US commercial paper or euro-commercial paper on behalf of the issuer (borrower). The dealership group does not underwrite the issue—which saves fees for the borrower—but undertakes to sell the paper to investors who plan to hold rather than trade it. Banks and investment banks tend to enter dealership arrangements only when they are confident of demand for the paper being issued.

dealing desk   see **desk**.

death duties   an unpopular tax which has now been almost entirely abolished in Australia at federal and State levels. Death duties were introduced in Australia in the 1850s as a tax on inheritances. So many ways developed of avoiding the tax (such as distributing wealth and property before death) that little revenue was being raised from this source. Death and estate duties attracted criticism because they unfairly penalised many people who inherited only small amounts of money. There is now some pressure to restore these taxes. Those who argue for a consumption tax (VAT) support death duties because an expenditure or consumption tax excludes savings and these could be taxed through death duties. Also **estate duties**.

debenture   a type of fixed-interest security, issued by companies (as borrowers) in return for medium- and long-term investment of funds. Debentures are issued to the general public through a prospectus and are secured by a trust deed which spells out the terms and conditions of the fundraising and the rights of the debenture holders. Typical issuers of debentures are finance companies and large industrial companies. Debenture holders' funds are invested with the borrowing company as secured loans, with the security usually in the form of a fixed or floating charge over the assets of the borrowing company. As secured lenders, debenture holders' claims to the company's assets rank ahead of those of ordinary shareholders, should the company be wound up; also, interest is payable on debentures whether the company makes a profit or not. Debentures are issued for fixed periods but if a debenture holder wants to get his or her money back the securities can be sold through a stockbroker. The word 'debenture' derives from the Latin *debeo* meaning 'I owe' as does 'debt'; the debenture is evidence of the borrowing company's debt to the lender.

debit   a bookkeeping and accounting term, indicating an entry made in the left-hand column of the ledger. Debit is the opposite of credit. In common use the phrase 'debit my account' is an instruction to charge a sum of money against the account. See **double-entry bookkeeping**.

debit card   a plastic card which can be used for purchases provided that there is money in the account against which the card is used. It is different from a credit card (though they can be similar in appearance): a credit card allows individuals and companies to incur a debt to be paid later; debit cards dispense with the need to carry cash—you can charge purchases against a nominated account. See **credit card, electronic funds transfer at point of sale**.

debt   an obligation by one individual or company to pay a specific amount of money to another party.

debtor   someone who owes money to someone else, who is thus a creditor. See **creditor**.

debt-to-equity ratio   a measure of a company's gearing (borrowing) which is calculated by dividing all financial debt by shareholders' funds (equity).

debt warrant   See **warrant**.

Dec (pronounced 'deck', 'deece' in the US)   futures market shorthand for December, as in 'I'll buy six decs at 85.00'. See **Sep**.

deed   a document which has been signed, sealed and delivered, proving or testifying the agreement of the signatories to its contents. Legal requirements still remain for particular documents to be deeds executed in this formal way before they are effective, for example conveyances of land (transfers under the *Real Property Act* are not executed as deeds but are deemed by the Act to have the same effect).

deep discount bonds   These bonds earn little interest because of their low coupons and they are sold at a large (deep) discount from face value. They are good for investors keen to fix their return over the life of the bond. An investor buys deep discount bonds at substantially less than face value and receives the capital gain on the investment when the bonds mature. If such bonds were acquired before 30 June 1982, the gain thus received is not liable to tax in the case of the ordinary individual (as against finance professionals). The change in the law at that time reflects the view of the Taxation Commissioner that the discount amount repaid to the investor on maturity of the bonds is assessable income for tax purposes. The advantage for the borrower issuing deep discount bonds is the lower rate of interest to be paid during the life of the bond (i.e. lower borrowing costs). Zero coupon bonds are the ultimate example of deep discount bonds. See **coupon, zero coupon bonds**.

de-escalate   careless jargon commonly understood to mean to move downward (of prices, rates or other statistics). Purists complain that escalators, of course, move both up and down.

defalcation   a grand legal term meaning misappropriation of money, usually applied to the misappropriation of funds held in trust.

default   failure to do what was legally or morally required, usually referring to the failure to pay a debt that has fallen due. Since anything is better for a lender than not being paid at all, banks which have advanced loans to organisations, or even countries, facing liquidity difficulties may avert default by reorganising the loans over longer terms. See **rescheduling**.

defeasance   a legal term that means to render an existing deed null and void, or to 'defease' that deed. It has been adopted in the finance world to describe the process of a borrowing company paying an amount (usually less than the existing obligation) to a third party, and in return the third party undertakes to repay obligations under the original borrowing as and when they fall due. For example, a bank could assume liability for the interest and principal owed by a borrowing company to debenture holders, in lieu of the company which earlier issued the debentures. Auditors will allow the company's debt to be 'defeased' or extinguished for reporting purposes provided that the preconditions specified in the US Accounting Standard SFAS No. 76 have been met. These preconditions require that monetary assets, which are essentially risk-free as to amount, timing and collection of principal and interest, be held irrevocably to satisfy the payments schedule of the original borrowing. The original borrower should face no more than a remote possibility of having to make future payments on that debt, even though the original debt obligation remains. Broadly, the aim of the company defeasing its debt is to achieve more efficient financial arrangements and a less debt-encumbered balance sheet. The process is also called **liability assumption**.

defensive strategy   see **matched book**.

deferred annuity   a type of annuity that pays an income starting from a future age or date. If the person who received a lump-sum payment is to continue to gain tax relief the deferred annuity must start paying a pension not later than the person's 65th birthday. Deferred annuities can only accept eligible termination payments such as lump sums from superannuation funds. This type of annuity was rarely used before the changes made by the federal government in 1983 to the tax legislation affecting superannuation, which encouraged the shift from lump-sum payouts to the creation of income in retirement. See **annuity, eligible termination payments**.

deferred delivery   a term to describe shares for which the scrip has not yet been issued. The shares are tradeable. *Abbrev.*: **dd**.

deferred dividend shares   shares issued with the stipulation that shareholders will only be entitled to receive dividends after a specified period, either because the issuing company is incurring losses or because it wants to use the funds for other purposes.

deficit   an excess of expenditure over revenue. For a country, a deficit in its balance of payments means that payments for imports, freight, etc., exceed receipts from exports, capital inflow and so on. For governments, a deficit is the amount by which their outlay exceeds revenue from taxes or charges. A deficit is financed by government borrowing from the general public or by printing money. Government deficits can be divided into:

- **a cyclical deficit** which is the portion of a deficit which is due to the current state of the economic cycle (deficits rise as unemployment increases because benefit payments go up while tax receipts fall);
- **a structural deficit** which refers to the portion of a deficit that would remain even if the economy were at full employment;
- **a seasonal deficit**. In Australia, the government's deficit reduces in the June quarter when provisional tax and a big proportion of company tax are due for payment.

deficit financing   the practice of financing expenditure by borrowings rather than by using current revenue. Governments indulge in this in the hope of stimulating an increase in economic activity (which would tend to cut the deficit back again) or to avoid the politically difficult alternative of raising taxes and charges. Most economists would not agree that it is desirable for the government to balance its budget. For example, it is only by running a deficit that the government can increase money supply and the amount of government securities (bonds) in the system. Also **pump-priming**. See **deficit spending**.

deficit spending   This occurs when a government spends more than it gathers in revenue. The shortfall has to be financed by government borrowing from the public, which can push interest rates higher, or by printing more money, which may increase inflation and, ultimately, also push interest rates higher in an effort to reduce the inflation. See **crowding out, deficit financing, Keynes, John Maynard** in **economists**.

deflation   the opposite of inflation, i.e. a fall in prices. It is sometimes applied to a situation where economic activity is falling. Deflation may be induced by a reduction in economic activity as a result of deliberate government policy, for example by reducing the amount of money in circulation either by raising taxes or cutting back on government spending. See **disinflation, inflation**.

delist   A company is delisted when its shares are permanently removed from a stock exchange listing, because it no longer complies with stock exchange listing requirements, for example if the company is taken over.

deliverables   stocks, such as bank bills of exchange or wool, which have been certified as acceptable for delivery under a Sydney Futures Exchange contract. For example, to be acceptable as deliverable, bank bills must mature within a specific range of dates.

delivery month   a future month, listed as one in which delivery can be given or taken for a contract traded on the Sydney Futures Exchange. Delivery months must be stipulated for all contracts traded on the exchange. See **futures markets**.

delta   this is a measure of the proportional change between two items. It is used to track the relationship between an option price and the underlying shares or futures contract price, to show the change in the option price for each one-point change in the underlying contract.

demand-pull inflation   see **inflation**.

demerger   the opposite of a merger (the practice of combining several companies under one corporate roof). A demerger hives off parts of a company into separate operations because it is believed they will perform better that way. See **float-off**.

demonetise   to end a commodity's role as a medium of exchange. For example, gold was demonetised in 1978, a move that ended its role as a medium of international settlement.

deposit   an amount of money placed with a financial institution either at call (redeemable or withdrawable on demand) or for a fixed period. In the latter case, the deposit would earn a higher rate of interest and be called a 'fixed' or 'term' deposit.

deposit margin   the amount paid by a trader in the futures market to cover against losses that might be incurred because of movements in the price of the commodity traded. It is a cash buffer set by the clearing house; the deposit is variable and represents an estimate by the clearing house of the minimum likely one-day price movement in the contract. If gold or interest rates are moving rapidly every day, the deposit margin would be increased to take account of the uncertainty. See **margin**.

depreciate   to fall in value; the opposite of appreciate. Currencies may depreciate against other currencies. In business, assets depreciate as they age and become less valuable. In the latter case there is a cost to the company or individual who bought the assets as they will have to be replaced by new, possibly more expensive, items. Depreciation is regarded as a genuine business expense and can normally be offset, for taxation purposes, against income. See **depreciation**.

depreciation   the accounting practice which the cost of fixed assets is systematically spread over the life of the assets. The amount of depreciation (termed an expense in accounting language) has the effect of reducing the profit or raising the loss figure for the periods during which the asset is used. As depreciation is a non-cash expense, it allows the money to be retained in the business, thus maintaining the capacity of the business to replace its assets. See **amortisation**.

depression   a time of low economic activity, distinguished from a recession by being prolonged and sustained; there are continuing falls in output, unemployment is high and rising, companies have unsold stocks because demand is low. Australia had a severe depression in the 1890s and again, with the rest of the industrialised world, in the 1930s—the period known as the Great Depression. The Great Depression brought widespread unemployment, as demand collapsed and businesses failed. The collapse of Wall Street and the New York stock market in 1929 set off a chain reaction of depression which lasted until well into the 1930s. The collapse of Wall Street determined the timing of the Great Depression but was not the sole—or even the main—cause of it.
Economists still argue about the cause; it is commonly accepted that one factor was the growing imbalance in world trade brought about by increased levels of primary production in more recently settled economies, such as Australia and Canada, in the face of inadequate growth in demand. At the same time, the earlier industrialised nations faced problems selling their increased output of manufactured goods. Monetarists see the large decline in the US money supply as an important cause; Keynesians focus on the reduction in spending by consumers and investors. It is generally agreed that the main cause in the Australian case was the fall in export prices and sales; other causes were the fall in overseas loans (which led to a reduction in government capital expenditure) and a slackening of residential construction. There is less argument about the duration of the Great Depression than about its source; between 1929 and 1932 industrial production in the capitalist world fell by 35 per cent, the volume of world trade fell by more than 40 per cent and unemployment rose to 30 million in 1932 in the four major capitalist economies. Recovery was slow and was still incomplete when World War II broke out in 1939. Australia was especially vulnerable because of its dependence on wheat and wool exports and on a high level of capital inflow.

derivative products   products constructed from existing products, such as options, swaps or forwards. The opposite of 'vanilla' or 'straight forward' products. See **vanilla product**.

derived measures see **implicit price deflator**.

desk in full, **dealing desk**; an all-embracing term for a company's trading team, who sit 'on the desk', work around the dealing desk — which is now really several desks representing the different areas traded, such as cash, bills or bonds. Those who are promoted to management level are 'taken off the desk' and often miss the cut and thrust of dealing.

devaluation the reduction in the value of one currency against another, either because the first currency weakened or because the second currency strengthened. If the Australian dollar were reduced in terms of the US dollar from 72 US cents to 70 US cents it would have been devalued against the US dollar. This could have been caused by a general weakening of the Australian dollar or by a burst of strength in the US currency. See **revaluation**.

diagonal spread see **option spread**.

DIGGERS see **zero coupon bond**.

diminishing returns Formally, this means that the increase in production obtained by adding an additional unit of labour will fall after a certain point as the number of units employed increases. Less formally, diminishing returns means that a point exists beyond which putting more into a venture will not produce a corresponding increase in output. The expression 'the law of diminishing returns' is frequently used loosely to mean that greater production does not necessarily bring higher profits: after the peak point of efficiency average return on capital stops rising or even falls.

DINGOS see **zero coupon bonds**.

direct investment taking a stake in a company or joint venture which brings a say in how the operation is run though it does not necessarily give a controlling interest. See **portfolio investment**.

director someone appointed to take responsibility for the policy formation and control of a company because of particular ability and expertise in an industry. Directors manage the company on behalf of the shareholders, who are the owners of the company. A public company must have at least three directors; a proprietary limited company must have at least two. Under a company's articles of association, directors undertake the supervision of management collectively as a board. They can delegate management functions to a managing director, but some activities require the board's participation, for example signing the annual accounts or authorising dividend payments.

direct quote   an exchange rate quoted in terms of the local currency, i.e. the number of units of local currency which equals one unit of a foreign currency. For example a quote which read that $US1 = $A1.176 would be a direct quote in Australia, but an indirect quote in the US. The $A is normally quoted indirectly, in terms of the $US price for one Australian dollar. See **indirect quote**.

dirty float   see **float**.

discount   a reduction in price either from the previous price or from face value. Securities are traded at a discount on the assumption that the buyer will receive face value when the securities mature. For example, a 180-day bank bill of exchange for $100 000 face value bought at a 10 per cent discount would cost $95 068.49 and the holder would receive $100 000 when the bill matures. The discount, then, is the rate of return calculated as simple interest (in this case $4931.51) on the face value of the investment ($100 000), expressed as a percentage per annum.

   To discount a security means to sell that security—a bill of exchange for example—at less than its face value. In the above example, the seller of the $100 000 180-day bank bill would have discounted that bill—i.e. sold it at a 10 per cent discount, for $95 068.49.

   Traders of securities such as bills of exchange must be aware of the difference between a discount and a yield calculation. The discount is the difference between the face value ($100 000) and the price for which the bill is sold ($95 068.49). The yield is the return on the amount invested —for example a 180-day bank bill bought at a yield of 10 per cent per annum, for face value of $100 000 would cost $95 300.26. When the bill matures, the holder would receive $4699.74, being the difference between the outlay and face value of the bill. It is a smaller amount than that earned by the investor who bought the bill at a discount, because in the case of a yield, the interest was earned on the proceeds ($95 300.26) and not on the face value of the bill ($100 000). (Those interested in the discount and yield formulae should consult a textbook.) In foreign exchange, discount is the opposite of premium. Currency quoted at a discount is worth less in the forward market than in the spot market. See **premium, yield**.

discounted cash flow   A method of measuring the return on capital or funds invested which takes into account the time value of money. Money can be shown to have a time value because, for example, $100 today invested at 10 per cent will yield $110 in one year's time. Conversely $110 to be received in one year would be worth $100 now.

discounted investment in government-guaranteed earnings return bonds   see **zero coupon bonds**.

discounted investment in negotiable government obligations   see **zero coupon bonds**.

discounted receipts of Australian government obligatory negotiable securities   see **zero coupon bonds**.

discount house   a member of the UK merchant banking elite. The London discount market consists of twelve members of the London Discount Market Association plus a few small firms of bill brokers. The primary function of the discount houses is borrowing and investing short-term money, particularly buying Treasury Bills (at a discount) from the government. The discount houses cover in full the weekly Treasury Bill tenders which form part of the UK government's short-term borrowings. The London discount houses are similar to the Australian authorised short-term money market dealers in that they have lender-of-last-resort borrowing facilities with the central bank and are active dealers in short-dated government securities, although recently they have diversified by holding a greater proportion of their assets in commercial bills and certificates of deposit. The Bank of England uses the discount houses as liquidity channels to ensure the market does not become too tight (short of money) or too liquid (too much money around).

discounting   in the context of *money*, reducing in price from an earlier level or from face value. In the context of *news*, taking good or bad news into account, in anticipation of its announcement. For example, traders are expecting news that will show inflation is rising, which has an adverse effect on interest rates, and will mark rates up ahead of the announcement. In the context of *wages*, not increasing wages to the extent necessary to keep pace with inflation, which results in a decrease in buying power. Unions have traditionally opposed discounting of wages, but recently a more flexible attitude has been apparent.

discount rate   the rate at which a bill of exchange or other security, such as a Treasury Note, is discounted (sold). The discount rate often refers to the rate at which central banks will buy paper from financial institutions, i.e. ease liquidity by exchanging cash for rediscounted (sold) securities. See **discount window, rediscount**.

discount securities   non-interest-bearing money market instruments which are issued at a discount from face value with the holder receiving face value when the security matures. Discount securities carry no coupon; examples are bills of exchange, promissory notes and Treasury Notes. See **discount**.

discount window   an anachronistic expression for the central bank's rediscount facility. The term dates back to the days when a clerk went to a specific window or counter at the central bank to sell (rediscount) his company's securities. See **rediscount**.

discretionary account   A client would set up a discretionary account with his or her broker, allowing the broker to decide fully or partly when and what to buy or sell on his or her behalf and at what price.

discretionary income   spare cash; what you have to spend after the other choices have been made for you by the tax man, your bank manager, credit card commitments and so on.

disinflation   Getting rid of inflation, either through deliberate government attempts or as a result of natural causes, for example as the result of an economic depression. See **deflation**.

disintermediation   cutting out the middleman so that borrowers and lenders deal directly with each other. In such direct financing, the borrower deals with the lender and vice versa; with intermediation a financial institution such as a merchant bank is involved so that the ultimate borrower and lender may not each know the other's identity. Disintermediation describes what happens when money is moved from banks or merchant banks and invested directly with, say, the government by the purchase of bonds. The Australian financial system is based largely on intermediation, whereas New Zealand, for example, has a greater degree of disintermediation which is a spin-off of its more regulated environment. Disintermediation is caused largely by interest rate controls; lenders want a higher return and borrowers who are rationed out are willing to pay a higher rate, and this gives them the incentive to get together directly. See **intermediation**, **reintermediation**.

disposable income   the portion of a person's income, including social service payments, that is left for spending or saving after the Taxation Department has taken its share.

dividend   what is paid out of company's profits to its shareholders, usually yearly (a **final dividend**) and sometimes half-yearly (an **interim dividend**). The annual dividend equals final dividend plus interim.

dividend cover   the number of times the amount of dividend paid by a company is covered by its earnings. It is calculated by dividing the net profit by the amount paid in dividends, or by dividing the earnings per share by the dividend in cents per share.

dividend imputation   this refers to a change in Australian tax legislation (effective 1 July 1987) designed to remove the 'double' taxation of company dividends. Previously dividends paid out of after-tax profits were taxable in the hands of the shareholders; that is, the company paid tax on its profits in the first instance, and paid dividends to the shareholders who in turn paid tax on the dividends. With imputation, dividends distributed by a company that has paid full company tax are not taxable in the shareholders' hands. Under the new system dividends will be taxed only once, either by the company or, if the company does not pay tax, by shareholders who receive the dividends. Shareholders will pay the tax at the relevant individual marginal rate.

See **franking account, franked dividends, unfranked dividends**.

dividend withholding tax see **withholding tax**.

dividend yield the theoretical return on an investment, assuming shares are bought on the market at the prevailing price and not taking into account charges such as brokerage. It is calculated by dividing the dividend per share by the current share price, expressed as a percentage.

dog-and-pony show a seminar or exhibition staged to introduce a new company or product, given by the salespeople of the investment bank/broking firm marketing the product, usually around the country and/or overseas; the financial markets version of the old travelling song-and-dance act.

dogs the term for a euromarket issue which is virtually unsellable. The *International Financing Review* lists 'Dogs of the Year', a summary of the worst issues on which underwriters lost most money.

dollars In wholesale money market jargon this is a synonym for one million. 'I'll buy five dollars of June 15 bills' means 'I'll buy $5 million of June 15 bills'.

don't sell notice an announcement, required by the stock exchange listing rules, made to the general public by directors of a company advising shareholders not to sell their shares, pending a further announcement. This procedure is common when takeover discussions are under way and a bid could push up the share price.

double dipping the practice of benefiting more than once from savings schemes such as superannuation. The payments are tax-deductible and the beneficiary may receive a tax-free lump sum at the end of the savings period. He or she might invest the proceeds for further gains in such a way that taxable income is minimised and eligibility for government pensions is maintained. Governments resent double dipping, but any legislation which affects low- and middle-income earners' pensions and superannuation plans is politically sensitive.

double-entry bookkeeping a system of recording all financial transactions, in which each transaction has two aspects, a debit and a credit, so that a complete record entails entering each transaction twice. Credit entries generally record the sources of funds and debit entries generally record the use made of the funds. This should not be confused with profits and losses (see **profit and loss account**).

The recording procedure of double-entry bookkeeping ensures that the balance sheet equation Assets (A) = Liabilities (L) + Owners' Equity (OE) is not violated. The rules are as follows:

Increase Assets = Dr.   Decrease Assets = Cr.
Decrease Liabilities = Dr.   Increase Liabilities = Cr.
Decrease Owners' Equity = Dr.   Increase OE = Cr.

Revenues and expenses are a subset of owners' equity thus:

Decrease = Dr.	Increase Revenue = Cr.
Increase Expense = Dr.	Decrease = Cr.

Example: you buy a car for $1000 cash:

Assets (car) increase $1000	Dr. Car account $1000
Assets (cash) decrease $1000	Cr. cash account $1000

Since one asset has increased and another decreased by a corresponding amount the balance sheet equation still holds.

Example: you buy a car for $1000 credit:

Assets (car) increase $1000	Dr. Car account $1000
Liabilities (debt payable) increase $1000	Cr. debt $1000

Since the asset increase of $1000 on the left-hand side of the balance sheet equation is matched by a $1000 increase in liabilities on the right-hand side, balance is preserved.

double taxation agreement   Australia has agreements with a number of countries which enable overseas companies with Australian subsidiaries to gain a tax credit in their own countries for tax paid in Australia. See **dual tax**.

Dow Jones index   a measure of the average price of shares on the New York stock market. The Dow Jones index is so-called after Charles Dow and Eddie Jones who first teamed up in 1882 to report stock market news to New York's financial community. The decision by the two men to launch a reporting firm distributing stock market news and analyses and gossip from a small Wall Street office sowed the seed of the *Wall Street Journal*, of which Charles Dow was the first editor. The Dow Jones takes the average of the closing prices of 30 representative stocks from 'mature' industries such as chemicals and steel, that is 'smokestack America', as against the more modern 'high-tech' industries. See **smokestack America**.

downside risk   the risk that prices/values might fall. The opposite of upside potential. See **upside potential**.

Down Under bonds   euromarkets term for $A and $NZ bonds.

DRAGONS   see **zero coupon bonds**.

draw   to draw a cheque or bill of exchange means to issue or write out a cheque or bill in someone else's favour.

drawdown   the actual use of funds provided under a borrowing facility. The borrowing facility would first be organised between the lender—bank or merchant bank—and client (the borrower), but the funds would not be used until the drawdown takes place. Once the client has used all or part of the funds, then the loan is 'drawn down'.

drawee   the person or company to whom a bill or cheque is addressed. On a cheque, the drawee is the bank on which the cheque is drawn. In the case of a bill of exchange it is the person who agrees to provide the specified sum of money, and who in signing the bill becomes the acceptor. See **bill of exchange**.

drawer   the person signing a cheque or bill of exchange. In normal banking, the drawer is the person who signs a cheque as the issuer, ordering his or her bank to pay out. With a bill of exchange, the drawer issues the bill and orders another party (the drawee) to pay the sum of money specified on the bill. See **bill of exchange**.

DRC   *abbrev.* **dual residency company**.

drop-lock security   a type of security, such as a debenture or bond, that gives some protection to the investor against interest rate movements. The security is issued with a floating or adjustable rate that is pegged to a benchmark rate (bank bill or interbank rate) and if the benchmark rate drops to a specific level, the security automatically switches to a fixed rate until it matures.

dual currency bonds   securities issued in one currency with interest payments in that currency but with the principal amount repayable in another currency at a specified exchange rate.

dual listing   listing a share or security on more than one stock exchange. For example a company could be listed on the Australian Stock Exchange and also on the Auckland exchange. Several **second board** companies have dual listing on more than one Australian exchange.

dual residency company   a company that qualifies as a resident in two countries, for example in Australia and new Zealand, so that its activities comply with regulations in each jurisdiction but the status allows it to maximise tax benefits in both. In a simple example Company X in New Zealand would incorporate a subsidiary in New Zealand, called Company Y. Y is resident in New Zealand but it operates in Australia, with Australian management, control and directors, so it also qualifies as a resident in Australia. Y borrows money to buy an Australian company, Company Z. It therefore acquires an asset (Company Z) and incurs an items of expense (the interest on borrowed funds). Companies X and Y are grouped together for tax purposes in New Zealand, and Y and Z are grouped together in Australia. The interest expense paid by Y can thus be offset against X in New Zealand and against Z in Australia. Australian tax legislation is expected to close this loophole. *abbrev.*: **DRC**.

dual tax   Where there is no double taxation agreement between countries, a company with a subsidiary abroad might have to pay tax both in its own country and the country in which the subsidiary operates. See **double taxation agreements**.

due date   the date at which payment has been contracted or agreed to be made. It can be the date on which a bill of exchange matures or on which repayment of a loan is scheduled to be made.

due diligence   Sufficient analysis has been carried out before recommending an investment or advancing a loan to a client. This is not technically a legal phrase, but is based on the notion of avoiding negligence when giving advice. See **duty of care**.

dumped   Stock is described as 'dumped' when it has been offloaded (sold) in large amounts at a bargain price that indicates the seller is indifferent to the loss made and to the depressing effect the transaction has on the stock's price. The seller just wants to get rid of the stock. *Dumping* in international finance means selling below cost to reduce a surplus or to irritate a competitor.

Dun and Bradstreet   a substantial international company which specialises in credit analysis. The company has been widely, but erroneously, credited with the origin of the term 'dunning' which means importuning persistently for the repayment of money. Dunners, people hired to do this, were at work in the seventeenth century. See **credit reference bureau**.

dunning   see **Dun and Bradstreet**.

dutch auction   a sale of securities in which the lowest price (highest yield) at which the whole offering could be sold is used as the price (yield) at which the securities are sold. In Australia the term has come to mean the practice (considered unethical) of requesting a price on a parcel of stock and then using that price as a lever to prompt other, more favourable, bids.

duty of care   a legal concept which means that companies or institutions or individual advisers must not be negligent when dealing with those affected by their advice. The party giving advice can be wrong, but would not be liable for damages provided it could be proved that sufficient care had been taken. The duty-of-care concept received some attention with the highlighting of borrowers taking out foreign currency loans only to find their liabilities substantially increased by the fall in the $A value against currencies such as the swiss franc and the yen. Banks and other lenders had to prove that they had observed their duty of care when dealing with borrowers who relied on their advice.

E

earnings before interest and tax   total earnings before provisions are deducted. This measures a company's performance and is often used in preference to net profit as it excludes the effects of borrowings and tax benefits and adjustments. *Abbrev.*: **EBIT**.

earnings per share   one of a number of gauges of a company's performance. It is calculated by dividing the company's earnings by the number of shares on issue to show the profit earned in terms of each share. For example, if a company with half a million shares issued has earnings of $1 million, the earnings per share is $2. *Abbrev.* **EPS**. See **price–earnings ratio**.

earnings yield   The earnings yield is achieved by dividing earnings per share by the share price and multiplying by 100 over one. It shows the relationship of earnings per share to the current share price and is the inverse of the price–earnings ratio. See **price–earnings ratio**.

easy money   market idiom for cheap money which is in ample supply. Opposite of tight money. Traders also talk of an 'easy day' meaning there was no shortage of cash and rates stayed low. Easy-money policies can mean the government wants to keep interest rates down; this can be inflationary in the long run. See **tight money**.

EBIT   *abbrev.* **earnings before interest and tax**.

econometrics   a specialist branch of economics which applies statistical and mathematical techniques to economic problems. It is sometimes said that if you lose your phone number, an econometrician will estimate it for you (plus or minus a margin of error). See **number cruncher**.

Economic Planning Advisory Council   a product of the National Economic Summit Conference held in April 1983 by the Hawke government. The council was established as a vehicle to continue the process of consultation and discussion on medium-term policies between the federal government and the trade union movement. A permanent secretariat of the council was set up and it is intended that an annual report will be produced on the Australian economy. *Abbrev.* **EPAC**.

economic rent   This is quite distinct from the usual meaning of 'rent'. Economic rent means a payment over that required to attract an individual (or capital) into a particular occupation; basically, it is a return above the opportunity cost of an asset or service. A simple example of this complex idea is a pop star (or merchant banker) who earns $100 000: in his or her original occupation as bank teller, he or she earned $15 000. If the only choice besides being a pop star or merchant banker were to remain as a bank teller, then any salary above $15 000 would persuade this person to stay with the big numbers—and his or her economic rent would be $85 000. This concept of rent is the basis of the resources rent tax. See **rent, resources rent tax**.

economics   the study of production possibilities, and the allocation of a society's resources. Thomas Carlyle referred to it as 'the dismal science'. A social science, it is often described by those who have studied it as commonsense, but for the uninitiated it is crammed with jargon and shrouded in mystique. Just as you think you have come to grips with economics, an economist will change the answers to the question. See **macroeconomics** and **microeconomics**.

economists   practitioners of economics. Economists study the allocation of resources (employment, income, trade) in the economy. Various definitions of economists have been advanced. They have been described at times in terms of grey suits and grey minds. Another suggestion is that an economist is 'someone who can draw a mathematically precise line from an unwarranted assumption to an incomprehensible conclusion'. Cynics have proposed 'soothsayer' or 'witchdoctor'.

For centuries many economists have created and enveloped themselves in a mystique marked by a proliferation of models, theories and jargon which explain some of the facts of life; in this process, they have tended to align themselves with schools of thought, many of which disagree, often bitterly, about causes and effects. Some of the major economists and thinkers whose studies and theories have been most influential are described briefly below.

Bentham, Jeremy (1748-1832)   UK philosopher and legal reformer, educated at Oxford. Bentham held that the utility (usefulness) of any law could be measured by the extent to which it promoted pleasure and happiness. This was the essence of utilitarianism, as expresed in his *Principles of Morals and Legislation* (1789). The object of all legislation, according to Bentham, should be the 'greatest happiness of the greatest number'. Bentham willed that after his death his body be stuffed and placed in University College, London. He is still there—a rotund figure in a glass case. Bentham attends, in body if not in spirit, the college's annual dinners, where he presides over much animated discussion.

Copland, Douglas Berry (1894-1971)   Copland is remembered as the major architect of the Premiers' Plan or Copland Plan of 1931 which provided the basis for policies aimed at dealing with the Depression.

Copland was born in New Zealand; he held a chair in economics at the University of Tasmania and later, in 1924, was appointed to the first chair in commerce at the University of Melbourne. He held this position and that of Dean of the Faculty of Commerce until 1944. During World War II he was Commonwealth Commissioner of Prices and an adviser to Prime Minister Curtin. His wartime experience softened his belief in laissez faire and in the early postwar period he was one of the most active supporters of Keynesian ideas. Copland was knighted in 1950 and officially designated founder of the Committee for the Economic Development of Australia.

Friedman, Milton (1912-)   a US economist, born in Brooklyn, New York, Friedman won the Nobel Prize for Economics in 1976. He is best known for his emphasis on money supply, for reviving the quantity theory of money which leads to an emphasis on monetary policy, as distinct from the Keynesian emphasis on fiscal policy. He is also well known for his free enterprise views. Despite Friedman's emphasis on empirical verification his critics have recently shown that his empirics (evidence) do not necessarily prove his main propositions. See **monetarist, quantity theory of money**.

Galbraith, John Kenneth (1908-)   leading US political economist. His major works include *The Great Crash 1929, The Affluent Society, Economics, Peace and Laughter, The New Industrial State,* and *Economics and the Public Purpose.* Galbraith emphasises the real world rather than theories; he promotes the idea of studying realities first and testing the theories against reality. Galbraith is known among economists as an institutionalist—someone who starts his or her studies with real-world economics. He is famous for his notion of 'private affluence, public squalor', and for coining the terms 'conventional wisdom' and 'technostructure'.

Giblin, Lyndhurst Falkiner (1872-1951)   Probably Australia's most original economist, Giblin achieved a place in the history of economic thought for his formulation of the idea of an export multiplier which provided a method by which fluctuations in our export income could be related to changes in national income. This idea was further developed by Keynes into a more general multiplier.

Giblin was much more than an economist. Born in Tasmania, son of the Premier of that State, he studied at Cambridge and then prospected on the Klondike, worked as a wharfie and timberworker, taught ju-jitsu in London, managed a Solomon Islands plantation and worked his way home as a cook to become a fruitgrower. He subsequently became a Labor MHA and won the MC and DSO in France. He then served as Tasmania's government statistician and later was the Ritchie Research Professor at the University of Melbourne, 1929-39.

Giblin was on the committee which formulated the Premiers' Plan to deal with the Great Depression, and he took considerable pains to explain the complexities of economics through his newspaper series Letters to John Smith. His work *Growth of a Central Bank* remains a landmark of Australian economic historiography. Giblin declined offers of a knighthood. See **multiplier**.

Keynes, John Maynard (1883-1946)   Famous as a UK economist, but more than that, Keynes was a man of eclectic interests, very different from today's specialists: pragmatic, flexible, not dogmatic. He was educated at Cambridge, where he studied mathematics and philosophy. He believed that production and employment and income levels are determined by the levels of total spending on goods and services. Keynes' ideas spread round the world and began to be seriously discussed in Australia in the 1930s (perhaps in response to the Great Depression). In his *Treatise of Money*, published in 1930, Keynes provided a critique of prevailing monetary theory and policy; he gave a fuller explanation in the *General Theory of Employment, Interest and Money* (1936).

Keynes provided a theoretical rationale for increased government intervention and he emphasised fiscal rather than monetary policies. He held that a fall in net income, lack of demand and rising unemployment should be met by increased government spending to stimulate the economy—'spending your way out of a recession', as it was expressed by his enemies. Keynesian ideas fell out of favour in the radically changed world of the 1970s, when recession joined forces with inflation. There was no simple Keynesian prescription for the 1970s and conditions favoured the monetarist revival. The discussion continues. See **Cambridge School, classical economics, crowding out, fiscal policy**.

Malthus, Thomas (1766-1834)   UK economist whose legacy to economic thought was contained in his *Essay on Population*, written in 1798, which developed the pessimistic idea that mankind was doomed to near-starvation because the population would increase and wipe out any increase in the availability of food. Malthus pushed for a lower birthrate, specifically advocating moral restraint. Speculation has favoured the explanation that a bad romance lay behind Malthus' theories; the study of political economy was widely suggested in his era as a cure for unhappy liaisons. Birth control, though, appears to have modified Malthus' problem, and technological development seems to have distanced us from his prediction of inevitable starvation. Theorists continue, however, to apply Malthusian fore-casts to Third World countries. See **classical economics**.

Marshall, Alfred (1842-1924)   Marshall combined the traditions of the English classical school of Smith and Ricardo with new ideas on demand and markets, so that he has been described as the English founder of neo-classical economics and his followers have become known as neo-classicists. He held a number of major economic posts but was mainly associated with the University of Cambridge, where he held the chair of political economy 1885-1908. His main work, *Principles of Economics*, was published in 1890 and went through eight editions in his lifetime.

Marshall maintained that one had to begin with an analysis of the behaviour of consumers and producers to understand the functioning of a market system. He held to the classical view of the importance of costs in determining prices but added a new dimension by emphasising the role of demand factors. He coined the term 'elasticity' to illustrate responses in demand to changes in prices.

It has been said that Marshall's wife reminded him each morning at breakfast to keep one eye on the real world. Unlike many modern economists, he believed in helping his readers by keeping the expression of his technical analysis as simple as possible. Unfortunately this meant he was often trying to translate the maths into English, which led to a number of confusions which would not have arisen had he stuck to the maths. See **Cambridge School, classical economics**.

Marx, Karl Heinrich (1818-1883)   German philosopher, economist, socialist and revolutionary. Marx studied at the University of Berlin and became a member of the Young Hegelians, an anti-religious radical group. Marx turned to journalism after his radicalism had proved to be an obstacle to a university career and in 1842 became editor of *Rheinische Zeitung*. The publication was suppressed. In 1844 he began a lifelong collaboration with Friedrich Engels. Marx was at different times expelled from Germany and France. He moved to England in 1849 and stayed there for the rest of his life. He was buried in Highgate Cemetery and there used to be a plaque on his favourite chair in the British Library reading room. Marx and Engels collaborated on the *Communist Manifesto*, published in 1848. Marx became a leading figure in the International Working Men's Association, later known as The First International. In 1867 the first volume of *Das Kapital* was published. The remainder was published after Marx's death, having been edited by Engels. Marx's ill-health prevented his meeting his deadline; his life-project was never really his triumph—it was Engels who published his jumbled, unfinished notes as *Das Kapital* vols 2 and 3.

Marx failed to solve all the analytical problems he had set himself. The brand of scientific socialism that became known as Marxism purports to explain the origins, development and demise of capitalism. Marxism promoted the concept of an inevitable transition, through gradual evolution, to a classless society—but the change required a violent overthrow of state power. The ideal classless society would be built on individual development through social cooperation, and state power would fade.

Mill, John Stuart (1806-1873)   British philosopher, political economist, exponent of utilitarianism, child prodigy. Mill was educated by his father and was a precocious student, reading Latin and Greek and studying algebra at the age of eight. He later had a nervous breakdown. He spent some time in France in 1820-21 with the Bentham family. Mill's major contribution was to synthesise the contributions of various members of the classical school, rather than to provide original concepts; he is described as the father of classical liberalism. See **classical economics**.

Quesnay, Francois (1694-1774)   economist and physician at the court of Louis XV, where his duties included attending Madame de Pompadour. Quesnay's contribution to economic thought and development is expressed in his *Tableau Economique*, published in 1758 and acknowledged as the first attempt at a macroeconomic input-output analysis (a matrix showing which industries the inputs to each industry come from and where the output of each industry goes). Quesnay was leader of the physiocrats, a school of thought that held sway in France in the 1660s and which claimed agriculture as the only truly productive sector of the economy. Manufacturers, according to the physiocrats, were 'sterile'; the fate of the economy rested on the agricultural sector which generated the physical surplus of output over inputs on which everything else depended. Physiocrats clashed with mercantilists in their views on agriculture versus manufacturing, though both focused on the importance of an economic surplus.

Ricardo, David (1772-1823)   an economist whose record in finance reads like every money market trader and stockbroker's dream: already working in the money market at the age of fourteen, Ricardo was smart enough despite a lack of formal education to have made his fortune by the age of 42 and to have retired to his country estate at Gatcombe Park (now Princess Anne's home) to write about economics. James Mill, the father of John Stuart Mill, encouraged Ricardo to publish. Ricardo's most important work, *The Principles of Political Economy and Taxation*, was published in 1817 and is highly regarded by classical economists.

Ricardo's basic concern was 'to determine the laws which regulate the distribution (among the different classes of landowners, capitalists and labour) of the produce of industry'. He argued that when real wages fall, firms tend to replace machinery with labour; and, when wages rise, capital-intensive goods become cheaper relative to labour-intensive goods. Ricardo constructed a theoretical model which he used to reason from particular abstract propositions to reach general conclusions about the real economy. He was the first to use abstract analysis of the economy to make decisions about the real world. So blame him, if you choose, for economists' preferences for abstract analysis. His work inspired generations of economists from Marx to Friedman but was cut short by his tragic death from an infected tooth. See **classical economics, free trade.**

Robinson, Joan (1903-1983)   British economist, one of the most influential of the post-Keynesian economic theorists. Professor Robinson taught at the University of Cambridge from 1931 to 1971. She was influenced by the works of Marx and Keynes and was a consistent critic of laissez faire economic theory. Major works include *The Economics of Perfect Competition* (1933) and *The Accumulation of Capital* (1956). Professor Robinson was at the forefront of heated debates over the meaning of 'capital' in the 1950s and 1960s and was a leading light among the Cambridge School which developed macroeconomic theories of growth and distribution. See **Cambridge School.**

Samuelson, Paul (1915-   )   Winner of the Nobel Prize for Economics in 1970, Professor Emeritus of economics at the Massachusetts Institute of Technology in Boston. He has contributed significantly to the development of mathematical economics, to the theory of equilibrium and consumer behaviour. His ubiquitous textbook *Economics* (of which there is an Australian edition) is the world's best seller and Samuelson became a millionaire from its royalties.

Schumpeter, Joseph (1883-1950)   Minister of Finance for Austria after World War I, Schumpeter held the chair of public finance at Bonn from 1925 to 1932, then moved to Harvard where he remained for the rest of his life. He stressed the importance of technical innovation for economic growth and cycles, arguing that without innovation an economy would reach a static equilibrium. Innovation in his view was the source of renewal for capitalism—but he predicted that increased competition among firms to innovate would produce 'gales of creative destruction' leading to the demise of capitalism. See **equilibrium.**

Smith, Adam (1723-1790)   Scottish philosopher and political economist. He lectured at Glasgow University between 1752 and 1763 in moral philosophy and is best known for his *Inquiry into the Nature and Causes of the Wealth of Nations*, published in 1776. Known more commonly as *The Wealth of Nations*, the work has become entrenched as a text for students of economics. Adam Smith is regarded as the intellectual father of the 'invisible hand' theory—i.e. leave it to market forces in the hope that that would allow everyone a fair go. Smith recognised the need for some government intervention, especially in the context of 'natural monopolies' such as water supply and road tolls. Smith was against too much government interference with foreign trade. See **classical economics, free trade, neo-classical economics, mercantilism.**

Walras, Marie Esprit Leon (1834–1910)   Walras held the chair of economics in the Faculty of Law at Lausanne, 1870–1892, when he was succeeded by Pareto. Walras is considered a founder of the branch of mathematical economics called 'the general equilibrium theory'; he favoured the theory of marginal utility and set out to demonstrate how the prices at which goods are bought and sold are influenced by the relative marginal utility (need) of those trading the goods. Despite his arcane mathematical interests, Walras was deeply interested in sociology and was a socialist by political leaning. See **general equilibrium theory, marginal utility, Pareto optimality.**

economy of scale   The bigger you are, the cheaper it comes, in the sense that the cost of producing or buying an extra unit falls. Although that is not always the case, economies of scale are usually achieved by making the most of size. Someone buying in bulk may often get a better price per item than someone buying single items. However, biggest is not always best; in theory, at some point a business activity will reach an optimum point of output and efficiency and after that the cost of producing additional units increases. Economies often arise, though, out of spreading overheads over a larger number of units. See **diminishing returns.**

ECU   *abbrev.* **European Currency Unit.**

Edge Act   US Federal law, enacted in December 1919 as Section 25(a) of the *Federal Reserve Act*, to allow US commercial banks to carry out international business across state borders — a departure from the rule that domestic US banks can only do business in the state in which they are chartered. Banks carry out their international business through chartered subsidiaries, called Edge Act corporations.

Edge Act corporation   a foreign banking organisation established under the terms of the Edge Act. See **Edge Act.**

EEC   *abbrev.* **European Economic Community.**

EFIC   *abbrev.* **Export Finance and Insurance Corporation**

EFP   *abbrev.* **Exchange for physical.**

EFT   *abbrev.* **electronic funds transfer.**

EFTPOS   *abbrev.* **electronic funds transfer at point of sale.**

elasticity   This measures the degree of response (the proportionate change) in one item to a given proportionate change in another. For example:

- **price elasticity of demand** (or supply) measures the extent of change in demand (or supply) in response to a change in price;
- **income elasticity of demand** shows how much demand changes when income changes;
- **cross elasticity** shows how the demand for (or supply of) one product responds to a change in the price of another;
- **substitution elasticity** shows how easily or otherwise one product (or input to a production process) can be substituted for another.

electronic funds transfer   banking of the future, already changing the present. With EFT, funds are transferred from one account to another by computer without the need for pieces of paper when making withdrawals, deposits or purchases. Automatic teller machines (ATMs) are an example of the application of EFT in banking. *Abbrev.:* **EFT**. See **electronic funds transfer at point of sale**.

electronic funds transfer at point of sale   new computer language that is invading the staid portals of banking. EFTPOS means you can shop using a plastic card which will debit the amount of your shopping bill to the bank or other account of your choice through a point-of-sale (checkout) terminal at the retail store. *Abbrev.:* **EFTPOS**. See **debit card**, **electronic funds transfer**.

11am call money   funds which can be recalled, repaid or renegotiated as to interest rate during a morning's money market trading, up to 11am, without the need for prior notice. These are distinct from 24-hour call money, on which notice must be given the previous day of any intention to recall, repay or renegotiate on rate. Eleven am call funds are also referred to as 'same-day cash' or 11am call money. See **24-hour call money**.

eligible termination payments   payments received on retirement, retrenchment, resignation or disablement. Many of these sums can be rolled over (converted) into investments on which tax is deferred, such as approved deposit funds, so that tax is not paid until the funds are withdrawn. This maximises the return on lump sum payouts. The eligible payouts include superannuation settlements, golden handshakes and other forms of severance pay. Long service leave does not qualify as an eligible termination payment. *Abbrev.* **ETP**. See **approved deposit fund**.

Elliott Wave Theory   a form of technical analysis (charting), named after Ralph Elliott, an American accountant who became fascinated by the behaviour of the sharemarket. He devised the theory in the early 1930s and first published the theory in 1939 in a series of articles in *Financial World*. The theory was originally applied to the major market averages and in its most basic form says that the market follows a repetitive rhythm of a five-wave advance followed by a three-wave decline. Elliott believed this theory was part of a much larger natural law governing all human activities whereby life and nature repeat themselves indefinitely in cycles. Those interested in studying his work should read the *Elliott Wave Principle* by Frost and Prechter. See **Fibonacci numbers**.

embargo   a restriction, sometimes enforceable by law, on goods or information, often applied for a finite period.

embezzlement   in quaint legalese, the crime of taking property as a servant, the property having been received by the servant on behalf of the master (employer). Embezzlement has a legal distinction from theft and larceny; it involves wilfully taking something belonging to someone who put you in a position of trust which gave you access to, say, the family silver or the company's reserves. Embezzlement entails a relationship between the wrongdoer and the wronged party. In practice, it is simply ripping off the boss.

empirical   based on experience or observation. History has been called 'empirical evidence'. In the conclusions of economists, empirical justifications are sometimes said to be wanting.

EMS   *abbrev*. **European Monetary System**.

endorse   in banking and finance, to write a signature on the back of a cheque or bill of exchange verifying ownership and confirming the legal capacity to transfer ownership to someone else. Also **indorse**.

endowment   Under endowment assurance policies, the sum assured plus any bonuses is paid out on the death of the policyholder or at the end of a stipulated period, whichever arrives first. Endowment policies carry higher premiums than either term insurance or whole-of-life policies, because payment is guaranteed either on reaching a specified age or on death. If the insured person dies before the endowment policy matures then his or her family, or whoever is named in a will as beneficiary, stands to inherit from the policy. The policies are so-called because 'endowment' means the provision of a permanent source of income, or a gift. See **term insurance, whole-of-life policy**.

entitlement issue   similar to a rights issue except that an entitlement issue is non-renounceable, i.e. the issue cannot be traded on to someone else. The shareholder being offered shares through an entitlement issue has the option of taking up the offer or allowing it to lapse. Small mining companies usually make entitlement, rather than rights, issues. See **bonus issue, new issue, rights issue**.

EPAC   *abbrev*. **Economic Planning Advisory Council**.

EPS   *abbrev*. **earnings per share**.

equilibrium   a favourite expression among economists for what the rest of us call 'balance'. Equilibrium is found more on the economist's blackboard than in the real world. In a market, equilibrium is achieved if supply exactly matches demand. On a more academic level, critics of the neo-classical use of the term argue that real-world economies are never in equilibrium. They say that the idea of an economy as a pendulum swinging from side to side (a notion borrowed from physics) is nonsense as there is no fulcrum (fixed pivot) to guarantee a return to an original position. Those who work in real-world situations should agree with this view: it is probably true that we are rarely in equilibrium because the equilibrium is always changing. Nevertheless the system always tends towards equilibrium and therefore it has an influence. See **general equilibrium theory**.

equitable estoppel   see **estoppel**.

equity   the part of something—asset, house or company—which you own; what the professionals like to call shares. If you lend a company money, you have made a loan and rank as a creditor who, under normal circumstances, would expect repayment of the loan plus interest at a future date. If you buy ordinary shares in a company you become an equityholder in that company, which means you share in its profits (and losses) and have a less clear-cut idea of your future return than does the lender. As an ordinary shareholder, you stand in line behind debenture-holders for settlement, should the company be wound up. You run the risk of loss, but in return for this you have a share in the company's surplus during good times, rather than a fixed return.

You also have equity in that part of the value of your house above the amount borrowed from the company which has a mortgage over the house.

Economists, as well as other people, use 'equity' in its original sense of fairness or impartiality.

equity accounting   a technique to account for a company's interest in an associated company, i.e. a company over which the investing company can exert influence but does not have control. (Usually the investing company would hold less than 50 per cent but more than 20 per cent of the shares.) The assets of a company with an investment in another are set out so that they include the investor's ownership interest in the associated company. Under this method, a company with an investment in an associated company will include in its annual report a share of the profit (loss) and reserves of the associated company, irrespective of whether the profits are distributed through dividend payments or retained by the associated company.

In the investing company's balance sheet this investment will be recorded at cost plus the investor's share of any post-acquisition increases in the associated company's net assets. Equity accounting is a specific accounting technique which contrasts with the traditional accounting method where holdings of 50 per cent or less in another company are shown at cost, and dividends received as the only recognition of the profits of the investment.

equity trust   a type of unit trust which gathers unitholders' funds and invests them in a range of shares through the stock market. See **unit trust**.

equity warrant   See **warrant**.

ESA   *abbrev.* **exchange settlement account**.

escalation clause   a clause in a contract which may entitle a seller to exact a higher price from a buyer than was originally agreed, should specified circumstances occur.

escape clause   a clause written into a contract, outlining a specified set of circumstances under which the rules of the contract would no longer apply or would be modified.

escrow   A document is in escrow if it has been delivered to and is held by a third party (the escrow agent) and is only to take effect as a deed when certain conditions have been met. One condition is often delivery of a similar document executed by another party to the contract it records.

estate duties   see **death duties**.

estoppel   a legal doctrine which has evolved over the past couple of centuries, which essentially means that an individual cannot deny the truth of a statement made by him or her, or the existence of facts on which other people have relied because of his or her words or behaviour. Estoppel broadly means that someone is stopped or prevented from saying, doing or contesting something. The word is derived from the old French *estoupail* meaning 'a cork'; the modern French *etouper* means 'to stop up'. A recent form of estoppel is 'equitable estoppel'; this would apply, for example, in the case of a neighbour building on your land, presuming it to be his. If you let him go ahead instead of telling him it is your land, equity would not allow you later to require him to remove the building from your land.

ETP   *abbrev.* **eligible termination payments**.

euro$A   Australian dollars held outside Australia.

eurobonds   a branch of the euromarkets, eurobonds took off in the 1960s. As with euromarkets, euro- refers to the characteristic of the bond being sold in Europe and outside the country of the issuer. The investment bank Morgan Guaranty defined the eurobond as 'a bond underwritten by an international syndicate and sold in countries other than the country of the currency in which the issue is denominated'. Eurobonds are used by top credit rate borrowers such as banks and big international companies, to raise medium- to long-term fixed-interest funds. See **euromarkets**.

eurocar   a euromarket, rather than $US domestic, issue of CARs. See **certificate for automobile receivables**.

Euroclear   a computerised settlement and deposit system for the safe custody, delivery and payment of eurobonds. Euroclear is the oldest settlement system and was originally sponsored by Morgan Guaranty. It is now operated under contract. See **Austraclear, Centrale de Livraison de Valeurs Mobilieres**.

euro-CP   *abbrev.* **euro-commercial paper**.

euro-commercial paper   commercial paper, usually in the form of bearer promissory notes or certificates of deposit, that is issued in the euromarket. *Abbrev.*: **euro-CP**.

eurocredits   These broadly refer to medium-term lending, usually by banks, which is made up of eurocurrencies. Eurocredits are generally large-scale loans and so are handled by a syndicate (group) of lenders. See **eurocurrency, eurolines, euromarkets**.

eurocurrency   To qualify as a eurocurrency, a currency must be on deposit or loan outside its own country. The eurodollar is the most common eurocurrency; other examples are eurosterling, euroyen, eurofrancs and so on. The eurocurrency market communicates by telephone and telex; dealings take place between banks (interbank transactions) and with institutions, companies and governments. The eurocurrency market was the first 'offshore' market; a more recent development has been the Asian Dollar Market. See **Asian Currency Unit, euromarkets, offshore**.

eurodollar $US held in banks outside the US, mostly in Europe. See **euromarkets**.

eurokiwi   bonds denominated in $NZ, issued in the euromarkets, i.e. outside New Zealand, designed for non–New Zealand investors.

eurolines   lines of credit denominated in eurocurrencies.

euromarkets   the markets for eurocredits, eurocurrencies and eurobonds — that is, currencies and securities held in Europe and outside their country of origin (euro- is equivalent to external in this context). The euromarkets took off in the 1950s, partly, it is said, as a reaction to the cold war between the US and the Soviet Union. This left the Soviet Union anxious about holding dollars in the US and so it placed them with European banks, who then lent them to customers. At the same time, US banks were operating under restrictions which led to their holding $US balances in Europe, particularly London. London was the first euromarket centre and is still the largest. See **eurobonds, eurocredits, eurocurrencies, eurodollars**.

euro-MTN   a medium-term note issued in eurodollars. See **medium-term note**.

euronote   the short-term version of the eurobond, issued with floating rates and usually with maturities of less than six months.

European currency unit   The unit of account within the European Economic Community, these form the basket of nine currencies used by the European Monetary System. The European currency unit is made up of all the eight currencies in the European Monetary System plus sterling. It forms part of the foreign exchange reserves of the European central banks and is also used as a currency in its own right: loans and investments are made in European currency units and companies invoice in them. *Abbrev.*: **ECU**.

European Economic Community   a body founded by the Treaty of Rome in 1957 as a customs union, popularly referred to as the Common Market, by France, West Germany, Italy, Belgium, the Netherlands and Luxembourg. The European Economic Community expanded in 1973 to include the UK, the Republic of Ireland, and Denmark, and grew again in 1981 with the addition of Greece. *Abbrev.*: **EEC**. See **Treaty of Rome**.

European Monetary System   An agreement between the EEC member countries to manage their currencies so that their exchange rates move closely in line with one another. It was hoped that this greater stability in exchange rates would facilitate the control of inflation in EEC countries and encourage economic growth. The currencies must be held within a band relative to agreed rates called 'central rates'; if any one currency moves significantly, attempts are made by its central bank to bring it into line. In addition there have been fairly regular general realignments of the eight currencies in the EMS (these are the deutschmark, French franc, Italian lira, Netherlands guilder, Belgian franc, Danish kroner, Irish pound, Luxembourg franc). The EMS agreement was adopted in December 1978 but the first central rates were established in March 1979. The EMS superseded the European Joint Float (popularly called the 'snake') which had been established in 1972. Participating currencies in the EMS are not exactly the same as those in the snake. See **snake**.

European option   an option that can be exercised before its expiry date but which is non-tradeable. This was the first type of option available on the Sydney Futures Exchange. Also known as **over-the-counter options**. See **American option**.

euroyen   Japanese currency held in term deposits in banks outside Japan, mostly in Europe. The yen are used in international transactions but settlement is made in Tokyo. Securities issued in euroyen pay interest in yen and the income is deposited in bank accounts held outside Japan.

euroyen bond   a bond denominated in Japanese currency, usually issued or held outside Japan. Euroyen bonds have been seen internationally since December 1984 when the US Treasury and Japan's Ministry of Finance agreed to open Japan's financial markets, thus increasing the importance of the yen in international finance. Before the emergence of euroyen bonds, multinational companies issued yen bonds in Japan.

exchange control   regulation at government level of activities such as money flows in and out of a country, and its transactions with the rest of the world. Exchange controls are usually maintained in the belief that they help to protect a country's currency and its foreign exchange reserves. The controls may restrict investments by residents overseas and non-residents' investments and participation in the local market. (Big international currency movements tend not to obey such controls.) Sometimes individuals are limited in the amount of currency they may take abroad for holidays. The UK abandoned exchange controls in 1979. In Australia, the exchange controls. which had persisted in one form or another since 1939 were almost totally removed in December 1983 by the Hawke Labor government.

exchange for physical   in futures trading, the practice of using the futures market as a pricing basis for instruments not traded on the futures exchange. The concept was introduced on the Sydney Futures Exchange in September 1981. It involves one party giving or taking delivery of, say, non-bank bills instead of bank-accepted bills, at a predetermined margin relative to the corresponding listed futures market contract price. The EFP is registered when the deal is first agreed but settlement takes place between the two parties and not through the futures market delivery process. The concept of EFP is well established in world futures markets. It is so-called because it allows a trader to exchange a futures position for a physical (cash market) position or vice versa. It is called 'ex-pit' trading on the Chicago Board of Trade. *Abbrev.*: **EFP**.

exchange of contracts   the penultimate stage when buying real estate. The exchange of contracts (a formal agreement between buyer and seller) is followed by the 'settlement period' which can give the buyer time to scurry about for more finance if that is needed. The settlement period usually lasts about six to eight weeks, depending on searches, surveys and other formalities. After exchange of contracts, buyer and seller should be able to sleep easily at night, as the deal is signed and sealed. However, hitches can arise, so save the champagne for settlement day.

exchange rate   What one currency is worth in terms of another, for example the $A might be worth 80 US cents or 205 yen. Currencies traded freely on foreign exchange markets have a spot (immediate) rate and a forward rate. Countries can determine their exchange rates in a variety of ways, the most common these days being:

- a **floating exchange rate system** where the currency finds its own level in the market;
- a **crawling or flexible peg system** which is a combination of an officially fixed rate and frequent, small adjustments which in theory work against a build-up of speculation about a revaluation or devaluation;
- a **fixed exchange rate system** where the value of the currency is set by the government and/or the central bank.

See **forward rate, spot rate.**

exchange settlement accounts   These refer to the accounts held with the Reserve Bank and used by the banks to settle transactions with each other. Funds in the exchange settlement accounts are quite distinct from 'uncleared' funds: they are the proceeds of the previous day's cheques which have been cleared at the banks' clearing house. They are also referred to as 'same-day' cash as the funds have immediate value. No interest is paid on exchange settlement account balances, so the banks monitor their levels very closely as there is little point in leaving surpluses that earn no interest. Banks are limited in the transactions that can be set directly against the exchange settlement accounts. These accounts handle immediate value transactions; other transactions go through the clearing house.

The authorised short-term money market dealers' accounts held with the Reserve Bank are also referred to as exchange settlement accounts. This is not strictly accurate but it is an accepted description. Bank deposits with authorised dealers can be transferred for same-day value from the dealers' accounts with the Reserve Bank to the banks' exchange settlement accounts, and vice versa. Neither the dealers' accounts nor the banks' exchange settlement accounts may be overdrawn at the end of the trading day. *Abbrev.*: **ESA**. See **clearing house, daylight overdraft, federal funds market, uncleared funds.**

exchange-traded options   options on the Sydney Futures Exchange which allow both the taker (buyer) and the grantor (seller) of an option to trade out of the option before expiry date. See **options.**

excise   a domestic tax levied on selected commodities by the federal government, which has exclusive power to impose excise duties. It is estimated that 98 per cent of excise falls on alcohol, tobacco and petroleum products. Excise is a specific tax, levied as a fixed sum of money per unit of the commodity taxed, as against an ad valorem tax which is expressed as a percentage of the value of the commodity taxed. See **ad valorem**.

ex-dividend   similar to ex-interest ('ex' means 'without' in money language), ex-divided identifies a quoted share or security as one on which the current dividend is earmarked for the seller, not the buyer. See **cum dividend**.

executive search   see **headhunter**.

executor   one who is appointed in a will to administer the distribution of a deceased person's estate (wealth and property) according to the wishes of the testator or testatrix (he or she who made the will).

exercise (of an option)   converting an option into its underlying futures contract or into the shares covered by the option, by paying the predetermined amount.

exercise price   see **strike price**.

Ex-Im Bank   *abbrev.* **Export-Import Bank of the United States.**

ex-interest   without interest. Bonds are quoted ex-interest fifteen days before coupon date so that interest can be paid to the registered holder.

ex officio   A position described as 'ex officio' is one that goes hand in hand with a particular office, not with the individual holding that office. Literally, it means 'by virtue of or according to office'. For example, the secretary of Federal Treasury is an 'ex officio' member of the board of the Reserve Bank, which means that whoever holds the office of secretary of the Treasury also sits on the Reserve Bank Board but ceases to do so when no longer secretary of the Treasury.

expenditure   accounting language for a payment made or to be made for an asset or service. See **capital expenditure**.

expense   US slang has converted this noun into a verb which means to treat a sum of money spent as an expense for accounting or tax reasons.

expense account   a tax-beneficial privilege given usually to business executives to recognise that almost everything they do is for the good (profit) of the company. It is expected that executives will consult clients and colleagues in gathering information and transacting deals and that any outlay should be met by the company as an investment in future profit. Expense accounts, often operated through credit cards, are used to pay for entertainment and travel. There is a close link between a person's status in the banking community and the size of his or her expense account. Under the new rules of the fringe benefits tax, expense accounts are no longer allowable tax deductions for the employer. See **convention, fringe benefits tax, Lunch, meeting.**

ex-pit trading   see **exchange for physical.**

export credits   the type of loans made by the Export-Import Bank to encourage exports. Export credit finance is often subsidised by the government to help it along.

Export Finance and Insurance Corporation   a statutory corporation established in 1974 to encourage Australia's overseas trade. *Abbrev.*: **EFIC.**

Export-Import Bank of Japan   Japan's export financing institution, set up in 1950.

Export-Import Bank of the United States   an independent federal banking corporation set up in 1934 to help in financing exports and imports between the US and other countries. The Export-Import Bank provides funds to borrowers outside the US, and offers export guarantees and insurance. *Abbrev.*: **Ex-Im Bank.**

export incentives   concessions to exporters to encourage them to sell more, for example export credits and other subsidies.

exposure   risk. Traders talk of 'exchange rate exposure' and 'interest rate exposure', which means they are at risk from potential variations in these rates. Nervousness about such vulnerability spawned markets which offer methods of protection such as hedging through futures trading or forward markets, borrowing in floating rate facilities and taking multicurrency loans.

ex-rights   a stock exchange term meaning that the price quoted for a share does not include the right to take up new stock that has just been offered or is about to be offered. The opposite is cum rights, which is stock sold with the rights to a new issue. See **cum rights.**

external account   This can be a bank account held by a resident with an overseas institution or it can refer to the overseas activities of a country, i.e. its trade with other nations and overseas borrowings. See **balance of payments.**

external debt   what is owed by a country's government and private sector to foreigners.

extraordinaries   see **extraordinary items.**

extraordinary general meeting   a meeting called for a specific purpose. See **annual general meeting, board room, director.**

extraordinary items   income or expenses which are quite outside the normal course of a company's business and which are shown separately from the annual profit or loss calculation. Also **extraordinaries**. See **operating profit/loss**.

F

face value the full amount of a security, loan or investment before interest is added on or discounted. Coupon interest is calculated on the face value of a loan or security; for example, a Commonwealth bond of $100 000 has a face value of $100 000 but would usually be bought at a discount (if market rates were higher than the bond's coupon rate) and the holder would receive face value when the bond matures. Australian Savings Bonds are sold at face value—you pay $100 for $100 worth of Aussie Bonds and get the same amount back when cashing them in, earning interest through the coupon while the bonds are held. Face value is the same as nominal value or par value. See **discount, nominal value, par value, yield to redemption**.

factor Originally referring to a steward or bailiff overseeing an estate, factor now has two meanings:
- the agent who takes over collecting another's debts. See **factoring**;
- one of the inputs to production, for example land or labour. See **factor cost**.

factor cost the cost of producing one item—including labour and ingredients—as distinct from its market price which would be affected by indirect taxes and subsidies.

factoring taking over the collection and supervision of a company's debts or receivables (what is owed to it). The factoring company buys, at a discount, all the trade debts due to a business as they arise, and provides an accounting and debt collection service. The factoring company makes early payment of a substantial percentage of the trade debts, thereby reducing the business's need to extend credit. The practice began in the US and spread elsewhere; it is very useful to small firms that are growing rapidly. See **factor**.

fall out of bed as in 'the $US fell out of bed', meaning the currency declined suddenly and substantially.

FANMAC *abbrev*. **First Australian National Mortgage Acceptance Corporation Ltd**.

Fannie Mae a security issued by the Federal National Mortgage Association of the US (say the initials FNMA out loud and you get Fannie Mae). An independent US agency, FNMA was established in 1938 and reviewed in 1954: its main business is to buy mortgages from banks, mortgage companies, savings and loan associations and insurance companies, and to help these lenders in their home financing. See **Annie Mae, Ginnie Mae.**

FASTBACs *abbrev.* **first automobile short-term bonds and certificates.**

FBT *abbrev.* **fringe benefits tax.**

featherbedding making conditions softer and more comfortable, implying a comfort that is not wholly deserved. Sometimes trade unions are accused of seeking to featherbed; that is, they use their industrial muscle to create jobs for members which are not wholly productive. Tariffs featherbed local manufacturers by making imports less competitive. A featherbedding executive is one who surrounds himself or herself with staff to reduce his or her need to work while creating the impression of running a large and vigorous organisation.

Fed *abbrev.* **Federal Reserve system.**

Federal Deposit Insurance Corporation a public corporation in the US created by the *Glass Steagall Act* to insure the deposits of banks, protecting depositors should a bank fail. See *Glass Steagall Act.*

federal funds market short-term interbank lending in the US. Federal funds are the reserve assets of the US commercial banks, which they hold with their Federal Reserve banks. Banks with surpluses lend to others who are short, usually only overnight. The situation where Australian banks lend their exchange settlement account surpluses to each other is referred to as the 'interbank market'. See **exchange settlement accounts, interbank market.**

federal funds rate the interest rate prevailing in the US federal funds market, that is the rates paid and charged on interbank lending of their reserve assets. The Federal Reserve can influence the federal funds rate through open market operations which increase or decrease member banks' reserves and therefore their ability to borrow or lend. The federal funds rate is thus closely watched as it can reflect the authorities' intentions on monetary policy and interest rates.

Federal Home Loan Mortgage Corporation Born in 1970, and owned by the twelve Federal Home Loan Banks, this organisation buys mortgages and resells them in the form of participation certificates (PCs), secured by pools of conventional mortgages. *Abbrev.*: **Freddie Mac.** See **participation certificates.**

Federal National Mortgage Association of the US see **Fannie Mae.** *Abbrev.*: **FNMA.**

Federal Open Market Committee a committee of the United States

Federal Reserve system which controls the purchases and sales of government securities and monitors the US foreign exchange market. It consists of seven members of the board of governors and heads of five of the twelve Federal Reserve banks, including the head of the Federal Reserve Bank of New York. The committee meets every three weeks and makes decisions which are carried out by the Federal Reserve Bank of New York. The minutes of its meetings are published six weeks after the event and are awaited with interest. No similar information is issued in Australia (at the time of writing, November 1984). *Abbrev.*: **FOMC.**

Federal Reserve system   the US central bank, established in 1913 by an Act of Congress, comprising the Federal Reserve Board, Federal Open Market Committee and the twelve Federal Reserve banks. The *Federal Reserve Act* 1913 divided the US into twelve regions (Federal Reserve districts), each with a Federal Reserve bank. The New York Fed is the most important. Federal Reserve banks hold the cash reserves of the member banks, rediscount bills and provide clearing facilities. The board is made up of seven full-time governors, each appointed for fourteen years, including the chairman, and a large permanent, professional (non-political) staff. *Abbrev.*: **Fed.**

Fed wire   the communications system linking all twelve Federal Reserve Banks in the US, their 24 branches, the Federal Reserve Board in Washington, US Treasury offices in Washington and Chicago. It has been called the central nervous system of money transfer in the US. Through the Fed wire the banks can transfer reserve balances for immediate credit, between banks and customers. Also **FedWire** or **Fedwire**. See **clearing house interbank payments system**.

Fibonacci numbers   a number sequence discovered by the thirteenth-century Italian mathematician, Leonardo Fibonacci de Pisa. The number sequence presented is 1, 1, 2, 3, 5, 8, 13, 21, 34 and so on to infinity. The numbers have several interesting properties, the most important being that the ratio of any number to its next higher number approaches 0.618 after the first four numbers. This and other ratios are often used in all markets to indicate likely retracement levels. The Fibonacci sequence of numbers is also referred to by Ralph Elliott as the mathematical basis for the Wave principle. See **Elliot Wave Theory**.

FID   *abbrev.* **financial institutions duty.**

fidelity fund   a form of insurance against the loss of money held in trust or on behalf of investors. Professional associations of lawyers, for example, may set up voluntary funds, provided by levies on members, to protect clients' interests. Every stock exchange must have one. The assets of the fidelity fund are the property of the exchange, held in trust. The responsibility for the fidelity fund rests with the stock exchange committee. Stock exchange member organisations contribute to the fund and initial contributions are required as a condition of membership of the exchange, with the exchange determining the amount to be lodged.

FIFO   *abbrev.* **first in, first out**

figure, the   foreign exchange dealers' shorthand meaning running off to the '00' at the end of a quote. For example, if the $US were quoted at 239.80/240 yen, the dealer would say the $US stood at 239.80/the figure. In the case of a $US/deutschmark quote, a price of 2.4580/2.4600 would read as 2.4580/the figure. See **big figure, the**.

fill or kill order   a futures market order, to be carried out immediately and if not, to be cancelled.

final dividend   see **dividend**.

finance company   a non-bank financial institution. Finance companies developed in Australia in the 1950s as sources of consumer finance at a time when bank credit was tight and bank loans hard to get. Australian trading banks bought into or established their own finance company subsidiaries and other financiers grew up independently of the banks to swell the availability of loans for a variety of purposes such as car or boat purchases, holidays and home improvements. Finance company rates are not cheap but the money is more often than not available; finance companies raise funds from the public through debenture and note prospectuses, taking funds for terms between three months and five years. See **non-bank financial institution**.

finance lease   a lease which effectively transfers from the lessor (owner) to the lessee the bulk of the risks and benefits that go with ownership of the leased property. See **operating lease**.

Financial Corporation Act 1974   The Act provides for the registration and direct regulation in Australia of a wide range of non-bank institutions. Its chief objectives are to supplement the information available to the authorities (Reserve Bank, Treasury, government) on non-bank financial institutions (NBFIs); and to provide an opportunity to control NBFIs for the purposes of monetary policy. Part IV of the *Financial Corporations Act*, which has not yet been proclaimed, would give the federal government, through the Reserve Bank, wide-ranging controls over the assets, interest rates and lending policies of NBFIs. These institutions are much relieved that successive governments have so far declined to put Part IV into practice. The main purpose of the *Financial Corporations Act* so far has been the acquisition of additional information and statistics on NBFIs. See **finance company, non-bank financial institution**.

financial engineering   see **zaiteku**.

financial futures   see **futures contract, futures markets.**

financial futures options   see **options.**

financial incentive   an offer of money, to induce you to improve your performance.

financial institutions duty   This State tax was introduced in January 1983 in New South Wales and Victoria and was subsequently adopted in South Australia, Western Australia and Tasmania. Financial institutions duty is a tax on the receipts of all financial institutions; the rate varies from State to State. It was thought initially that the tax would deflect money market business from Sydney and Melbourne to tax-exempt centres, but this has not proved to be the case. The rates applied are fairly low, for example 0.3 per cent on a transaction; short-term money market transactions fall into a special category because of the heavy turnover.

financial instrument   a document such as a bill of exchange, bond, Treasury Note or promissory note. See **instrument.**

financial jargon   what this book is all about.

financial supermarket   one-stop money shop, offering the full range of financial services, from deposits and loans to insurance and travel. The opposite of boutique bank. See **boutique, niche.**

Financial Times index   the UK equivalent of the Australian all ordinaries index and the US Dow Jones; the measure of the average value of shares on the London Stock Exchange. The FT index is compiled and published daily in the *Financial Times*, the UK's financial bible. It measures the movements in the shares of 30 representative industrial companies. *Abbrev.*: **FT index.**

financial year   In Australia the financial year, for government and taxation purposes, runs from 1 July to 30 June. Many companies use the same period as their financial year; some companies, however, operate in different time frames and may end their financial year in September or December to conform with an overseas parent. A financial year can also refer to 360 days (twelve months each of 30 days), a scale used as the basis for interest calculations in a number of countries. Financial year time frames differ from country to country. Also **fiscal year.**

fine rate   Traders in the money market talk of 'fine rates' when they mean low, or the most favourable rates available. Top-name companies can borrow at fine rates.

fine-tuning   In managing the economy, a government may fine-tune, or make small adjustments, in reponse to economic indicators which suggest some action to correct trends or anomalies. This was trendy in the 1950s and 1960s but has not proved so effective in recent years.

FIRB   *abbrev.* **Foreign Investment Review Board.**

fire sale value   a measure of the worth of assets that marks them down to the price they might fetch if sold quickly. A price will usually be well below their book value. See **book value.**

firm   a business, partnership, company or proprietary company. The phrase **go firm** (on a deal) means a trader can assure the other party that the transaction will take place at the prices and volumes discussed. In share trading, prices are said to **firm** meaning they rise; confusingly, when interest rates rise on fixed-interest investments, this means the prices fall.

First Australian National Mortgage Acceptance Corporation Ltd
Incorporated in September 1984 and known by its acronym FANMAC, the company is headquartered in Sydney and is a product of a combined New South Wales government and finance industry study on the possibility of developing a secondary mortgage market. FANMAC operates as a commercial financial organisation purchasing mortgages in Australia and issuing securities in domestic and overseas markets; it mobilises funds for the housing market from non-traditional sources such as superannuation funds and life companies and provides investors with a new form of marketable security. FANMAC is 26 per cent owned by the New South Wales government, with the remaining equity held by a range of banks, merchant and investment banks, credit unions and insurance companies. *Abbrev.*: **FANMAC.**

first automobile short-term bonds and certificates   issued by Drexel Burnham Lambert Inc. and similar to Salomons' **CARs.** They are pass-through securities issued by a trust against a pool of car loans. The certificates and bonds are bought and traded by institutions. *Abbrev.*: **FASTBACs.**

first in, first out   an accounting technique for valuing a company's stock in which it is assumed that goods are used in the same sequence in which they were bought. The goods on hand represent those last purchased and are valued at the latest purchase price. This has drawbacks: if prices are rising, the technique overstates profit, if prices are falling, profits are understated. *Abbrev.*: **FIFO.** See **LIFO.**

fiscal drag   the reason you do not seem to have more money to spend, even though your salary has been increased. At the same time as your salary was raised, inflation is moving people into higher tax brackets, on a progressive scale. Fiscal drag refers to the weight of higher taxes on higher incomes so that after-tax incomes do not reflect the extent of a wage rise. Private sector growth and activity is dampened down because after-tax incomes are not rising.

fiscal policy   the arm of government policy (the other is monetary policy) which influences the economy through the budget by changes in tax and welfare payments and government expenditure. Monetarists claim that fiscal 'fine-tuning' of the economy is ultimately destabilising; they say that fiscal policy is less effective than monetary policy or not effective at all. Supporters of fine-tuning disagree, of course, saying that the relative stability of the late 1950s and 1960s was due to fine-tuning. Because of 'crowding out' problems, political constraints and 'budget cycles', fiscal policy is generally less flexible than monetary policy. See **budget cycle, crowding out, fine-tuning, monetarist**.

fiscal year   see **financial year**.

fixed charge   see **charge**.

fixed deposit   the same as a term or time deposit. Money may be placed with a bank, merchant bank, building society or credit union for a fixed term at a fixed rate of interest which will remain unchanged during the period of the deposit. Depositors may have to accept an interest penalty if they break the deposit, i.e. ask to take the money out before the agreed period has expired. See **term deposit**.

fixed interest   interest paid on investments such as bonds and debentures, paid at a predetermined and unchanging rate for a specified period of time. See **bond, debenture**.

fixed parity   the system in foreign exchange by which all exchange rates were set officially—by governments or central banks—and usually changed only at intervals. Following the creation of the Bretton Woods system, all currencies were fixed in relation to the $US, which was in turn tied to gold. This rigid system was abandoned in favour of a system of floating exchange rates under which, theoretically at least, the price of a currency is determined by market forces of supply and demand. See **Bretton Woods, parity**.

fixed-rate loan   a loan that has been made at a specific rate which will prevail for the term of the financing.

flat rate of interest   interest charged on the full amount of a loan throughout the entire term of the loan. The flat rate takes no account of the fact that periodic repayments, which include both interest and principal, gradually reduce the amount owed. Personal loan repayments are usually calculated on a flat rate of interest. The effective interest rate is considerably higher than it first appears. A rough rule is that 9 per cent flat equates to about 17 per cent effective per annum; that is, double the flat rate minus one per cent, although this varies with the term of the loan. See **compound interest, simple interest**.

flat tax   a single-rate tax on personal income which applies at the same rate irrespective of the level of income earned. If the flat tax rate were, say, 25 per cent of income, then all wage and salary earners would have one-quarter of their income deducted for tax, instead of the present situation where tax is levied on a progressive scale with lower income earners paying a lower proportion in tax than those on higher salaries.

flesh pedlar   see **headhunter**.

flexible annuity   a term-certain annuity which provides regular income and flexibility of income payments so that the annuitant (the person receiving payments, who (usually) earlier invested the funds in the annuity) has a choice of income level. The annuitant has access to the capital and can withdraw funds from the annuity. The initial capital and interest payments made are guaranteed, but the flexible annuity does not provide a guarantee on future interest payments. See **annuity, term-certain annuity**.

flexible peg   see **exchange rate**.

flight to quality   what happens when investors become nervous of private sector creditworthiness and decide to sacrifice potentially higher returns to achieve security, for example taking their money out of private sector investments such as, say, promissory notes or corporate debentures, and buying government bonds.

float   This word can be used in different contexts. For example, currencies can float, which means their exchange rates or values against other currencies fluctuate in line with supply and demand in the market as against being set by government. A company can float shares (a share flotation), which means it offers its shares for sale, and loans can be written at a rate that floats at a margin above or below a benchmark rate which means the loan's rate moves in line with the benchmark rate. The noun 'float' refers to these activities.

Major nations moved to a system of **floating currencies** in 1971 when it became clear that the prevailing system of fixed parities was not working effectively. The UK floated the pound sterling in 1972, i.e. allowed it to trade freely in foreign exchange markets instead of having its rate determined by the government; Australia decided to float the $A in December 1983. The shift to allow currencies to float was made so that currencies could find their own levels in the markets, with supply-and-demand and speculative forces being the main determining factors.

Most floats still entail some degree of government intervention, though floats differ in the extent to which they are managed. A true **free float** is also called a **clean float**. Probably the closest to this is in the US, where the Federal Reserve has intervened only rarely and has declared its action after the event. More heavily managed floats are referred to as **dirty floats**, indicating that the country's central bank intervenes fairly regularly to influence the currency's level by buying or selling.

Australia's float appears to have aimed for a very lightly managed system with the Reserve Bank retaining the right to intervene from time to time 'to smooth out disorderly markets', as central banks say.

A float in banking terms means the amount of funds still in the process of being cleared. Smart operators write cheques against the float in their accounts, relying on outstanding cheques not having yet 'hit' so that they have time to deposit funds to cover the cheques written. New banking technology has cut down the length of time available for using floats this way. See **central bank intervention, fixed parity, flotation, hit**.

floating charge see **charge**.

floating currency see **float**.

floating-rate finance money that is provided at a rate set at a margin above (rarely below) a benchmark rate so that the rate charged for the funds moves in line with the benchmark rate instead of staying fixed throughout the term for which the money has been provided.

floating-rate notes securities, popular in euromarkets and adopted elsewhere. They are usually issued for five years or more and carry a variable interest rate which is adjusted every six months by a margin against a benchmark rate, such as LIBOR. FRNs became popular in recent years because of the increased volatility of interest rates which left lenders and borrowers reluctant to commit funds for a fixed period at a fixed rate. It is estimated that about 20 per cent of all Eurodollar issues are in the form of FRNs. *Abbrev*.: **FRNs**. See **LIBOR**.

float-off see **demerger**.

floor 1. A member of the **cap** and **collar** family, a floor guarantees a minimum rate of return but leaves the investor free to participate in rising interest rates above the agreed floor level. 2. in full, **trading floor**; where traders meet to transact business, as in the stock exchange or futures exchange floor. See **floor trader**.

floor price the level below which the price of a commodity or security will not fall because no seller will accept less, for example the reserve price at an auction. Often a government authority, such as the Australian Wool Corporation, is involved, setting a level which stops prices falling too far, i.e. below the floor price for wool. See **ceiling price**.

floor trader the person on the floor of an exchange such as a stock exchange or futures exchange who executes orders as the representative of a member firm. See **stock exchange**.

flotation (of shares) When a company floats its shares it is offering shares to the public to raise cash. See **float**.

flow of funds the movement of money; who is borrowing or lending, from or to whom, how much and how often. For flow-of-funds purposes the economy is divided into four sectors: government, households (including unincorporated businesses), companies and foreigners. A study of the flow of funds can show the level of enthusiasm for saving or spending, what levels of interest rates dampen demand for credit and what levels attract most deposits. Flow-of-funds studies highlight patterns, rather than determine reasons. (See the Financial Flow Accounts Supplement to the *Reserve Bank of Australia Bulletin* for Australia's flow-of-funds statistics.)

FNMA   *abbrev.* **Federal National Mortgage Association of the US.** See **Fannie Mae**.

FOB/fob   *abbrev.* **free on board.**

FOMC   *abbrev.* **Federal Open Market Committee (US).**

Footsie   This stands for FT-SE (pronounced Footsie) — the London Financial Times Stock Exchange Index which lists the 100 largest public company shares traded on the London Stock Exchange. It is the UK equivalent of the US's Dow Jones.

forced savings   technically, saving that takes place because of a shortage of goods on which to spend, rather than a preference for saving. In common usage, demands on your income such as superannuation payments or overpayment of PAYE would be classed as forced saving—though more correctly these are called 'contractual savings'. The effect is similar in that you are prevented from spending the money—at least until it is reimbursed.

force majeure   circumstances beyond anyone's control that present an obstacle to the completion of a deal or contract.

foreign exchange   cash or other claims (such as bank deposits and bonds) on another country, held in the currency of that country; what you get when you exchange your Australian cash or travellers' cheques abroad; what the Reserve Bank holds in its 'official reserves'; what is usually earned from a nation's exports.

Foreign Investment Review Board   a body responsible for advising the federal government (Treasurer) on foreign investment matters. It examines and makes recommendations on individual investment proposals that fall under the *Foreign Takeovers Act* 1975 and other areas of foreign investment policy. The Foreign Investment Review Board consists of a chairman and deputy chairman who are part-time members, and an executive member who is the First Assistant Secretary of the Foreign Investment Division of Treasury. Executive services are provided for the board by this Treasury Division. *Abbrev.*: **FIRB**.

foreign tax credit system   a change, first applicable in the 1987/88 financial year, to the tax treatment of foreign income earned by Australian residents. Previously such income was exempt from Australian tax where it had been taxed in the country of source, irrespective of the level of foreign tax. This created an advantage for Australian residents earning income in another country. From 1 July 1987 an Australian resident taxpayer is subject to tax on the worldwide income derived by the taxpayer. A credit will be allowable in respect of any foreign tax paid.

forex   market shorthand for foreign exchange.

forfaiting   a form of fixed-rate trade finance. Forfaiting involves the purchase by a financial institution—the forfaiter—of an exporter's debts. These debts are usually in the form of bank bills of exchange or promissory notes and have been accepted by the exporter as deferred payment for goods sold to foreign buyers. The exporter sells the bills or notes at a discount, for cash, and passes all commercial and political risks and responsibilities for collection to the forfaiter. The exporter protects himself by including the words 'without recourse' in endorsing the bill. Forfaiting is commonly used in Europe, Latin America, North Africa and the Far East. The word derives from the French *a forfait* (surrendering rights).

forfeited shares   shares in a no-liability company which are forfeited (lost) to the previous owner because of non-payment of the call on the shares. See **company**.

forward   a word referring to future commitments, prices, etc., whose terms are established in the present.

forward exchange   the purchase or sale of foreign exchange for delivery at a future date at a predetermined price. This is used as a method of protection against variations in the exchange rate. See **forward margin, forward market, forward rate**.

forward margin   the difference between today's rate or price for a commodity, such as a foreign currency, and that commodity's projected future rate or price. The forward margin on a currency is expressed as a number of points above or below the spot (present) rate and is called a discount or a premium. The spot rate plus or minus the forward margin is called the forward rate. See **discount, forward rate, premium**.

forward market   a market where traders and speculators can take out contracts for purchases or sales of commodities at a future date, in specified volumes and at specified prices. Futures trading is an example of a forward market. See **forward rate, spot market, swaps**.

forward rate   the price for a commodity, such as a foreign currency, for other than prompt delivery. Forward rates in currencies are expressed at a premium or discount to the spot rate. See **forward margin, spot rate**.

forward rate agreement   an interest rate hedge which allows borrowers and lenders to lock into future interest rates without exchanging the principal amounts of the borrowing or loan. A forward rate agreement is a contract struck between a client and a bank or merchant bank, which fixes the interest rate relating to an expected loan or deposit, for an agreed amount, term and date. The bank or merchant bank quotes a forward rate using a benchmark reference rate such as the bank-accepted bill rate, for a specified period. On the agreed future date the difference between the rate struck under the contract and the prevailing market rate is settled between client and bank. Where the client has locked in a borrowing rate that proves to be lower than the bank bill rate at the end of the agreed period, the bank pays the difference to the client; conversely if the rates set under the forward rate agreement prove to be higher than prevailing interest rates the client pays the difference to the bank or merchant bank. *Abbrev.*: **FRA**.

forward with optional exit   a form of break-forward marketed by the Hambros Bank. *Abbrev.*: **FOX**. See **break-forward**.

FOX   *abbrev.* **forward with optional exit**.

FRA   *abbrev.* **forward rate agreement**.

franchise   a system of distributing goods and services in which one organisation (the **franchisor**) grants the right to another (the **franchisee**) to produce, sell or use its developed product, service or brand. A franchisee is a retailer who is licensed—franchised—to sell or use the franchisor's products. McDonald's Family Restaurant and the Kentucky Fried Chicken chains are examples of franchisors who let various outlets sell their products.

franked dividends   dividends paid out of company profits on which the full Australian tax has been paid, at the rate of 49 per cent, so that the dividends are tax-free in the hands of shareholders. See **dividend imputation, unfranked dividends**.

franking account   a record-keeping account required purely for tax purposes. The balance in the account represents the notional amount of after-tax profits that can be distributed to shareholders, without the shareholders having to pay further tax. See **franked dividends, dividend imputation**.

Freddie Mac   *abbrev.* **Federal Home Loan Mortgage Corporation**.

free enterprise   doing your own thing, and being allowed to do so; an entrepreneurial economic environment. A free enterprise company or individual operates without government interference or control in a system characterised by private ownership.

free lunch   Something, theoretically, that you don't have to pay for. 'There is no such thing as a free lunch' is a fine piece of rhetoric that is food for hours of argument. Usually, even with a so-called 'free lunch' you have to pay in some form for what you are given.

free market   a market that is left alone to set its own prices, unhindered by government or central bank intervention.

free on board   This applies to the valuation of goods as they are exported and represents what the exporter earns. It is the figure used by the Australian Bureau of Statistics when calculating the value of Australia's exports. Transport and insurance costs are excluded and entered to the importer's account; hence they are transported (on board ship) 'free' from the exporter's point of view. *Abbrev.*: **FOB** or **fob**.

free port   a port where no duty or taxes are paid on imports or exports.

free trade   a doctrine of free trade popularised by the Manchester School in the UK (1820-1850). The school believed in political and economic freedom with the minimum of government control and claimed that the economic welfare of all countries would be maximised if international trade were unhindered by government controls. The Manchester School drew on the earlier views of Adam Smith and David Ricardo for support for its arguments. Essentially, free trade is the absence of tariffs and government restrictions which could interrupt trade flows. Although in the short run nations may gain from the introduction of tariffs, economists now tend to feel that this view of self-interest is misguided, for example that tariffs are harmful as they can encourage an inefficient operation. The General Agreement on Tariffs and Trade was introduced to lay down some rules. Bad times tend to turn a nation's mind back to the notion of protecting its own backyard (the 1930s saw a jump in tariffs and the recession of the early 1980s revived interest in forms of protection). See **Smith, Adam** and **Ricardo, David** in **economists, General Agreement on Tariffs and Trade**.

freeze   to fix wages and prices by legislation or agreement, so that they do not move from the levels prevailing when the freeze is implemented. A wages and prices freeze is a way of trying to control inflation.

Friedman, Milton   see **economists**.

friendly society   Founded in Australia last century (the first in 1840), friendly societies were groups of workers who made small periodic contributions to a common fund which could be used when needed for funerals, sickness and so on. Friendly societies predate modern social services such as pension schemes and retirement benefits. They were formed on the basis of group interests, such as craft or religion. Now friendly societies operating in each State offer benefits such as funeral or sickness insurance, hospital cover and sometimes retirement benefits through savings and investments.

fringe benefits tax   Fringe benefits tax legislation sets out the taxes to be paid by employers on the amount of fringe benefits provided to employees. That taxable value is determined by specific rules detailed in the legislation and, with few exceptions, all benefits such as concessional housing loans, cars and so on are taxable. Entertainment expenses are no longer allowable as deductible expenses but they do not form part of fringe benefits tax legislation. *abbrev.* **FBT.**

FRNs   *abbrev.* **floating-rate notes.**

front end   the beginning of a transaction or process. For example, front-end development of a mining venture means the first stages of exploration, the setting up of infrastructure and so on.

front-end fee   the fee paid by a borrower to a lender at the beginning of a loan facility, or the cost to an investor of buying into a unit trust such as an equity trust or property trust. Front-end fees vary substantially, so it is advisable to check what amount applies in each case. Also **front-end loading.**

frozen account   Transactions through such an account are suspended pending legal examination or action. A deceased person's bank account is frozen until new ownership of the asset is established according to the terms of a will or until the probate process is complete. A bankrupt person's account is frozen until a receiver or manager is given authority over the bankrupt's affairs.
    At the time of writing (November 1984) banking regulations stipulate that the Australian trading banks must hold a percentage of their deposits 'frozen' in statutory reserve deposit accounts with the Reserve Bank. See **statutory reserve deposit.**

frozen assets   These assets cannot be used until legal action is out of the way. A company in receivership or a person declared bankrupt would have assets such as bank accounts frozen pending the receiver or trustee taking over administration of the company or the bankrupt estate.

FT index   *abbrev.* **Financial Times index.**

full   A trader is described as 'full with a client' when the maximum amount of credit exposure (for example through lending and foreign exchange transactions) has been carried out with that client, according to the trader's company's board directives.

fully paid shares   shares on which no uncalled capital is due.

fundamentalism   a creed which places faith in economic theory when analysing, say, the position of a company or country, the state of the economy and the balance of payments, rather than relying on trends to determine investment decisions. Fundamentalists use economic theory rather than statistics. People who make educated guesses are not infallible; neither are fundamentalists. See **chartists**.

funds   another word for money.

fungible   When one unit of a commodity is equal to any other like unit (such as grains of wheat or corn), these are termed fungible, i.e. one could be substituted for the other with no change in value. Dollar notes of the same amount (unless rare collector's specimen) are fungible, but bills of exchange and coins of different values are not. Fungibility of securities such as bills is an important consideration for computerised clearing systems such as Austraclear, CEDEL and Euroclear. 'Fungible' derives from the same Latin word as 'function'—hence fungibles are units of a commodity whose functions are interchangeable.

funny money   money won from dubious sources—'laundered' funds or the cash economy. It can also refer to currency produced by running the nation's money-printing press in the belief that it will pay the bills and solve all economic ills. This belief is still held in some political circles.

futures contract   an agreement to buy or sell a standard quantity of a commodity—such as gold, $US or bank bills of exchange—on a specific future date at an agreed price determined at the time the contract is made on the futures exchange trading floor. It is a binding contract, enforceable at law.
   Futures contracts are traded by open outcry on the floor of the futures exchange—in the case of Australia, the Sydney Futures Exchange—in a similar fashion to share market trading. Generally, someone wishing to trade in futures contracts would arrange to buy or sell a particular contract with a futures broker who is a member of the exchange. Contracts are for a specific amount and quality of a given commodity or financial instrument, for delivery at a specified time in the future. All futures contracts are registered with the clearing house, which monitors the market and sets deposit margins and margin calls. The bulk of futures contracts are not held to delivery but are closed out ahead of delivery date. About 2 per cent of contracts are held to delivery. See **clearing house, contract, futures markets**.

futures markets   Futures markets have existed for centuries but evolved in their present form in the US in the nineteenth century. Chicago, in the midst of the grain and farming belt, emerged as the home of futures trading. The Chicago Board of Trade, established in 1850, focused on grain; the Chicago Mercantile Exchange took off soon after, dealing in butter and eggs. The exchanges provided traders with the means to take out protection against vagaries in the prices of their commodities over which they had no control but which dramatically affected their income. The exchanges also provided speculators with a new outlet. The Sydney Futures Exchange began trading in 1960 as the Sydney Greasy Wool Futures Exchange, and wool was the only commodity traded until the live cattle contract was introduced in 1975. This was followed by the gold futures contract in 1978. Futures trading stuck with commodities, including products such as pork bellies and soya beans, until the 1970s when interest rate uncertainty, following the new floating currency system, focused attention on financial futures.

Financial futures offer the chance to hedge or protect against movements in interest rates and currencies. They have been a boom industry in the past decade as investors, traders and speculators seized on a new method to protect themselves against, or make money out of, increasingly volatile interest rates and exchange rates. Financial futures took off in the US in the early 1970s; currency futures started trading in 1972 in Chicago and interest rate futures followed in 1976. The Sydney Futures Exchange was the first outside the US to move into financial futures with the launch of bank bill futures in October 1979. Since then financial futures trading in Australia has expanded to encompass **currency futures, share price index futures** and a **Commonwealth bond futures contract**. The Sydney Futures Exchange plans to introduce **eurodollar futures** and **exchange-traded options**. Recent innovations at the Sydney Futures Exchange have been the introduction of 'locals' as traders, negotiated commissions and the switch from a ring to a pit system on the trading floor. See **exchange-traded options, futures contract, LIFFE, local, options, pit, Sydney Futures Exchange**.

G

Galbraith, John Kenneth see **economists**.

gapping taking advantage of a time difference. An example is borrowing short to lend long because that achieves a better interest rate return for the lender (in a normal market where short-term rates are lower than those in the longer term).

garnishee to attach someone's money or property to someone else, by order of a court (garnishment). If a court makes a garnishment against your employer (which it may do if so requested by one of your creditors) then your boss must send part of your pay to the people to whom you owe money. Other sources of money, including bank accounts, can be garnisheed. The garnishment procedure enables a creditor to get his or her hands on the money directly. 'Garnishee' as a noun refers to the person served with a garnishment.

GATT *abbrev.* **General Agreement on Tariffs and Trade.**

gazump a word that came into vogue with a buoyant real estate market, lending a new term to an ancient practice: doing someone down on a deal. In gazumping the seller raises the price—usually of a house and in response to a better offer—just before the deal is clinched. It is unethical, but legal and not unknown, especially when the housing market is booming; buyers are keen and sellers are greedy. Suggestions about the origins of the term include the Yiddish *gezumph* meaning 'to swindle' and a London barrow boys' expression meaning to 'short change'.

GDP *abbrev.* **gross domestic product.**

gearing The relationship between a company's shareholders' funds and some form of outside borrowing. Gearing is generally expressed as a ratio. A company is described as 'highly geared' if borrowed funds are high in relation to shareholders' funds. Analysts talk of a company's gearing when referring to its solvency and its ability to take on new commitments. An Australian bank's gearing is typically 20:1—that is, its borrowings are around twenty times shareholders' funds. An example of regulated gearing is that of the authorised short-term money market dealers; their gearing is imposed by the Reserve Bank and set at a maximum of 33:1 which means they can borrow up to 33 times their shareholders' funds. See **leasing, negative gearing.**

General Agreement on Tariffs and Trade an organisation begun in 1949, established under the terms of an international agreement; its secretariat is in Geneva, Switzerland. Through international meetings and moral suasion, it aims to minimise barriers to trade, and to reduce tariffs and preferential trade agreements. *Abbrev.*: **GATT**. See **Geneva Trade Conference**.

general equilibrium theory This theory describes the relationship among all the entities in an economy—consumers, producers and the markets in which they exchange products. These relationships determine all prices and incomes in the economy. The **partial equilibrium theory** describes the analysis of a single member, assuming that prices of all other products remain fixed. The partial equilibrium theory tends to be used more than the general equilibrium theory as it has wider application.

Geneva Trade Conference This conference, held in 1947, was the starting point for the General Agreement on Tariffs and Trade, the purpose of which is to promote free and uninterrupted world trade. See **General Agreement on Tariffs and Trade**.

gensaki First approved in 1976, this is a yen repurchase agreement based on Japanese securities. The rates on *gensaki* agreements are set in line with the yen certificates of deposit market rate. *Gensaki* refers only to repurchase agreements available in Japan, not in overseas markets. See **repurchase agreements**.

Giblin, Lyndhurst Falkiner see **economists**.

gilt-edged a quaint nineteenth-century description of government securities, still in use, intended to underscore their safety as an investment.

gilts Initially used as shorthand for UK government securities, especially the longer maturities, this term has come to be used to describe government securities of other countries. For example the Australian gilt curve means the Australian Commonwealth government bond curve.

Ginnie Mae a US security issued by the Government National Mortgage Association, an agency of the US Department of Housing and Urban Development. Ginnie Maes were the first interest-rate futures contract introduced on the Chicago Board of Trade in 1976, and are actively traded on all major US securities markets. See **Annie Mae, Fannie Mae**.

give-up In Australia this refers to the price a seller has to give up to sell a security such as a bond; it is the selling price. For example, a buyer wants 10.25 per cent yield for a 90-day bank bill. A seller's price is 10.2 per cent but the buyer won't budge, so the seller moves to the buyer's price and has to give up a yield of 10.25 per cent.

glamour stocks   The stock exchange is not immune from trends, and 'glamour stocks' are the trendies of the market. They are popular and are perceived to offer growth potential, so everyone climbs on the bandwagon, though often without much careful analysis of the true values. For example, Poseidon was a glamour stock of its time.

Glass Steagall Act   an Act by US Congress in 1933, aimed at improving banking practices. It prohibited commercial banks and trust companies in the US from investment banking and established the Federal Deposit Insurance Corporation to protect bank depositors' funds. See **Federal Deposit Insurance Corporation**.

globalised   business jargon for 'worldwide'. A bank or company which has become globalised operates internationally.

global note facility   a development of the note issuance facility which combines the ability to issue euronotes with the ability to gain access to the US commercial paper market, if necessary with the support of a letter of credit of a highly rated bank. The global note facility concept has been extended to cover access to markets other than the US. See **multi-option facility, note issuance facility**.

GNMA   *abbrev.* **Government National Mortgage Association**. See **Ginnie Mae**.

gnome loans   loans taken out in Swiss francs. These were popular with many Australian and New Zealand borrowers in the early 1980s because the Swiss interest rates were well below domestic rates in both countries (around 5 per cent compared to double figures). Borrowers who failed to pay attention to the exchange rate risk suffered badly when the Australian and New Zealand currencies fell sharply against the strong Swiss franc.

Gnomes of Zurich   a colloquialism referring originally to Swiss but now also to other European bankers dealing in currencies and gold.

GNP   *abbrev.* **gross national product**.

going concern   A business described as a 'going concern' is one which is in operation and is viable.

going concern value   a measure of a company's worth, based on the assumption that the business will continue to operate, thus giving a higher value to the assets than would be attributed by a fire sale value. See **fire sale value**.

going public   This is what a private company does when it decides to change its image and status and issue shares to the general public, often to raise money for an expanding business. Generally private companies contemplating going public take professional advice from a stockbroker or merchant bank, who will advise and help organise the issue of shares. If it wishes to become publicly listed, a company must also sign the stock exchange listing agreement, which imposes certain obligations about the disclosure of information to the investing public. 'Going public' could be regarded as the corporate equivalent of coming out of the closet, in that it implies a degree of confidence that one is ready to launch oneself into the public arena.

gold-convertible bonds   bonds that are convertible into gold. They are typically issued by gold-mining companies and bought by investors who want a longer-term investment in gold without buying, storing and insuring the metal. The issuing company gives the right to convert the bonds into gold and in return raises funds at a fairly low coupon or interest rate; at the same time it establishes a potential forward sale of gold. The investor offsets a fairly low rate of return against the benefits of having a foot in the gold market without the problems of storage or insurance.

golden circle   a form of collusive dealing in a market such as foreign exchange, by which traders successfully channel profits into their own pockets at the expense of a client or their employer. The dealers make a profit by buying and selling currencies at different prices, in a way that ensures they, or the sham company they have formed, take a profit from the difference in prices.

golden handcuffs   handsome payments made provided the employer stays with the company. Banks, investment banks, merchant banks and broking firms operate with a formula so that a given amount is paid initially and the remainder paid along the way according to track record and performance.

golden handshake   a substantial gift made by a company to an employee (often of long standing) either to soften the blow of premature departure from the company (not necessarily voluntary) or to recognise services rendered throughout a long and productive career.

golden hello   a generous upfront payment made by a company to an incoming employee. Similar to a signing-on fee.

golden parachute   termination or retirement benefits provided for top executives as a reward for the responsibilities they have carried. The golden parachute—cash settlement or shares or options on shares —is structured to soften the blow if the executive and employer part company for any reason; for example, a hostile takeover could result in job losses.

gold futures contract   see **futures markets, Sydney Futures Exchange**.

gold reserves   what the Reserve Bank of Australia or official bodies in other countries hold as part of their total gold and foreign exchange reserves to help meet the demands of foreign trade and financial transactions.

gold standard   An international monetary system where, in theory, the values of different currencies were kept constant in terms of gold. Each currency was convertible into gold; therefore exchange rates between currencies were fixed and international debts were settled in gold. (In practice, though, reserve currencies did exist, such as sterling.) Under the gold standard, internal adjustments to domestic disturbances were forced by balance of payments flows; the value of a country's money supply had to be related to the level of gold held in the community. The gold standard has been officially abolished but gold is still very important and debate on the pros and cons of the gold standard continues. Exchange rates were based on the gold standard before World War I.

The system was revived in the 1920s and lasted, in a different form, until 1933. The disrupting effect of the Great Depression was the immediate cause of the collapse of the gold standard; in the longer run its demise was due to its costly mechanism of adjustment and to the decline in Britain's relative economic strength and the accompanying changes in the trade and capital movements on which it had been based. The US took its dollar off convertibility to gold in 1933 and reintroduced a more restricted form of convertibility a year later. The gold standard survived in a limited fashion after World War II; the decisions of the Bretton Woods conference in 1944 tied most currencies to the $US, which in turn was tied to gold. By 1971 the $US was no longer convertible to gold and any attempts to fix the major currencies' exchange rates were abandoned in 1973 in favour of floating exchange rates. See **Bretton Woods, float, specie**.

goods and services   anything—tangible and intangible—which makes a contribution to well-being. It is impossible to read even the most simple textbook on economics without hitting the phrase 'goods and services' several times. It is a favourite portmanteau term used by economists (it crops up in this book, too) to cover all items of production (what you buy) and all services ranging from banking and investment to the local garbage collection.

goods and services tax   an indirect tax, introduced in New Zealand on 1 October 1986, at a rate of 10 per cent, as a broadly based consumption tax. From the consumer's point of view this has a similar effect to the European value-added tax. *Abbrev.*: **GST**. See **value-added tax**.

good till cancelled   an expression used in share market and futures trading indicating to a broker that an order is to hold valid until the client cancels it. *Abbrev.*: **GTC**.

goodwill   an intangible asset. It is the good reputation enjoyed by a company, individual or product; the asset constituted by the tendency of the customers or clients of a business or professional practice to deal with that business or practice despite a change of personnel operating it—i.e. the attachment of existing customers. See **intangible assets**.

Government National Mortgage Association   *Abbrev.*: **GNMA**. See **Ginnie Mae**.

government paper   see **paper**.

Gramm Rudman Act   named after Senator Phil Gramm and Senator Warren Rudman, the congressional sponsors of a US Budget Reform Bill, signed into law in December 1985. The Act sets targets for cuts in government spending designed to eliminate the deficit by 1991 and incorporate procedures to trigger automatic expenditure cuts if deficit targets are not met.

grandfather clause   a clause in a legal agreement which says that situations already in existence when new legislation comes into effect are exempted from the new rules—previous generations are untouched.

Granny bonds   see **indexed bonds**.

grantor   a seller (in the context of option trading). See **options**.

Great Depression   see **depression**.

greenback   a colloquialism for the US dollar which is derived from the colour of the ink used to print the dollar notes. 'Greenbacks' were first issued as Treasury Notes or 'legal tender' during the American Civil War, in 1862-63, as an emergency measure. Some were withdrawn after the war but that move met with opposition and some of the greenbacks were left in circulation. 'Greenbacks' at that time also referred to a political party, on the US scene in 1874, which opposed the withdrawal of the notes and, among other aims, wanted some of the US debt to be paid in greenbacks instead of gold. See **gold standard**.

greenmail   a practice used in takeovers, where the company threatened with a takeover bombards the aggressor company with money. The target company buys off the bidder. The process is called greenmail because the company making the bid is hit with greenbacks ($US).

Gresham's law   This has been enshrined in the maxim that 'bad money drives out good'. Gresham's law held that if two coins are in circulation and their relative face value differs from their bullion value, the coin of the higher bullion value will be stored or melted down so that eventually it will be out of circulation. Originator of the law, Sir Thomas Gresham, was a sixteenth-century English philanthropist and financier (unusual combination) whose money went to found Gresham College and who paid for the building of the first Royal Exchange in London.

gross   whole or total, before any deductions have been made; the opposite of 'net'. See **net**.

gross domestic product   a measurement of the flow of goods and services produced in an economy. In calculating GDP, an attempt is made to put values on these goods and services and by doing so to provide a national aggregate. To avoid 'double counting', only goods used for final consumption or capital goods are included. For example, the value of the flour used by a bakery would be included in the value of the bread which is the final product. It is a gross measure because no deduction is made for depreciation of capital goods, machinery and so on. It would be impossible to calculate accurately the value of all depreciation in a modern economy. GDP describes domestic product because it does not include income earned outside the country. By adding up the value of all domestically produced goods and services, you arrive at GDP at market prices.
A form of measurement that is easier to carry out involves starting from a different angle: GDP at factor cost is estimated by adding up the returns paid to the factors of production—though this method has its hurdles too. GDP at factor cost equals GDP at market prices minus indirect taxes plus subsidies. This method is thus an attempt to eliminate that part of prices paid which is in fact tax, and to add subsidies.
In Australia, the government statistician uses these two distinct methods for calculating GDP: one uses expenditure, the other income. By convention the latter is taken as the GDP and any discrepancy between the two is then added on to the former to make the national accounts consistent. During the 1970s this 'statistical discrepancy' grew from a figure of less than one quarter of 1 per cent to more than 1½ per cent of GDP. This led the more iconoclastic souls in the economics profession to ask: 'How do we know where we are going if we don't know where we've been?' Readers who are still in the dark or who are anxious for more detail are now referred to a macroeconomics textbook. (Explaining GDP is no simple task. In the 1950s a machine was invented to help demonstrate the idea to undergraduates. According to legend, the machine consisted of intricate arrays of pipes filled with coloured water—but it was scrapped when the taxation pipes kept springing leaks.) *Abbrev.*: **GDP**. See **factor cost, gross national product**.

gross interest   the interest on an investment before tax is deducted.

gross national product   This is GDP plus any income earned by residents from their investments overseas, minus any income earned domestically but due to non-residents. *Abbrev.*: **GNP**. See **gross domestic product**.

gross yield   the return on an investment before tax is deducted.

group accounts   see **consolidated accounts**.

Group of Five   the informal tag given to meetings of the finance ministers of the US, West Germany, the UK, Japan and France, who meet to discuss international monetary and exchange rate matters and coordination and cooperation on policies. Also **G-5**. See **Group of Ten**.

Group of Ten   the ten major capitalist country members of the International Monetary Fund, plus Switzerland (still not a member). It will shortly become known as the Group of Eleven to reflect Switzerland's involvement. The Group of Ten is a less formal arrangement than the IMF, although it is a branch of that body. It tends to meet ad hoc when the need arises. The Group of Ten plays an effective role in the allocation of big IMF loans, and has a role in the Bank for International Settlements. Member countries are the US, UK, West Germany, France, Belgium, the Netherlands, Italy, Sweden, Canada and Japan. *Abbrev.*: **G-10**. See **International Monetary Fund**.

Group of 24   a group of finance ministers from 24 developing country members of the International Monetary Fund. *Abbrev.*: **G-24**.

growth recession   Under this environment economic activity still increases but at a rate that is too low to produce a lift in employment so that unemployment rises instead. See **recession**.

growth stock   a share in a company which is expected to increase in capital value rather than provide an immediate high return.

GRUF   a global RUF. A GRUF usually involves other borrowing options, such as US commercial paper, bankers' acceptances, advances or letters of credit for which the GRUF acts as a backdrop. See **revolving underwriting facility**.

GST   *abbrev.* **goods and services tax**.

GTC   *abbrev.* **good till cancelled**.

guarantee   a statement (contract) to perform an obligation or discharge a liability of another person should that person fail to do so. It must be written to be legally enforceable. It is a fundamental security in business and monetary transactions by which a company of clear substance, such as a bank or parent company, agrees to pay the debt of a less creditworthy company to facilitate a borrowing or other deal by that latter company. A guarantee is sometimes confused with a warranty (where applying to goods sold). The essential difference is that a guarantee involves a third party; a warranty does not. (The two words

115

derive from different spellings, in two French dialects, of the same word.) See **warranty**.

guarantor   one who makes a guarantee or agrees to be answerable or responsible for another's debts. Legally, the guarantor makes a contract with the lender. If you are young or earning a low salary, a lending institution might agree to advance you money only if someone substantially more creditworthy 'goes guarantor' (as the Americans say)—that is, he or she agrees to stand ready to fork out if you fail to repay the loan or fulfil the obligation. See **indemnity, guarantee**.

H

half a bar   Australian money market jargon for $500 000—half a million dollars.

handkerchief transaction   similar to a round robin, a process where at every stage a sum of money appears as an asset in different hands. Popular at balance dates to window-dress the balance sheet. Misleading to those reading the balance sheet which has been inflated by the handkerchief transaction. See **round robin**.

Hang Seng Index   the Hong Kong Stock Exchange's equivalent of the US's Dow Jones.

hard currency   an example of journalese which has come to mean a stable currency, well supported by reserves, in demand in world markets and therefore fairly easy to convert into another currency.

harmless warrant   Also **wedding warrant**. See **warrant**.

headhunter   a colloquial expression for an individual or agency which specialises in finding executives for organisations in return for a fee or commission. A more refined description is 'executive search' but on the other hand 'flesh pedlar' is colourful and popularly used.

hedge contracts   see **hedge market**.

hedge market   an alternative market in Australia for covering exchange rate risk; the hedge market is based on offsetting, non-deliverable contracts, called **hedge contracts**. The hedge market was widely used for years by those whose transactions, for one reason or another, were ineligible for cover in the banks' official forward market. The authorisation of 40 non-bank financial institutions as foreign exchange traders in June 1984 and allowing the banks' market to cover capital transactions (instead of being restricted to trade transactions as before) altered the picture. At the time of writing (November 1984) the hedge market is still regarded as a useful adjunct and likely to continue to have a role for longer-term transactions.

hedge settlement rate   the rate used as the basis for settlement of hedge contracts maturing that day. At present the rate is calculated as the average of the trading banks' spot $US/$A prices quoted at 9.45am each business day. Before December 1983 and the $A float it was based on the Reserve Bank's daily announced mid-rate for the $A in terms of the $US. See **hedge market**.

hedge spot rate   the two-day-value hedge market price.

hedging   taking steps to protect against, or at least reduce, a risk; a form of insurance. The term is common in futures and foreign exchange markets where traders use facilities available to protect themselves against future price or exchange rate variations. If someone bulk-buys scotch whisky ahead of the budget in anticipation of a price rise in the budget, then he or she is also hedging (provided the whisky is drunk—if it were bought to be onsold, then the buyer is speculating).

HIBOR   *abbrev*. **Hong Kong Inter Bank Offered Rate**.

hidden reserves   assets or wealth of a company that cannot easily be detected from reading its balance sheet, such as undervalued assets or overstated expense provisions that might never be needed. Traditionally the term has been used with reference to banks that were allowed by regulatory authorities to understate the book value of certain assets by an undisclosed amount and hence to understate the amount of their reserves. This allowed the banks to transfer profits and losses to and from such hidden reserves without disclosing them in the profit and loss account.

hire purchase   buying goods through instalment payments so that the 'hirer' is buying the goods at the same time as having the use of them, but not becoming the owner of the goods until all instalments have been paid. This has also been called the 'never-never' because the payments seem to be never-ending—the buyer feels he or she will never own the goods. See **credit, instalment payments**.

historical cost accounting   the traditional method of accounting, where assets are valued at their original cost, less accumulated depreciation. This method of accounting is the most widely used in Australia today. However, it is usually modified in its application by the revaluation of fixed assets such as land and buildings. See **current cost accounting, inflation accounting**.

hit   A cheque hits your account when your account has been debited for the amount for which the cheque was written.

hit on the screen   A dealer who has been 'hit on the screen' has to deal at the rate displayed as his or her buy/sell quote whether or not that is still the prevailing market rate.

HLIC   *abbrev*. **Housing Loans Insurance Corporation**.

holder in due course   a person who buys a bill of exchange in good faith and without notice of any defect in the title of the person from whom the bill was bought, becomes the holder in due course. Every holder is presumed to be a holder in due course until the contrary is proved.

holding company   a company owning a controlling amount of shares in one or more other companies. Such a company plays a custodial role; it is concerned with the financial control, management and marketing of its subsidiaries. It does not hold the shares merely as an investment. The holding company can have a controlling interest in a subsidiary through its power to appoint directors or managers to it. All companies in which an investor owns more than 50 per cent of the issued share capital are subsidiaries; if 100 per cent of the share capital is owned, then the company is referred to as a 'wholly owned subsidiary'.

HOMES   *abbrev.* **home-owner mortgage eurosecurities** issued by Salomons. These are securities issued in the UK and backed by mortgages.

Hong Kong Inter Bank Offered Rate   the rate offered on interbank deposits in Hong Kong. It is the Hong Kong version of LIBOR. *Abbrev.*: **HIBOR**.

horizontal spread   See **option spread**.

host bond   a security, such as a bond, which is issued simultaneously with and related or linked to an issue of warrants. It is the underlying bond to a warrant (or option). See **warrant**.

hot money   money that is hard to hold; the bucks that stop only briefly (often just overnight) and move on for the best rate. Hot money changes hands frequently, looking for the most lucrative home either in the domestic market or for large-scale international speculation which would take into account interest rates and exchange rate expectations.

house account   an account handled by a brokerage firm acting on its own behalf, as principal; an account traded by a merchant bank on behalf of an in-house person, as distinct from an account managed by the firm on behalf of a client.

household sector   This includes all the individuals in Australia and unincorporated organisations such as partnerships and sole traders, including farming ventures. The term is generally used to indicate small-time investors as against the big-time wholesale money market.

housing finance   loans for housing. The great Australian dream is to be able to afford housing finance and buy your own home rather than pay rent. The average home loan at the time of writing (November 1984) is $35 000 for 25 years and its repayments make a substantial dent in the average pay-packet—but everyone hopes for the capital gain over time. A rise or fall in the home finance rate always makes headlines; it is the most important 0.25 per cent in anyone's language—politicians, bankers, mortgagors and mortgagees.

Housing Loans Insurance Corporation   This was established in 1965 to fill a perceived gap in the mortgage insurance market, by covering lenders of housing finance when they made loans beyond the normal limits. The HLIC covers lenders against losses on loans related to owner-occupied housing, land or home building. It handles the bulk of Australia's mortgage insurance, though a number of private mortgage insurance companies have grown up in recent years. The federal government in 1979 (then the Fraser Liberal-Country Party coalition government) indicated that it saw grounds to sell the HLIC into private hands, but so far nothing has happened along these lines. *Abbrev.:* **HLIC.**

hurt money your own money — the portion of funds provided by a borrower in a transaction that is a combination of the client's own money and a loan from another party. For example, a bank or merchant bank lends an individual or a company a sum of money to buy shares, but insists that a proportion of the funds required is provided by the borrowing client. If the value of the shares falls, the lender will demand additional funds or security from the client — more 'hurt' money.

hyperinflation Alarm bells ring for a country's economy with hyper-inflation — though it is hard to say exactly when rising or galloping inflation shifts into higher gear and becomes hyper- (from the Greek meaning 'excess') inflation. Germany experienced hyperinflation in the early 1920s and many countries now live with inflation rates above 100 per cent. Such a level frequently brings social as well as economic disruption and is said to be one of the factors leading to a breakdown in democracy.

hypothecation see **letter of hypothecation.**

I

IAC   *abbrev.* **Industries Assistance Commission.**

IBF   *abbrev.* **international banking facility.**

ICCH   *abbrev.* **International Commodities Clearing House.**

ICONs   *abbrev.* **indexed currency option notes.**

IMF   *abbrev.* **International Monetary Fund.**

IMM   *abbrev.* **International Monetary Market.**

imperfect market   a market where individual buyers and sellers are able to influence prices. This might be because sellers are few or because information available to buyers about prices or products is deficient. Most markets are imperfect markets as they lack the characteristics assumed in the theoretical concept of perfect competition. See **perfect competition.**

implicit price deflator   a measure of average prices. It is calculated by dividing a current price value by its corresponding constant price value—for example, the ratio of an aggregate such as GDP measured in current prices, to that aggregate measured in constant prices. Implicit price deflators are termed 'derived' measures by the Australian Bureau of Statistics and are not normally the direct measures of price change by which current price estimates are converted to estimates at constant prices. A source of detailed information on implicit price deflators is Appendix B of *Australian National Accounts: Concepts, Sources and Methods* put out by the Australian Bureau of Statistics.

import tariffs   see **tariffs.**

imports   what is purchased from other countries for use in one's own country. Visible imports are items such as clothing, cars and wine; invisible imports are items such as freight payments, dividend payments and royalties.

imputation   see **dividend imputation.**

in and out like a dirty brown trout   Australian money market expression to indicate someone who buys and sells securities within a very short space of time, often within minutes.

incentive   carrot-and-stick psychology; a payment tied to results. Employers offer incentives to cultivate loyalty and productivity among workers; governments offer them, in the form of subsidies or taxation concessions, to encourage industrial development or exportable products.

income tax   tax levied directly on personal income. See **taxation**.

incorporated   An organisation described as 'incorporated' is one which has gone through the legal process necessary to form a company. The word is abbreviated in the US to 'inc' after a company's name. See **incorporation**.

incorporation   the process of forming a company. Incorporation is carried out by lodging the necessary documents—memorandum and articles of association, notice of registered office, list of directors—with your local Corporate Affairs Commission and paying the necessary fees and stamp duty. The date shown on the certificate of incorporation is the date at which the company starts to exist and has corporate status. See **corporation, incorporated**.

increment   a fancy term for a regular proportionate increase, usually applied to salary rates; a popular buzzword with personnel managers, who are really talking about pay rises. It means getting a bit more than you had before. Increments also tend to be automatic, whereas a rise may not be.

indemnity   an undertaking (in the form of a contract) to make good someone else's loss. Sometimes it is a term in a bilateral contract; sometimes it is similar to a guarantee. The person with the benefit of the indemnity does not first have to demand payment from the person who caused the loss, before claiming on the person who gave the indemnity. See **guarantor**.

index   a numerical measure of the way a variable has changed over some base period. A popular way to use it is to say that in a given year the index is 100, so that differentials in other years can be expressed as percentage rises or falls from the base 100. Anything, from dogfood production to the incidence of nosebleeds in the under 3-year-olds, can be given an index if an expert is interested enough. Most currencies use an index based in 1971 at the time of the Smithsonian Agreement as a yardstick against which to measure movements in their trade-weighted baskets. The $A trade-weighted index published in the monthly *Reserve Bank Bulletin* tracks the currency from a May 1970 base of 100. See **basket, consumer price index, retail price index**.

indexation   usually a system of adjusting such items as wages, prices or taxation and other living costs or investments to the rate of inflation. See **inflation**.

indexed bonds   bonds in which the value of the dividend (resulting from the coupon) and/or the capital value of the investment on maturity would not be fixed when the bonds are issued but would be linked (indexed) to a specified variable, usually the inflation rate. The UK introduced these in the form of 'Granny bonds' a few years ago and the federal government in Australia has announced its intention to offer indexed bonds.

indexed currency option notes   a euronote issue that includes a currency option, first seen in 1985 and issued, serviced and redeemed in $US. *Abbrev.*: **ICONs**.

indirect quote   In Australia, an indirect quote is the US dollar price of one Australian dollar. A direct quote is the Australian dollar price of one US dollar. One is the reciprocal of the other. For example, the traditional (indirect) quote for the $A is that it is worth, say, 85 US cents. A direct quote in Australia would be to express the quote as one US dollar is worth $A1.176, which would be calculated by dividing one by 0.85.

indirect taxation   The distinction between direct and indirect tax is still used, though its usefulness is strongly debated. Direct tax implies taxes paid by people on whom they are levied, but since it has become apparent that all taxes can be shifted to hit different people and not necessarily those at whom they were originally pitched, it follows that taxes (except probably income tax) are really indirect. Economists study the shifting of taxes—for example they ask if company tax is borne by companies or by their customers in the form of higher prices. When people talk of 'indirect tax' they generally mean charges other than income tax; sales tax is an example of an indirect tax. The difference between direct and indirect tax is important in national accounting, to distinguish between GDP at factor cost from GDP at market prices. In the Australian national accounts, indirect taxes are defined as 'taxes assessed on producers, i.e. enterprises and general government, in respect of the production, sale, purchase or use of goods and services, which are charged to the expenses of production'. See **factor cost, gross domestic product, taxation**.

individual retirement account   a US term describing the account allowed by the Internal Revenue Service to each US citizen, into which the individual can take $US2000 annually tax-free off his or her salary and invest these funds on the basis of deferred tax until the minimum age of 59½. *Abbrev.*: **IRA**.

indorse   see **endorse**.

Industries Assistance Commission   Established in 1973 legislation to take over and extend the role of the Tariff Board, the Commission began operating in 1974. It makes recommendations to the federal government on levels of subsidy or other assistance to Australian industries; it has prime responsibility for determining tariff levels. Like the Tariff Board, which had been created in 1921, the IAC is an advisory board, but it has wider scope than the Tariff Board and wider powers to examine government aid to particular industries. *Abbrev.*: **IAC**.

inelasticity (of demand)   the characteristic of a product for which demand changes less than proportionately in response to a given change in its price; such changes are usually in opposite directions. For example, the price of beer rises dramatically but drinkers do not lower their demand proportionately.

inflation   a sustained increase in the price level—a given amount of money buys less and less. People on fixed incomes, such as pensioners, suffer most when inflation is rising, unless their pensions or incomes are fully indexed to the inflation rate. Economists suggest various causes and solutions for inflation (see **monetary policy**). For convenience, economists have identified two types of inflation:

- **demand-pull**   where aggregate demand exceeds aggregate supply —i.e. everyone is trying to buy more than is available or can be produced and competition for scarce products pushes up their price. (Monetarists argue that the excess of aggregate demand is due to an inappropriately rapid expansion in the money supply);
- **cost-push**   where increases in wages or other costs push prices up. Prices are related to unit labour cost. See **unit cost, unit labour cost**.

inflation accounting   an attempt to assess a company's progress after adjusting for the effects of inflation. Historical cost accounting does not accurately reflect changing values of money and assets. For example, if you bought an item for $10 and then sold it for $15, historical cost accounting would calculate your profit to be $5. If, however, it costs you $20 to replace that item then you have really made a loss of $5 (which would be shown up by the inflation accounting method). See **current cost accounting, historical cost accounting**.

infrastructure   community services, for example septic tanks, bus routes, phone services and water supply—a catch-all term applied to the services we consider necessary for comfort and convenience or essential for production, such as transport. The word means a framework on which an industry, etc., can be built.

injunction   a writ or court order forcing you (**mandatory injunction**) to do something or restraining you (**restrictive injunction**) from doing something as your course of action could be harmful or detrimental to others. If you break the injunction—i.e. go ahead as planned—you could be punished for contempt of court.

inscribed stock   The owner of this stock does not hold the securities: ownership is recorded in a registry and the owner gets a certificate which is not itself transferable. The stock has to be transferred using appropriate forms. The Reserve Bank records ownership of government stock in its registries and each listed company holds a register where its shareholders' names are inscribed. This relieves holders of the risk of carrying bearer securities. See **bearer.**

inside lag   see **leads and lags.**

insider trading   dealing for profit in areas in which the person dealing has privileged information; frowned upon and unlawful, but not unknown.

inside the fees   Securities that trade inside the fees are selling at a price that allows the underwriter to make money from the agreement to underwrite and distribute an issue of securities. See **outside the fees.**

insolvency   a situation where the value of liabilities exceeds the value of assets and a person is unable to pay debts as they fall due. A company or an individual can be insolvent.

instalment payments   The reality of the never-never, these are the regular (usually monthly) payments you have to make to repay a borrowing (hire purchase, personal loan, mortgage and so on). You can opt for relatively high instalment payments and pay the loan off more quickly; lower instalment payments are easier on immediate cash flow but are spread over a longer period. See **credit, hire purchase.**

Institute of Chartered Accountants in Australia   Formed in 1928 as the professional organisation representing accountants, the Institute now has about 15 000 members, most of whom would be in practice as accountants, rather than in industry. There is considerable overlap of membership between the Institute and the Australian Society of Accountants, with whom the Institute jointly sponsors and funds the Australian Accounting Research Foundation. The Foundation issues the accounting standards. See **accounting standards, Accounting Standards Review Board, Australian Accounting Research Foundation, Australian Society of Accountants.**

institutional buy-out   see **leveraged buy-out.**

instrument   Traders and economists talk of 'instruments' when they are referring to documents or securities such as bills of exchange or promissory notes, bonds, Treasury Notes or letters of credit.

insurance   protection against possible hazard; you take out an insurance policy against an event which may or may not happen, for example a burglary, your house burning down, or going to hospital. Such policies are commonly known as 'general insurance' and can cover your house, its contents, a factory, shops, legal liability, a car, livestock, crops etc., against specified events or disasters; they also cover sickness and accidents, providing an income during a period of disability and medical and hospital funds. Any form of insurance cover entails payment of a sum (premium) to the insurance company; this is often split into regular instalments, and covers the specified item or items insured, up to a specified value. It is essential to read the small print in your policy carefully. Life insurance is also referred to as **life assurance** (see **assurance**) and comes in various forms. See **annuity, endowment, superannuation, term insurance, whole-of-life policy**.

insurance bonds   life insurance policies backed by investments in a life office statutory fund. The bonds do not pay income or dividends to bondholders but accumulate income for further investment. Insurance bonds fall into two groups:

- **capital-guaranteed bonds,**   which tend to invest in government and fixed-interest securities. These are secure and less volatile than investment-linked bonds;
- **investment-linked bonds**   which offer greater longer-term growth.

The tax treatment of insurance bonds makes them attractive investments: the bonds are free of capital gains tax and free from income tax if held for ten years or more. Income tax is levied progressively, depending on the term for which the bonds are held. For example, one-third of the profit is taxed at the marginal rate of the bondholder and the rest is tax-free if the bonds are held for more than nine years but less than ten; two-thirds of the profit is taxed at the marginal rate and the rest tax-free if the bonds are held for more than eight years but less than nine. A tax-paying investor making a withdrawal within the first eight years is liable to tax on the profit component of the amount withdrawn but is eligible for a tax rebate of 29 cents in the dollar, or 29 per cent of that profit component.

intangible assets   a company's resources which have no easily measurable dollar value but which nonetheless are valuable, such as a good reputation, or goodwill. Generally, intangible assets cannot be sold separately from the business as a whole. See **goodwill**.

interbank market   In Australia this refers to short-term, often overnight, borrowing and lending between banks, as distinct from banks' business with their corporate clients or other financial institutions. See **exchange settlement accounts, federal funds market**.

interbank rate   the rate of interest charged on loans between banks. See **federal funds rate, London Inter Bank Offered Rate**.

interdelivery spread   This strategy is similar to a calendar or horizontal spread but is used with futures contracts as well as in options trading. It involves buying one month of a contract and selling a different month of the same contract, for example buying the December contract in bonds and at the same time selling the March contract in bonds, with the objective of making a profit from the price differential between the two contract months. See **option spread**.

interest   the charge on borrowed money or the return earned on funds out on loan or invested. Interest rates vary with the demand for and supply of credit; they are influenced by people's expectations of inflation and can vary from borrower to borrower according to credit status. See **compound interest, simple interest, usury**.

interest cover   the number of times the total interest payments made by a company on its borrowings are exceeded by its earnings.

interest-only funds   With these funds, the borrower pays interest (like a rent), for the use of the money, usually for a comparatively short period such as one to three years. The money is relatively expensive, the debt non-reducible (unlike credit foncier and mortgage payments). None of the capital is paid back during the term of the loan; that has to be repaid at the end unless the borrower negotiates with the lender to roll the loan on for a further terms. Solicitors' funds are a common source of interest-only funds. See **credit foncier, mortgage, solicitors' funds**.

interest rate condom   see **cap**.

interest rate futures   Futures contracts based on financial instruments such as bank bills of exchange or Commonwealth bonds which allow traders and investors to take out protection against likely future movements in interest rates. In Australia, interest rate futures are traded on the Sydney Futures Exchange. See **futures markets, Sydney Futures Exchange**.

interest rate swap   see **swap**.

interest rate swap options   another stage of the interest rate swap, not yet widely used in Australia. Swap options allow a borrower to take an option to enter into a future interest rate swap at an agreed rate. Also known as **swaptions**.

interface   a word of the 1980s, which has expanded from its conventional meaning (of the boundary or area common to two adjacent things) to indicate interaction between computer systems or communication between different groups of people. In its current usage it simply means people or systems being able to understand and talk to each other.

interim dividend   see **dividend**.

intermarket   a description for trading that takes place between like instruments and different markets.

intermediation   the opposite of disintermediation: borrowing from a saver to onlend to an ultimate borrower; being the middleman. The advantages of intermediation are economies of management costs, spreading out risk of default, a degree of liquidity management allowing mismatch of maturities (borrowing short, lending long). See **disintermediation, reintermediation**.

internal rate of return   the return from an investment, calculated to show the rate at which the present value of future cash flows from an investment is equal to the cost of the investment. *Abbrev.*: **IRR**.

Internal Revenue Service   the US Federal agency responsible for collecting federal taxes on income (individual and company) and for investigating any infringement of US tax regulations. *Abbrev.*: **IRS**.

International Bank for Reconstruction and Development   see **World Bank**.

international banking facility   a US class of bank similar to an offshore banking unit which allows a bank to operate in international banking without some of the restrictions that usually apply to domestic banks. IBFs would typically be exempt from restrictions covering reserve requirements and would operate with a concessionary tax rate. *Abbrev.*: **IBF**.

International Commodities Clearing House   This provides clearing services for the Sydney Futures Exchange. It has provided clearing and guaranteeing services for London futures markets since 1888, when it was established as The London Produce Clearing House. Its name was changed in 1973 to reflect its broader and more international role. The ICCH's identity is quite separate from that of the Sydney Futures Exchange; its main role is to provide a registration service for all contracts and to guarantee the performance of each contract to its members. *Abbrev.*: **ICCH**. See **futures contract, Sydney Futures Exchange**.

International Monetary Fund   This was established by the Bretton Woods agreement of 1944. (Keynes had a major involvement in Bretton Woods and played a role in the formation of the International Monetary Fund.) The IMF began operations in 1947 to encourage policies, including exchange rate policies, to keep the balances of payments between countries in overall balance. Member countries (presently numbering 126) contribute to the IMF, via quotas, which are determined in relation to the size of each IMF member's economy; this pool of funds is used to make loans to member countries with balance of payments problems.

On being approached by a country experiencing such problems, the IMF examines the difficulties; if an agreement can be reached with the government concerned about the cause of, and solution to, the problems, a letter of intent is signed. This commits the IMF to a programme of assistance to the country, usually over a period of about three years, provided that the country carries out the IMF's proposals to correct its balance of payments problems.

The IMF is located in Washington, and operates with a board of directors and a managing director. Its annual report makes informative reading. *Abbrev.*: **IMF**.

International Monetary Market   Established in 1972 as a division of the Chicago Mercantile Exchange, the International Monetary Market concentrates on futures contracts in financial instruments, currencies and gold. *Abbrev.*: **IMM**. See **Chicago Mercantile Exchange.**

international monetary system   This term describes whatever is the current predominant set of arrangements among countries for determining the relative values of currencies. There is no formal system, since each country sets its own policy on how the value of its own currency will be allowed to move against other currencies. At the beginning of this century the gold standard was important, with most currencies tied to a value in terms of gold; these arrangements fell apart and a formal attempt at an international monetary system was made at Bretton Woods in 1944, which resulted in currencies being tied to the $US, which was in turn tied to gold. The Bretton Woods era lasted till 1971 when fixed exchange rates bit the dust in favour of floating. See **Bretton Woods, float, gold standard.**

intervention   see **central bank intervention.**

intestate   a term used to describe the situation when someone has died without leaving a will.

in the money   a term used to describe an option that can be exercised at a profit. The option contract's current market price is higher than the strike price of a call option or lower than the strike price of a put option. A call option on a commodity or share would be in the money at a strike price of 50 if the underlying commodity or share were selling for 51 or more; a put option at a strike price of 50 would be in the money if the share or commodity were selling at 49 or less. See **at the money, intrinsic value, out of the money.**

intraday trading   entering into and closing out a position within the same day. Also known as **jobbing.** See **close out.**

intramarket   the description for trading different months in the same commodity, for example buying December and selling June bank bill futures contracts.

intrinsic value   In the context of options trading, this refers to the amount by which an option is in the money. In the case of a call option, intrinsic value is the current futures price less the strike price. For a put option the intrinsic value is the strike price less the futures price. If the difference between the prices is not positive in either case then the intrinsic value is zero. See **time value**.

inventory   a list of what you have. In company accounts, inventory usually refers to the value of stocks, as distinct from fixed assets. Included in an inventory would be assets which are held for sale in the ordinary course of business or are in the process of production for such sale—or which are to be used in production of goods or services which will be available for sale.

inverse yield curve   see **yield curve**.

inverted market   see **backwardation**.

investment allowance   This allows a taxpayer a deduction of up to 18 per cent from assessable income in the year that eligible new machinery or plant is acquired. It is an upfront, once-off deduction and has traditionally been a method of stimulating investment in new plant. Eligible property on which the investment allowance is claimed has to be held for twelve months, must have cost more than $500 and must be used solely in Australia to produce assessable income for the taxpayer concerned. In December 1981 the-then federal Treasurer John Howard said the income tax law was to be amended so that the investment allowance under leveraged lease arrangements entered into after that date would be withheld if the end-user of the leased property was a tax-exempt organisation. The investment allowance ceased in June 1983 for tax-exempt organisations but will continue for tax-paying entities until June 1985, for the signing of eligible contracts, with the deadline for plant installation set at 30 June 1987.

investment bank   a financial intermediary which operates at the wholesale (not retail) end of the financial markets, as a middleman between companies raising funds by issuing securities and the investors who buy the paper. Investment banks help their clients by underwriting and distributing securities and devising innovative finance packages (in return for fees). Investment banking skills rely on market knowledge and expertise rather than on the strength of the bank's balance sheet. Investment banks generally do not take deposits and make loans and here they differ from deposit-taking and loan-making merchant banks and trading banks. They do, though, compete with the merchant and trading banks in the securities markets. In the US the term investment banking overlaps with broking, in Australia with merchant banking. See **merchant bank**.

investment grade   the description used by ratings agencies for securities such as bonds and notes that are of sufficient quality to be classed as sound investments. For example, Standard & Poor's consider their top four categories, AAA to BB, to qualify as investment grade. Securities ranked below investment grade are known as junk bonds. See **junk bonds.**

investment-linked bonds   see **insurance bonds.**

investor   a person who shows confidence in a company or government by putting his or her money into its hands in the expectation of earning interest and/or reaping a capital gain (profit) on the funds invested.

invisibles   as in 'invisible exports and imports', transactions in services such as insurance, banking and foreign travel; intangibles, which are included in the current account of a country's balance of payments. See **balance of payments.**

IOU   an abbreviation of 'I owe you'; a piece of paper which stands as written evidence of a debt.

IRA   *abbrev.* **individual retirement account.**

issued capital   the portion of authorised capital which has been issued to shareholders. If the shares are not fully paid, there remains an uncalled element for which shareholders are liable, except in a company designated 'NL' (no liability). Share capital could be divided thus:

authorised	$20 000 000
issued	10 000 000
paid-up	5 000 000
uncalled	5 000 000

See **authorised capital, no liability, share capital.**

IRR   *abbrev.* **internal rate of return.**

IRS   *abbrev.* **Internal Revenue Service.**

issuing house   a London merchant bank specialising in arranging and underwriting share and securities issues. It is one of the three main classes of UK merchant banks, the other two being discount houses and accepting houses. Some merchant banks are both accepting and issuing houses. In Australia, the Issuing Houses Association merged with the Accepting Houses Association in 1979 to form the Australian Merchant Bankers Association. See **Australian Merchant Bankers Association.**

J

Jackson Committee   a committee established in 1974 by the Whitlam government. It was chaired by R. G. Jackson, who was then general manager and director of CSR Ltd, and was to advise on policies for Australian manufacturing industry. The report advocated that Australia move towards a more open economy and that gradual structural adjustment of the nation's manufacturing sector be carried out. As has proved typical with such reports, little was done to put its recommendations into practice. The report's main novelty was its provision for a timetable for tariff reform. It was criticised, though, for its call for increased financial assistance to the manufacturing sector in the form of bigger grants and tax concessions and for its suggestion that exchange rate policy should offer more support for that sector. A 1977 White Paper reiterated its theme.

jargon   slang, argot, colloquialisms, clique talk. Every industry and specialty is guilty of it. Using jargon makes the participants feel comfortable and important and excludes non-participants who, God forbid, might one day learn the jargon and see through the mystique. Economists and financiers are particularly adept at creating their personalised patois, although the new ascendant of the genre is computerspeak. Jargon can also be useful shorthand for communication among specialists in any field.

Japanese offshore market   the Japanese version of the OBU and the US's IBF. This market began in December 1986 but operates under stricter conditions than an IBF, with stamp duty imposed and controls on the volume of funds between offshore and domestic market. *Abbrev.*: **JOM**. See **international banking facility, offshore banking unit**.

jawboning   see **moral suasion**.

J-curve   the curve drawn to illustrate the performance of a country's balance of payments after its currency has been devalued. The immediate effect of a devaluation is to raise the cost of imports, reduce the value of exports so that the current account deteriorates. Gradually, though, the volume of exports increases because they are cheaper and the volume of imports should correspondingly fall because they have become more expensive. This should rectify the current account balance, turning it into a surplus.

jobber   a UK stock exchange personality who deals in shares and acts as principal, dealing directly with sharebrokers, not with clients. In the Australian futures trading context, jobbing is the same as daytrading. See **daytrading**.

jobbing the market   see **daytrading**.

joint stock company   a nineteenth-century term for a public company whose shares are transferable.

joint venture   cooperation between two or more companies or countries, or any parties, on the one project to produce mutually agreeable results. It can be cooperation between private sector and public sector institutions in situations where the private sector is short of funds and needs public sector assistance. A joint venture is similar to a partnership except that it is not necessarily a continuing one—the association in the case of a joint venture might last only as long as the project takes to complete.

JOM   *abbrev.* **Japanese offshore market**.

junk bond   a high-yield bond that earns high interest for the holder but could prove worthless if the company whose name is etched on the bond cannot pay out when the bond matures. Junk bonds offer a higher-than-usual yield but also carry a higher-than-usual risk. The investor earns an attractive rate of interest to compensate for the risk; the borrowing company (which issued the bond) has to pay a high rate of return on its borrowings to win investors' funds. The so-called junk bonds were pioneered in the US by the Wall Street investment bank Drexel Burnham Lambert. They are termed junk bonds for technical reasons associated with credit rating in the US, where securities rated less than, say, BB, are known as sub-investment grade bonds. See **investment grade**.

K

Kansas City Board of Trade   Founded in 1876, this is the second largest grain exchange in the world and was the first exchange to trade stock index (share price index) futures. See **Chicago Board of Trade**.

kerb market   a US term to denote trading in shares of companies not listed on the main stock exchange board. In Australia 'kerb' market has been used to describe the 'second board' or 'junior market' catering for shares which see little turnover.

Kerb, the   the New Zealand Futures Exchange's Futures Industry Information Centre, located at the exchange's head office in Auckland. The public can watch the course of trading on the futures exchange and other domestic and international markets, on screens located in the centre. The Kerb offers a wide range of educational material designed for the individual trader. See **New Zealand Futures Exchange**.

Keynes, John Maynard   see **economists**.

kick-back   a slice of a fee or salary or commission given to a third party for its assistance, cooperation or non-interference in a commercial arrangement; usually accompanied by a nudge and a wink and often illegal or unethical, or both.

killer warrant   See **warrant**.

killing   as in 'making a killing'—turning in a handsome profit in a short space of time, a profit big enough to boast about.

kite   UK market slang for an accommodation bill of exchange. See **kite flying**.

kite flying   a UK expression to describe the use of bills of exchange or other instruments to raise funds to give the appearance of being creditworthy.

Kiwi bonds   New Zealand government securities denominated in $NZ, issued in New Zealand to household investors. They are the New Zealand equivalent of Australia's Aussie Bonds and, as with the Australian version, they are par securities, i.e. they are not sold at a discount from face value. See **Australian Savings Bond (Aussie Bond)**.

Kondratieff cycle   a trade cycle that lasts a long time. It is named after the Russian economist, Nikolai Kondratieff, who identified 50- to 60-year cycles of economic activity and who is noted for his important contribution to the analysis of long-term fluctuations. His analysis, though, did not help the search for a conclusive explanation for the post-1973 recession. Also **long (Kondratieff) cycle**.

L

Laffer curve   Arthur Laffer of the University of Southern California developed the Laffer curve in the 1970s. The curve is said to demonstrate that governments raise more revenue by cutting taxes than by increasing them; others argue that the opposite is the case. Laffer's concept has become somewhat dated now and anyway he did not provide enough evidence to justify his claim conclusively.

lag   see **leads and lags**.

laissez faire   'hands off'. Literally, it is French for 'let act'. Adam Smith (1776 *Wealth of Nations*) was largely responsible for the development of this concept. Laissez faire is a system in which economic activity is able to proceed almost entirely free of government rules and regulations. Advocates of pure laissez faire believe that the unhindered forces of supply and demand and self-interest will achieve balance in society, leading to the most efficient use of resources and therefore the highest level of production and income. The Great Depression of the 1930s and continuing high levels of unemployment in the 1980s cast doubt on this belief. See **Smith, Adam** in **economists**.

last in, first out   an accounting method which values a company's stock on the basis that the latest items purchased are the first to be used in production or sales. Goods on hand represent earliest purchases and are valued at the earlier prices. If prices are rising, inventory values will be understated and if prices are falling they will be overstated. This method is not accepted in Australia as it is believed to lead to the undervaluation of stocks and has the effect of reducing reported profits in times of inflation. *Abbrev*.: **LIFO**. See **first in, first out**.

laundered funds   ill-gotten gains that have been 'washed'; that is invested with a 'respectable' institution to disguise their dubious source. See **funny money**.

laying off   see **reinsurance**.

LBO   *abbrev*. **leveraged buy-out**.

L/C   see **letter of credit**.

LDC   *abbrev*. **less developed country**.

lead manager   see **mandate**.

leads and lags   In the context of international payments, these are

136

gaps between shipments and payments. These gaps can be exaggerated as importers and exporters try to advance or delay their payments and receipts according to how they think exchange rates will move. If a devaluation (of the domestic currency) is forecast, importers with a foreign currency obligation will hurry to pay otherwise they would need more local currency to pay later—they 'lead' their payments. Exporters on the other hand would benefit in that situation by delaying converting foreign currency receipts into the local currency—they 'lag'. Until the virtual abolition of exchange controls in Australia in December 1983 leads and lags could not be used extensively, for example exporters had to convert foreign exchange receipts into $A within 30 days of receiving the funds.

Leads and lags are also used in a variety of economic models, for example investment this year might be determined by profits last year. Economists talk of the **policy lag**: in this context the **inside lag** is the recognition that some change is needed in policy stance and the time taken to implement that change; the **outside lag** is the time the change takes to affect the economy once implemented.

league ladder a performance gauge used in various markets to measure the volume of deals underwritten by banks and investment banks as managers and co-managers. Also **league table**.

lease an agreement between two parties under which one is granted the right to use the property of the other for a specified period of time in return for a series of payments by the user to the owner. See **leasing**.

leasing Buildings, cars, photocopiers—a whole range of items—can be leased (let) for a number of years under lease agreements. The lessee (person taking out a lease) agrees to pay a number of instalments (often fixed though they can be flexible) over an agreed period to the lessor, who remains the owner of the asset (item) throughout the period of the lease. Probably the chief attraction of leasing, from the lessee's point of view, is that it can offer tax advantages while leaving more money for other purposes than would be the case with an outright purchase. Also, by leasing rather than buying an asset a company does not affect its gearing because leased assets and the corresponding liabilities have not been shown in the balance sheet; changes to accounting standards are due to be published which are likely to alter leasing to a balance sheet item. At the end of the lease period, the lessee can either re-lease for a further period, trade in the goods or equipment and buy something else or offer to buy the leased goods or equipment from the lessor. If the lessee chooses to buy the leased item(s) then he or she would usually find the lessor willing to sell them at the residual value that was agreed on at the start of the lease. Traditional sources of lease financing are trading banks, some merchant banks, specialist leasing companies, finance companies and leasing companies which are offshoots of big equipment suppliers. See **gearing, leveraged leasing, off-balance-sheet financing, residual value**.

left-hand side   a foreign exchange term meaning the rate at which a bank will offer currency against, say, the $US. A quote reading 239.20/40 yen indicates the bank's selling rate of 239.20 yen against the $US; the bank will buy at 239.40 yen to the $US—the theory being 'sell low, buy high' (in directly quoted currencies). The expression 'trading on the left-hand side' means there is selling pressure on the currency. See **trading on the right-hand side**.

leg in the air   a colourful phrase to describe a futures trader looking to complete a straddle; the trader may take a view on market movements that suggests doing one leg of the straddle first (hence leg in the air) and completing the second leg later the same day. Both 'legs' of the straddle have to be executed within one day to qualify as a straddle. Traders talk of 'lifting a leg', which means planning the above. If you get caught with a 'leg in the air' you have to get out as best you can. See **straddle**.

legal tender   officially recognised money which cannot be refused when given in payment.

Lehman investment opportunity notes   stripped zero-coupon securities issued by Shearson Lehman in the US. These are similar to Merrill Lynch's TIGRs and Salomon Brothers' CATS, being securities representing future principal/coupon payments to be made on specified issues of US Treasury Bonds. *Abbrev.*: **LIONs**.

lender-of-last-resort   the common term applied to certain types of borrowing facilities provided by central banks to selected financial institutions (in Australia the authorised dealers and the trading banks). These selected institutions in turn have to comply with a number of regulations imposed by the central bank.

Lender-of-last-resort loans have been used to different degrees by the two sectors in Australia. For the authorised dealers the facility has at times been one dimension in a range of trading options and therefore been frequently used—though the introduction in August 1984 of repurchase agreements will put the facility back to one of 'last resort' in favour of greater use of repurchase agreements.

Central bank loans to the major trading banks are available under strictly defined conditions, still rarely made, and only in the context of the LGS (liquid assets and government securities) convention. See **liquid assets and government securities convention, repurchase agreements**.

less developed country   a country characterised by a poverty level of income, a growing population, high unemployment and a high level of agricultural employment, and few exports. Such countries were classified as Third World countries; this category has recently been redefined to accommodate changed conditions in some so-called less developed countries. *Abbrev*.: **LDC**. See **Third World**.

lessee   the person to whom a lease is granted and who pays the instalments (rent) due under the lease agreement to the lessor.

lessor   the grantor of the lease, who remains the owner of the leased property throughout the term of the lease and who receives lease payments from the lessee.

letter of credit   an irrevocable and unconditional undertaking by an international bank (sometimes local banks also issue letters of credit) to repay the principle and interest of a loan in the event of default by the borrower. Letters of credit help the flow of trade and financing by giving added assurance to a lender that a loan will be repaid or goods paid for. In Australia letters of credit are frequently used by finance companies which are local subsidiaries of overseas banks and which borrow using the backup of the parent company L/C. L/Cs can also be used to back a lessee in a leveraged lease deal or the borrower in a promissory note issue. Modern use of the letter of credit is an extension of the century-old custom by which a traveller was provided with a letter of credit from his or her bank, addressed to another bank, to ensure access to funds when away from home. *Abbrev*.: **L/C**

letter of comfort   a letter, often issued by a parent company on behalf of a subsidiary operating in a different country. The parent company issuing the letter (Company A) agrees to make every effort to ensure that Company B (the subsidiary) will comply with the terms of a given contract, but Company A is not committed to perform B's obligations if B cannot do so or defaults.

letter of hypothecation   a letter, for example between a broker and client, pledging securities as collateral for loans made to buy shares. Such a letter does not transfer title of the securities pledged, but it does give the broker the right to sell the securities detailed by the letter of hypothecation, should the client default.

leverage   the relationship between a company's debt and the capital issued. See **gearing**.

leveraged buy-out   a method of buying a company using borrowed money, generally undertaken by the company's existing management. Those carrying out the takeover might not have the necessary funds but are convinced of the merits of the deal; the lending institution, which either provides money or takes an equity position, expects to be repaid principal plus interest or to make a profit on the equity. Also known as **institutional buy-out** in the UK. *Abbrev*.: **LBO**. See **management buy-out**.

leveraged leasing   a specialised form of leasing. It effectively uses certain taxation concessions relating to plant and equipment, for example depreciation and investment allowance (where applicable) which the lessee may not otherwise have been able to use fully. This method results in a lower cost of funds and it is therefore often used to cope with the financing of high-cost 'big ticket' items such as planes or plant. 'Leveraging' simply means borrowing on the strength of an asset; it is a US expression that has come into wider use. Leveraged leasing involves a third party in addition to the lessor and the lessee; this third party is the 'credit provider' who makes available the bulk of the funds needed to acquire what is being leased. Finance is made available to the lessor under a non-recourse loan which is often secured by a mortgage over the leased property or assignment over the lease and the lease rentals. For the lessee nothing changes under a leveraged lease agreement except, of course, that the lease rate available is cheaper than other forms of finance. See **big ticket, leasing**.

LGS   *abbrev.* **liquid assets and government securities convention**.

liabilities   the opposite of assets. Liabilities generally refer to a person's debts, or in the case of a company, to its debts and the dividends payable to shareholders.

liability assumption   see **defeasance**.

libertarianism   This branch of economic thought represents a shift away from the belief that governments can solve everything, in favour of a greater role for market forces in the allocation of resources. Governments and statutory authorities would play correspondingly reduced roles. A libertarian therefore is a free-enterprise economist who believes that economic activity should operate with the minimum of regulation. Such ideas are often associated with the so-called Chicago School which has supported the idea of unfettered markets rather than government interference. See **Chicago School**.

LIBID   *abbrev.* **London Inter Bank Bid Rate**.

LIBOR   *abbrev.* **London Inter Bank Offered Rate**.

lien   the right to hold property of another as security for the performance of an obligation. A lien is basically a security which requires the security holder to have possession of the goods or assets over which the security is claimed (a **possessory lien**). A simple example of a possessory lien would be the case of a person leaving his or her car at the garage for repairs; the garage proprietor who has physical possession of the car would have a lien over it till paid for repairs carried out. There are some liens created by statute (**statutory liens**) which are misnomers because possession of the object of the security is not necessary. An example of a statutory lien is a crop lien—a lender holding a crop lien will have a security over the crop without having possession of it.

life assurance/insurance   see **assurance, insurance.**

life-cycle hypothesis   This tries to show why people divide their money as they do, for example between saving and spending, why older people (who normally earn more than young people) tend to save a greater proportion of their income than do the young, and why. Once retired, older people revert more to the youthful pattern, spending a larger proportion of their money.

life insurance office   see **life office.**

life office   A large financial institution whose chief function is mobilising funds from the household sector to provide various forms of life assurance. Many life offices also operate superannuation funds. See **annuity, insurance, superannuation.**

LIFFE   *abbrev.* **London International Financial Futures Exchange.**

LIFO   *abbrev.* **last in, first out.**

lifting a leg   see **leg in the air.**

LIMEAN   the average (mean) of LIBID and LIBOR. See **LIBID, LIBOR.**

limited liability   a legal concept which protects shareholders in a limited liability company by limiting their liabilities to the value of their shares in the company, even if the company has debts exceeding the value of those shares. The limited liability company is the basic commercial structure developed during the nineteenth century to allow individuals to carry on a business without exposing all their personal assets to the risk of the business failing, as this could lead to personal bankruptcy. See **company, no liability.**

limited recourse finance   funds that have been arranged on the understanding that the lender has recourse to the borrower in certain circumstances only. For example a lender providing funds for minerals exploration might have no recourse to the borrower if minerals were not found in sufficient quantity.

line of credit   a flexible loan from a bank or merchant bank, which allows the customer (client) access to funds over a given period but does not entail regular fixed instalment repayments. A line of credit is more like an overdraft in that the amount the client chooses to use is left to his or her discretion, within the limit of the line of credit. For example, a bank might grant a client a line of credit for $3000, but the client may not use all the funds at once—they are available as needed. Banks regularly review the level of use of a line of credit and if the funds are not being used then the line could be cut back as banks do not like to see their funds allocated but not usefully employed, i.e. earning them interest. A line of credit can include an option to draw bills of exchange, rather than the funds being advanced in cash. Bank charges have to be taken into account when calculating the overall cost of a line of credit.

Lion Notes   Issued in Australia by Lion Securities, a subsidiary of the investment bank and broking firm J.B. Were and Son, these are bearer promissory notes created by securitising debt. Lion Securities was formed to manage a trust for these pass-through securities, similar to the structure used to create mortgage-backed certificates in the US, and more recently in Australia. The notes are issued at a discount, for terms between 30 and 185 days and are backed by a pool of bank-guaranteed assets.

LIONs   *abbrev.* **Lehman investment opportunity notes.**

liquid assets   assets which can be turned into cash easily or swiftly and with minimum capital loss. See **liquidity.**

liquid assets and government securities convention   an understanding reached in 1956 between the major Australian trading banks and the central bank, under which the banks agree to observe a minimum ratio of liquid assets and government securities to their deposits and if necessary to borrow from the central bank (now the Reserve Bank) to maintain this ratio. At the time of writing (November 1984) the ratio is 18 per cent. The convention typically refers to currency, deposits with the Reserve Bank (except statutory reserve deposits), Treasury Notes and other Commonwealth government securities. *Abbrev.*: **LGS.** See **lender-of-last-resort, statutory reserve deposit.**

liquidation   A company which is put into liquidation (either by its members or by its creditors) is one whose business is to be wound up. The assets are sold, liabilities settled as far as possible, and any remaining cash returned to shareholders. A company can be liquidated even though it is viable (i.e. able to pay its debts) if it is felt better to distribute funds to shareholders than to carry on the business. This can be done by shareholders or by the company's creditors.

liquidator   a person appointed to see to the winding up and liquidation of a company. A **provisional liquidator** is appointed by a court, normally as a matter of urgency because it is feared that the assets of the company may be 'dissipated'. Normally it can take up to three weeks to have a liquidator appointed and creditors may feel this to be too long to protect their interests. The powers of a liquidator may occasionally be limited by order of the court.

liquidity   the capacity to be converted easily and with minimum loss into cash; 'liquid times' in the money market means there is plenty of money around. A liquid investment is one that is easily turned into cash with minimum capital loss and minimum delay, for example ultra-short-dated Treasury Notes.

liquidity ratio　Financial institutions hold a proportion of their assets in liquid (easily cashable) form, as a matter of internal control and/or because liquidity ratios are imposed on them by the monetary authorities, as in the case of central banks imposing liquidity ratios on banks for prudential reasons.

liquid ratio　a measure of the relationship between the current assets held by a company and its current liabilities. Also **acid test, quick test**. See **current ratio**.

liquid yield option notes　notes issued by Merrill Lynch in the US. These are zero-coupon convertible securities, with an option to sell the debt after a fixed period. *Abbrev.*: **LYONs**.

listed company　a company whose shares are quoted on the stock exchange and are available to be bought and sold by the general public. See **going public, Stock Exchange**.

Little Mo　see **cash base**.

loan shark　a term used to describe unlicensed moneylenders who lend (usually) small amounts of money at much higher rates of interest than those charged by conventional lending institutions. See **moneylender**.

local　(in futures markets) a person who trades on the futures exchange floor on his or her own personal account, not as a broker. The Sydney Futures Exchange introduced 'locals' as a new class of membership in June 1984. See **futures markets, Sydney Futures Exchange**.

loco　a term used in commodity markets, meaning 'at'. Typically a trader would talk of gold traded 'loco London' (from the Latin *locus*, 'place'), as in 'locate' and 'local'.

Lombard rate　the Bundesbank (West Germany's central bank) rate charged to the commercial banks—the equivalent of the US discount rate.

London Inter-Bank Bid Rate　the rate of interest bid by the big London banks on $US call money loans traded among themselves. It is the other side of a LIBOR quote. *Abbrev.*: **LIBID**. See **LIBOR**.

London Inter Bank Offered Rate　This rate is used as a benchmark in Eurodollar lending, with the borrower agreeing to a margin over the London Inter Bank Offered Rate (rarely under). It represents the rate of interest charged by the major London banks on call money loans made among themselves. The margin or spread paid varies according to the borrower's credit standing in the market. The lender stipulates which period is to apply, whether for three or six months or so on. *Abbrev.*: **LIBOR**. See **HIBOR, LIMEAN, TIBOR**.

London International Financial Futures Exchange   This exchange began trading in 1982; it is located in the historic Royal Exchange Building in the heart of the City of London. The success of financial futures in the US, notably in Chicago, and in Sydney, encouraged the launching of futures exchanges elsewhere in the world. The London International Financial Futures Exchange offers traders and speculators opportunities in eurodollar interest rate futures, a range of currency futures contracts, a long sterling gilt (bond) futures contract and a contract based on the Financial Times 100 share market index. *Abbrev.*: **LIFFE**. See **futures contract, futures markets, Sydney Futures Exchange**.

long (Kondratieff) cycle   see **Kondratieff cycle**.

long   In foreign exchange and share market trading, long denotes a net asset position, i.e. a trader has bought more of a commodity than he or she has sold. 'Borrowing long' means borrowing in the long term. See **long position**.

long position   A trader holding a long position in a currency or commodity has overbought in that currency or commodity; traders talk of a long position to indicate an excess of purchases over sales. For example a trader might say 'I've got a long position in $US' instead of saying 'I've overbought in $US'. Traders might even shorten the sentence further and say 'I've gone long $US'. See **short, short position**.

long term   The opposite of short term and equally imprecise. The definition of long term is fairly arbitrary but it would be safe to assume that, say, a long-term investment implied an investment that would last at least more than one year and probably more than five. See **short term**.

Lorenz curve   hard to define without constructing the graph—those specifically interested should consult an economics textbook. As a simple illustration, the Lorenz curve is often used to illustrate inequality in income distribution, showing what percentage of the national cake goes to the top ten per cent and what goes to bottom ten per cent. It is named after the Italian economist Max Lorenz.

loss leader   a trader or business person who sells goods at less than their cost to attract enough business to other products so that they will make up what they lost through low prices by selling other goods at a profit.

loss pricing   holding down prices, despite the loss this may entail, in the hope of wooing customers from a competitor.

Lunch   a tribal ritual deeply ingrained in the culture of the business community. Lunch is performed by two or more people between the hours of 12.30pm and 3pm. It is a carefully ordered ceremony, the phases of which are marked by the appearance and disappearance of glasses of gin, chardonnay, cabernet sauvignon and vintage port. The performance of Lunch is often orchestrated by polite gentlemen in bow ties with names like Edouard or Francois who murmur suggestions about combinations of *saumon fumé* and *poisson du jour* which go well with the chardonnay and so on. Many separate Lunches may be celebrated simultaneously in places called restaurants, which are dedicated to the cultivation of the ritual. The names of these restaurants frequently start with La or Le. Lunch takes on a further dimension in the power play games of the city when it involves men AND women; power traditionally rests with the host or hostess, since he or she initiated the Lunch, chose the restaurant, will select the appropriate wines and will foot the bill. This simple convention becomes blurred when Lunch guests (and Edouard/Francois looking after them) are confronted with a female. People performing Lunch will often spend much of their time observing others and speculating on why who is Lunching with whom, who invited whom (which will become clear when the bill is paid). Business is sometimes discussed. The fringe benefits tax has curtailed this form of non-salary benefit. See **expense account, free lunch, fringe benefits tax, working breakfast, working lunch.**

LYONs   *abbrev.* **liquid yield option notes.**

M

M & A   *abbrev.* **merger and acquisition.**

macroeconomics   the big screen (*makros* is Greek for 'large'). Macroeconomics focuses on the major aggregates such as gross domestic product, the balance of payments, and the links between them in the context of the national economy. It examines the effects of fiscal, monetary and foreign exchange policies on those aggregates (in contrast to microeconomics which is the study of markets, the behaviour of buyers and sellers in response to changes in demand, supply, costs and other factors). Macroeconomists accuse microeconomists of being unable to see the forest for the trees (and vice versa). It has been said that the two types live in separate worlds, not even connected by a rope ladder across the chasm between.

main board   the stock exchange board on which the larger and more established company shares are traded. Listing requirements are more onerous than for the smaller companies which list on the second board. See **second board.**

Malthus, Thomas   see **economists.**

Manchester School   see **free trade.**

mandate   the authority to act for another party. It is a term commonly used in the euromarkets: a borrower who wants to discuss a fundraising proposal will talk to various banks about terms, then appoint a lead manager who will be awarded the mandate or authority to arrange the finance.

management and investment companies   These are fairly new companies, formed under the *Management and Investment Companies Act* 1983. The object of the Act is to encourage the development of a venture capital market in Australia. Management and investment companies are intermediaries, raising funds to lend to high-tech industries, and those who invest in them get a tax benefit for doing so. *Abbrev.*: **MICs.**

management buy-out   A change of ownership takes place in a company so that the significant shareholders become those who are involved in running the business. Management believes the company could improve under their ownership so they buy out the existing owners. Most management buy-outs include some leverage (borrowing).

See **leveraged buy-out**.

MAPS *abbrev.* **market auction preferred stock.**

margin the difference between a benchmark rate and the rate charged to individual borrowers; it is sometimes called spread. In the Euro-markets LIBOR is used as a base rate and borrowers pay a margin above (rarely below) with the size of the margin geared to the borrower's perceived creditworthiness. A margin can also be used when taking security against a loan; the lender can request a margin of oversecuring, to cover interest due not yet paid or to cover potential risk. See **London Inter Bank Offered Rate, spread.**

margin account A trader operating a margin account does so partly using funds borrowed from his or her stockbroker, futures broker or bank—from the party with whom the trader has the margin account. See **margin trading.**

marginal buyer someone who is happy to buy at the present price but who would be deterred by an increase in price.

marginal utility This concept measures the increase in total utility (satisfaction, use or need) of consumption of a good which is produced by increasing the quantity consumed by one unit. The marginal utility of any good or commodity—even beer or ice-cream—is said to diminish as successive units (portions of it) are consumed, while consumption of other commodities is held constant. Critics say the concept of marginal utility cannot be measured. See **utility.**

margin call a request for more funds to cover an adverse movement in price in the futures market. Margin calls are set by the clearing house each day for its members; if a trader fails to meet a margin call then the clearing house can close out that clearing member's position in the marketplace, and if a loss is made, the trader has to wear it. There are two stages involved in a margin call: the clearing house calls the broker (member) in the morning, who in turn calls the client. It is the broker who is liable to the clearing house for the funds involved—the clearing house recognises the obligations of the broker, not those of the client. Margin call money must be lodged by 2pm.

margin trading trading using a margin account, i.e. using money partly borrowed from your broker or bank. For example, share margin trading allows an investor with limited cash reserves to buy more shares than would be possible using his or her own resources; the trader can 'gear up' using borrowed funds.

market the key to the free-enterprise system; a generic term for the arrangements in which people buy and sell a vast range of items, preferably at a profit. Some markets have a physical location—fruit markets, the stock market, the futures market; others such as the money market and foreign exchange are a network of traders connected by telephones and telexes.

marketable securities   see **securities**.

market auction preferred stock   a method of issuing shares in the US, where the paper is issued at a dividend rate that is changed every 49 days by a Dutch auction. Holders who are unhappy with the new rate can redeem their shares at face value. *Abbrev*.: **MAPS**.

market capitalisation   the stock market's assessment of a company's value, calculated by multiplying the number of shares on issue by the individual share price.

market forces   This generally refers to the terrible twins, supply and demand, which are held to determine the price of a product and the volume in which it will be sold. Letting market forces prevail suggests everything will sort itself out. This is not necessarily true, but there is more support these days for letting market forces prevail than there is for heavy government regulation or interference.

market-if-touched order   an order that is based on the market price reaching a specified level. Once the specified price level is reached, it becomes a market order and is carried out. For example a trader might place a market-if-touched order to buy bank-accepted bills at 85.00 when the bills are selling for 86.00; once the price drops to 85.00 the trade would be executed on the buyer's behalf as a market order. Used widely in futures trading. Also called a **board order**.

market on close   buying or selling at the market price at the close of the day's trading. *Abbrev*.: **moc**.

market operations   see **open market operations**.

market order   an instruction to buy or sell a commodity or share at the current market price. Also **at market order**.

market raid   see **raid**.

market share   the proportion of the total amount of a service or product—banking or air-conditioners—that is provided by one organisation. Sometimes companies focus on capturing a big share of the market rather than making a profit.

market value   what you would get for an asset if you were to sell it. That might be quite different from what it cost you, what you have recorded as its book value, or its insured value or replacement cost.

Marshall, Alfred   see **economists**.

Martin Committee (Review Group)   The Labor government established this committee in May 1983, under the chairmanship of Vic Martin, to examine the proposals of the Campbell Committee in the light of Labor's economic and social objectives. Vic Martin was formerly managing director of the Commercial Banking Company of Sydney Ltd (now merged to form the National Australia Bank) and is presently executive chairman of the Mutual Life & Citizens Assurance Co Ltd and chairman of Amro Australia Ltd. Other committee members were: Professor K. Hancock, Vice-Chancellor, Flinders University; Richard M. Beetham, First Assistant Secretary, Treasury; Des Cleary, deputy chief manager, Reserve Bank of Australia. See **Campbell Committee.**

Marx, Karl Heinrich   see **economists.**

MAS   *abbrev.* **Monetary Authority of Singapore.**

matched book   Traders talk of their book being matched when their borrowings and loans are equal in so far as borrowing costs are offset by the interest earned on loans, and the book is also evenly balanced as to liquidity and maturities. A trader running a book that was matched in all respects would be said to have a **defensive strategy**.

match-out   A trader who is holding both bought and sold contracts in the same futures contract month will close out his or her position through a clearing house match-out which will result in the trader offsetting the two open positions.

matrix   a rectangular arrangement of numbers or figures which help in assessing their significance. An understanding of matrix algebra is required if one wishes to understand some of the more sophisticated economic modelling of our era. The first use of the idea in economics was made by Francois Quesnay in his *Tableau Economique*, which was a diagrammatic presentation of a matrix drawn long before matrix algebra had been developed. See **Quesnay, Francois**, in **economists.**

maturity   the date on which a debt or borrowing is due to be repaid. For example, a 90-day bank bill of exchange is due for payment 90 days after its issue date; it has a 90-day maturity. A borrower repays a lender when a loan matures—when the predetermined payment date arrives. Bondholders get paid out when the bonds they are holding mature; bonuses due under insurance policies are paid out when the policies mature.

May Day   1 May 1975, the day that fixed brokerage commissions ended in the US. Brokerage became negotiable. Precursor of the UK's **Big Bang**.

mean   In the arithmetic sense, this is an alternative for 'average'. The arithmetic mean is one of the simpler versions of average, being the total divided by the number of components; for example, if ten pairs of shoes cost $800 then the mean cost would be $80. The geometric mean is the Nth root of the product of a series of numbers; this is used to calculate rates of growth of, say, bank deposits. See **median, mode.**

media   newspapers, magazines, television, radio and any other channel of information. A knowledge of the media is useful to business executives who are so often torn between trying to get things into the press and trying to keep them out. Many companies delegate their relations with the media to public relations or advertising consultants, most of whom started as journalists, which should give them a start in understanding journalists' quirky minds. Good media relations means telling them everything they want to know; effective media relations means telling them what *you* want them to know. Also **mass media.**

median   an alternative measure of the typical value of a group of numbers. Median differs from mean: it is the middle value in a listing of numbers in order of magnitude. If five individuals earn respectively $200, $250, $300, $1000 and $2000 per week, the mean would be $750 but the median wage is $300 because half earn more and half earn less than this amount. In the range of numbers 3, 4, 6, 7, 9, the median is 6. The median has the advantage that it is not as affected by extreme values in one direction as the mean. See **mean, mode.**

medium-term note   intermediate-term debt securities, issued for three to 30 years and continuously offered. They are not underwritten. *Abbrev.*: **MTN**. See **COLTS.**

meeting   a gathering of two or more people at which something is discussed. In the corporate lexicon the word has taken on a new value as a catch-all euphemism for any absence or activity which is better not described in plain words. Depending on the context, meeting can be used thus: 'he's in a meeting' = a secretary's way of saying the boss does not want to talk to you; 'let's have a meeting' = 'let's have lunch'; 'we'd better have a meeting on this' = the boss doesn't understand the problem and needs time to ask his secretary; 'I have to be in Melbourne for a meeting' = 'it's Melbourne Cup week'; 'I think we should have another meeting with our corporate finance people' = 'we've got you over a barrel and we're going to screw you'.

members' scheme   see **scheme of arrangement.**

memo   a memorandum—a written communication. Ideally, a way of getting information on to the record, or of circulating information widely and quickly. In practice, a device for creating files, and therefore an impression of efficient activity. Memos can be cleverly worded to confuse the recipient where the purpose is to slow down unwelcome work; they can be employed to divert the embarrassment of ignorance

('It's a complex situation—I'd better give you a memo on it'); they can be invented to disguise dereliction ('But I sent you a memo on that yesterday—that mail room's a mess'). A large proportion of memos are unncessary. Many good managers never write them—they simply scribble on other people's.

memorandum of association   a company document which sets out the basis on which a company is established, gives its name, objectives (though that is no longer compulsory), capital and the extent of the liabilities of its members. The memorandum of association covers the company's external dealings, as against the articles of association which spell out the company's internal rules. Together the memorandum and articles of a company set out its constitution. See **articles of association**.

mercantilism   an economic theory and practice common in sixteenth- and seventeenth-century Europe which stressed the importance of the bullion reserves built up as a result of an economy's balance of trade. Mercantilism promoted government regulation of a nation's economy to increase state power at the expense of rival nations. Modern protectionism is founded on beliefs similar to the mercantilist doctrines of safeguarding a nation's wealth through protection, tariffs, hoarding gold, i.e. we should have a surplus in our balance of payments (hence 'neo-mercantilism'). Adam Smith, in his *Wealth of Nations*, strongly criticised mercantilists: Smith and other supporters of laissez faire did not go along with the idea that one nation should or could grow rich at the expense of others; they emphasised the two-way aspects of trade. Mercantilism suited colonising nations and empire-builders, who believed that the colonies should be markets for the mother countries' exports and suppliers of raw materials for the mother countries, which would have a monopoly over the commerical activities of the colonial possessions. As with the gold standard, there are gaps between the theory and practice of mercantilism—hence the huge academic debate. See **laissez faire, Smith, Adam** in **economists**.

merchant bank   a UK and Australian term denoting a financial institution which specialises in providing financial services rather than lending its own funds. The use of the term differs between countries. In Australia some merchant banks have tended towards a greater degree of direct borrowing and lending than their UK counterparts, though this may change following the trading banks' greater freedom at the short end of the money market.

Merchant banks go back to the sixteenth century in Europe, when they financed trade—the banking and finance side of their business developed as an adjunct to their trading activities. Merchant banks appeared in Australia in the 1950s and became an important sector of the capital-markets, filling a gap left by the trading banks who were for years subject to heavy government regulation (and, some would say, were innately conservative). The Australian merchant banks equate approximately to the US investment banks and in recent years some have moved towards more of an investment banking style and away from direct lending. The Australian merchant banks' activities are generally spread among trading in money, securities and futures markets, organising longer-term finance for corporate clients, and advising and assisting clients with foreign exchange management. The merchant banks also advise on mergers and takeovers; sometimes they undertake project financing and investment management, or underwrite short- and medium-term corporate debt. Emphasis on different areas varies from company to company.

Popular adjectives to describe merchant bankers are 'innovative' (their favourite), 'aggressive', 'entrepreneurial', 'highly paid'.

merger and acquisition   the combining of two companies to form one, suggesting a balance of strength and willingness between the two to join forces. This is not necessarily always the case. Companies talk of mergers and acquisitions when they really mean takeovers but the former term is more sensitive to the feelings of the target company. *Abbrev.*: **M & A**. See **takeover**.

mezzanine debt   a security that falls halfway between debt and equity.

microeconomics   the study of markets and individual units in the economy (from the Greek *mikros* meaning 'small'). Microeconomists study consumers, firms, households, to see their effects on prices, productivity and so on. See **macroeconomics**.

MICS   *abbrev.* **management and investment companies.**

MidAmerica Commodity Exchange   Founded in 1868, this is Chicago's third commodity exchange. It is the fourth largest in the US, providing futures contracts mostly in agricultural products such as pigs, oats and soya beans, in precious metals and recently also in some financial futures.

midrate   the middle rate between buy/sell quotes in foreign exchange; for example, if the $US/yen quote were to read 238.20/238.60 yen, the midrate would be 238.40 yen. From the mid-1970s until October 1983, the Reserve Bank announced the midrate of the $A in terms of the $US at 9.30am each business day. Between October and December 1983 it announced an 'indicative' $A/$US rate, at 5pm each business day. This short-lived regime was replaced on 12 December 1983 with a floating exchange rate system which leaves the $A rate determined by the market.

Mill, John Stuart   see **economists**.

mini-budget   see **budget.**

mini-max   a capital markets instrument whose interest rate floats within a specified band, i.e. the interest rate is subject to both a **cap** and a **floor**.

minimum lending rate   From 1972 to 1981 this was the rate at which the Bank of England made funds available to members of the UK discount market, against the security of Treasury Bills. the MLR replaced the bank rate in October 1972 and was itself abandoned in 1981. *Abbrev.*: **MLR.**

Ministry of Finance   Japan's eqivalent of Australia's Treasury. This department has many functions including the control of the budget, tax matters, monetary policy (in cooperation with the Bank of Japan), and control over financial institutions (banks, insurance and securities companies). *Abbrev.*: **MOF.**

Ministry of International Trade and Industry   A powerful section of the Japanese government, this department oversees the manufacturing sector in the same way that the Ministry of Finance supervises the financial sector. *Abbrev.*: **MITI.**

mint   The Royal Australian Mint, located in Canberra, is a part of Treasury and produces Australia's coins. The mint sells the coins to the Reserve Bank, which in turn issues them to the banks.

minutes   detailed records of business meetings, some of which take hours.

mismatch   a situation where assets and liabilities do not match in maturity. This may be brought about deliberately, for example when gapping (taking advantage of different rates applying to different maturities). A mismatch in, for example, foreign exchange, could involve no net exposure against the domestic currency but an exposure between third (foreign) currencies. Mismatching is typical of a financial intermediary. See **gapping.**

missing the market   what brokers try to avoid. A broker who missed the market for a client would have lost the opportunity for a favourable trade. If the broker carries out the trade at a later time and on less favourable terms, he or she could be asked to make up the difference to the client.

MITI   *abbrev.* **Ministry of International Trade and Industry** in Japan.

mixed economy   an economy that contains features of capitalism and socialism and is illustrated by a typical Western economy which is neither pure capitalist nor pure socialist. It is said to be a concept invented by writers of high-school economics textbooks. Socialist countries have degrees of free enterprise and capitalist countries operate with state-owned organisations. Australia is a mixed economy with major state-owned enterprises in communications, air and sea transport, banking, energy generation, mining, insurance and health services, as well as privately owned and controlled enterprises in these areas.

MLR   *abbrev.* **minimum lending rate.**

MMC   *abbrev.* **money market certificate.**

minority interest   the proportion of a company's profit or loss attributable to outside shareholders in subsidiary companies which are not wholly owned.

minority shareholders   small-scale shareholders who have shares (equity) in a subsidiary company. In the case of a takeover, those shareholders who have not accepted the offer after the offeror company has received 90 per cent acceptance may be called outstanding minority shareholders.

moc   *abbrev.* **market on close.**

mode   another measure of the typical value in a series of numbers: the mode is the item which occurs most frequently in a group. For example, if four cups are red, one blue and one white, then the mode is red. See **mean, median.**

MOF   *abbrev.* 1. **Ministry of Finance (Japan).** 2. **multi-option facility.**

monetarist   a follower of the school of thought called monetarism which asserts that inflation is caused by too rapid growth in the money supply and that therefore keeping money supply growth within a desired band should be the aim of anti-inflationary policy.
   Extreme monetarists believe that monetary expansion has no effect on real economic activity (employment, spending, production etc.). More realistic versions of monetarism acknowledge that the links between money and inflation are imprecise and long-term and that, in the short run, monetary expansion can stimulate the economy. Monetarists tend to denigrate the efficacy of income policies to curb inflation, advocating a steady reduction in the growth of money to beat inflation. They also tend to oppose frequent changes in policy in attempts to 'fine-tune' the economy, believing that if only governments would stick to steady, non-inflationary policies and stop fiddling with it, the economy would tend towards full employment of its own accord. Monetarism has its origins in the quantity theory of money, and was revived by Milton Friedman and others in the 1960s. It was favoured by policymakers in the 1970s when targets for monetary growth were adopted in many countries, including Australia. See **fine-tuning, monetary policy, money supply,**

quantity theory of money, rational expectations.

Monetary Authority of Singapore   an organisation carrying out the functions of a central bank in Singapore. *Abbrev.*: **MAS**.

monetary base   see **cash base**.

monetary policy   the branch of economic policy which is concerned with the behaviour or the money supply, interest rates and financial conditions generally. The tools of monetary policy include open market operations by the central bank in securities markets, intervention in the foreign exchange market and various controls over financial institutions (for example restrictions on interest rates, lending asset ratios). In the 1950s and 1960s governments tended to focus on fiscal policy, on prices and income levels. Surging inflation in the 1970s brought monetary policy into greater prominence since control of monetary growth is generally considered necessary, if not sufficient, to beat inflation. That did not turn out to be a panacea either. See **fiscal policy, monetarism, money supply**.

monetise   to convert into money.

money   what we all need and never feel we have in sufficient quantity. An enigmatic textbook description of money says that 'money is what money does'. Money is often equated merely with notes and coins, but it is more complicated than that. More explicitly, money is held to have three functions:

- as a means of exchange, more convenient than the old barter system;
- as a unit of account, i.e. money can be measured in dollars and cents so that you know how much you are paying in total for your lunch or your new shoes;
- as a store of value: you can store your savings in the form of money and it will last (inflation aside) and not melt in the sun or rot in the rain.

Money as we know it today in notes and coins is the modern exchange medium, more convenient than a bag of salt (the Roman soldiers' payment, hence the word 'salary' from the Latin *sal*, 'salt') or gold bars. Money in some form has always existed. Primitive tribes recognised the need for a medium of exchange; cattle was popular, being self-transporting, but had the drawback of being large and of varying quality. The Lydians used money in the form of precious metal in the seventh century BC; the Chinese were using paper money in 800 AD. Future generations, of course, will be using plastic money and will discuss our quaint fondness for dirty bits of paper and coins.

money base   see **cash base, money supply**.

money broker   a firm borrowing parcels of money as agent and lending those funds to another company, charging a fee for bringing borrower and lender together.

money centre bank   a large US bank, usually found in a key city location, that trades and issues securities. The big international banking names that are to be found in the world's financial centres (London, New York, Paris, Tokyo) are money centre banks. They lend, borrow and trade financial instruments on a grand scale and thus play an important role in international finance and economics.

moneylender   This used to be a pejorative term to indicate someone lending at rates of interest well above those charged by 'traditional' lending institutions such as banks, building societies, credit unions and finance companies. Over the years the term 'moneylender' has come to mean any person or organisation whose business is the lending of money and as such is covered by the 1984 *Credit Act* in the category of 'providers of credit'. See **loan shark**.

money market   the 'shorter' end (i.e. the short-term area) of the capital market, where banks, finance companies, merchant banks, large corporations, savings banks, building societies and credit unions, life offices and superannuation funds trade short-term securities (often called money market securities) and borrow and lend cash for short periods of time (i.e. generally less than 12 months). Much of the money market borrowing and lending of funds is overnight, though long-term finance is arranged too. See **capital markets, merchant bank, short, short-term money market**.

money market certificate   a savings instrument in the US, offering an interest rate that is tied to the US Treasury Bill rate. *Abbrev.*: **MMC**.

money market mutual funds   the US equivalent and forerunner of Australia's cash management trusts. A boom industry of the late 1970s and early 1980s when interest rates were high. The US Savings and Loan Associations and commercial banks operated with restrictions on interest rates which left them limited in the rates they could offer depositors (Regulation Q) whereas the new money market funds were able to offer investors a high rate of return, by investing in short-term high-yielding securities. US banks are now freer, interest rates have settled down, the banks set up their own funds and brought an edge of competition to the money market funds.

money shops   as in 'one-stop money shops', a recent US innovation, aiming to provide the full range of consumer financial services, from mortgages to savings and investment advice, under one roof. They are usually open longer and more accessible than the traditional lending institutions.

money supply   Broadly this is the amount of cash in the hands of the public plus deposits with banks; the term became popular in the 1960s and 1970s with the rise of monetarism. Australian money supply measures range from the narrowest category, money base, to the widest measure, called broad money. In between come M1, M2 and M3. The money (or cash) base consists of currency in circulation and the deposits of the banks with the Reserve Bank; broad money covers M3 plus borrowings by non-banks, including cash management trusts.

- M1 = deposits in cheque accounts at trading banks plus the public's holdings of notes and coins;
- M2 = M1 plus other deposits of the private sector at trading banks;
- M3 = M2 plus the deposits of the private sector at savings banks.

Other Ms have crept into the picture in recent years:

- M4 which is M3 plus building societies;
- M5 which is M4 plus finance companies;
- M6 which is M5 plus funds with money market corporations.

The UK uses a narrow M1 which is the total amount of cash and current accounts; M3 which is broader and is M1 plus deposit accounts. There is also Sterling M3 which is M1 plus term deposits of the UK private sector and sterling deposits of the UK public and private sectors. The UK also uses PSL 2 (private sector liquidity) = money in circulation, all sterling deposits, money market instruments such as Treasury Bills and bank bills of exchange, building society deposits.

The US has three categories of monetary aggregates:

- M1 which is the narrowest, being money in circulation, traveller's cheques, call deposits at banks and thrift institutions and mutual savings banks;
- M2 which is all of M1 plus some term deposits, banks' overnight deposits, overnight Eurodollars held by US residents and money market funds' balances;
- M3 which is M2 plus big term deposits, corporations' repurchase agreements with banks and savings and loan associations, and institutional money market funds' balances.

See **broad money.**

monopoly   In a monopoly, production and sale of a product is in the hands of one firm, company or individual who therefore controls its market and its price. Trade practices and anti-trust laws, though, could judge a company to be a monopolist even though it has less than 100 per cent of market share. Natural monopoly occurs in industries where there can really only be one seller, for example the telephone system or the postal service.

monopsony   the other side of monopoly: where there is only one buyer.

Moody's Investor Services   a reputable US corporate credit ratings agency, founded in 1903 by John Moody, merged in 1961 with Dun and Bradstreet. See **Australian Ratings, Dun and Bradstreet, Standard and Poor's.**

moonlighting   holding down more than one job—the second job is done by moonlight.

moral suasion   the language of politicians and central bankers, used to make others conform to their wishes without enforcing rules directly to that effect. The Reserve Bank of Australia has shown a preference for operating through moral suasion even when direct controls might have been used. Often just called 'suasion' (in Japan it is known as 'window guidance') it has been used to persuade banks and other financial institutions to keep to offical guidelines; the 'moral' stems from pressing on the targets of the suasion their 'moral responsibility' to operate in a way that is consistent with furthering national benefit. In the US it is called 'jawboning'—exercising the persuasive powers of the jawbone rather than legislation.

mortgage   a form of security. In the case of a mortgage under Old System title, the borrower in effect transfers (conveys) title to the lender subject to the borrower's right to redeem, i.e. to have title transferred back to the borrower once the debt has been paid off. The *Real Property Act* defines a mortgage under the Act as 'any charge on land created merely for securing the payment of a debt'. In the case of a mortgage under this Act title stays with the borrower and the lender has a registered charge over the land or property to secure the payment of the debt.
   Banks and building societies provide funds, based on a proportion of the purchase price, for houses or land on the security of a mortgage to individuals and companies. The property is mortgaged until the debt is paid off. See **charge, Old System title, security, Torrens title.**

mortgage-backed certificate   a security (piece of paper) that is similar to a bond and represents an interest in a pool of mortgages. Such certificates are issued in the US by the Federal National Mortgage Association, the Government National Mortgage Association and a number of large banking institutions. The principal issuers of mortgage-backed certificates in Australia are AusNat Mortgage Pool Agency and the National Mortgage Market Corporation. See **Annie Mae, Aussie Mac, Fannie Mae, Ginnie Mae.**

Mortgage Bankers Association of Australia   the industry body of mortgage bankers, formed in 1982 as a national association of members whose business is predominantly based on providing secured mortgage loans. See **mortgage banking**.

mortgage banking   the business of originating secured mortgage loans, either as principal or agent, managing and servicing the loans and, where appropriate, selling the loans to other investors.

mortgagee   the lender of funds under a mortgage, for example a bank or building society.

mortgage pool   a portfolio of mortgages. See **pass-through security**.

mortgage trust   A form of managed investment, a mortgage trust is a unit trust that pools investors' funds and invests them in residential, commercial and industrial property mortgages, usually for terms of three to five years and offering a variable rate of return. See **unit trust**.

mortgagor   the borrower of funds under a mortgage.

moving average   the average of a sequence of numbers over a specific period. The average 'moves' as new numbers are added to the sequence, replacing earlier numbers.

MTN   *abbrev.* **medium-term note**.

multi-currency loan   finance that is provided with the option of using different currencies; some loans are written with a multi-currency option so that the borrower could start off with, say, all funds in $US, but at a designated stage review the borrowings and perhaps take a portion in yen or deutschmarks if that looks desirable; other loans may allow the borrower to use several currencies at once.

multinationals   companies operating in more than one country, often in several countries, producing a significant proportion of total output in countries other than their own. (The Singer Sewing Machine Company was probably the first.) Multinationals make their decisions against the background of their global operations rather than in the light of what might necessarily be best for the individual countries in which they operate. This led to some conflict of interest; multinationals have frequently been blamed for avoiding tax and exploiting the countries in which they operate, though the trend for heaping blame for the world's economic problems on multinationals has diminished. Multinationals are now showing greater willingness than before to work alongside local companies and integrate themselves to a greater degree with the local scene. They would have got better press if they had been more widely understood. The ogre image prevails to a degree; they are still newsworthy and would probably hit the headlines more often if a shorter name could be found for them.

multi-option facility   This covers a facility with a wider range of funding options than the standard underwritten euronote, sometimes involving the underwriters' carrying a contingent liability for short-term instruments such as bankers' acceptances or for cash advances as well as the euronote issue. *Abbrev.*: **MOF**.

multiplier, the   a term used by Keynes to describe the effect on the national income of a one-dollar change in one component of aggregate demand. Some economists have argued that this was the single most important tool to come out of the Keynesian revolution but as a measuring device it has come under extensive criticism.

The concept is best illustrated by textbook exercises but can be explained basically as the relationship between an initial change in one of the components of aggregate demand (for example consumption or investment) and the total change in national income which results from it. Investment multipliers are the most important. Suppose, for example, that during a period of some unemployment a firm decides to build a new factory with a total cost of $1 million; the incomes of the contractors who carry out the building and provide services and machinery will thus rise, as will the wages of workers who had previously been unemployed. The size of or change in the multiplier will depend on the proportion of extra income saved by these income earners. Thus if the income generated is all kept under the bed then the impact will be minimal. If one-fifth of the $1 million is saved—in other words the marginal propensity to save is one-fifth—then the multiplier will be equal to five. The higher the multiplier, the greater the impact of the initial increase. In this example, if $800 000 is spent, while $200 000 is saved this means an increase by the same amount in national income. In the next round, four-fifths of that total, or $640 000 will be spent. Eventually the process ends when the last dollar of the increased income has been saved.

The idea of the multiplier is still useful and is still used, though the formula cannot be exact because of time lags, leakage from increased savings, taxes and imports, and because of further changes in investment which are a product of other forces. See **Giblin, Lyndhurst Falkiner** in **economists, trickle down**.

mutual fund   US term for a unit trust. See **unit trust**.

N

naked position   A trader who has bought or sold securities and not taken out some protection would hold a naked (uncovered) position. Such a trader stands to gain more if trends are favourable (no hedge costs) but would lose more if prices move adversely to the position held (no protection).

naked warrant   See **warrant**.

narrowing the spread   closing the gap between the bid and asking (buy and sell) prices of a commodity or share. For example the bid price of a share, which is the highest a buyer is willing to pay, might be $20 and the asking price, which is the lowest price a seller will accept, might be $21. A broker making an offer to buy at $20.50, assuming the asking price remains $21, would be narrowing the spread between the bid and asked prices from $1.00 to $0.50. The term is also used with reference to spread/straddle trading, for example the June–September spread narrows from four points to two. See **bid and ask, spread, straddle**.

NASD   *abbrev.* **National Association of Securities Dealers**.

NASDAQ   *abbrev.* **National Association of Securities Dealers Automated Quotations**.

national accounts   Australia's national accounts were first constructed in response to World War II and were first published in 1945 with the commonwealth budget. They are a by-product of the Keynesian revolution and the introduction of macroeconomics in its present form. The national accounts are published annually, with quarterly estimates also released. These accounts are classified in several ways. Essentially they summarise income and expenditure for the economy as a whole and for various sectors of it. They provide useful information for economic analysis and are the source of estimates of gross domestic product (GDP). The national accounts are subject to constant, long-term revision which makes using them a little tricky.

National Association of Securities Dealers   Members of this US organisation include the investment houses and broking firms that deal in securities. The association is supervised by the Securities and Exchange Commission and aims to ensure that ethical standards and practices are maintained in securities trading. *Abbrev.*: **NASD**.

National Association of Securities Dealers Automated Quotations
a computerised system that provides brokers with the prices of shares
and securities traded on the New York stock exchange and over the
counter. The quotes are published daily in several newspapers.
NASDAQ is owned and operated by the National Association of Securities
Dealers. *Abbrev.*: **NASDAQ**.

National Companies and Securities Commission   This regulatory body
was established in 1979 to streamline and standardise the administration of cooperative law and the regulation of securities markets in
Australia nationally rather than State by State. The NCSC was set up
by the *National Companies and Securities Commission Act* 1979 and is
responsible for the administration of the cooperative legislation on
companies and the regulation of securities industries. The aims of the
NCSC are essentially:

* greater uniformity in the law and its administration;
* promotion of commercial certainty;
* reduction in business costs;
* increased efficiency in capital markets;
* improvement in investors' confidence in securities markets by
  ensuring relevant information is available and accurate to facilitate
  investment decisions.

The NCSC works through the State corporate affairs commissions. It
is not intended that the NCSC become involved in day-to-day detailed
administrative work; the powers of delegation by the NCSC to the CACs
are incorporated in the NCSC Act. The NCSC has general responsibility
for policy direction and administration but delegates day-to-day
administration of the cooperative companies and securities legislation to
the various State authorities. The concept of establishing a nationally
operating supervisory body for the securities industry dates from the
mid-1970s. The framework for what is known as the Formal Agreement
between the commonwealth and the six States, and which formed the
basis for the established of the NCSC, was summed up in 1977 by the
then federal Minister for Business and Consumer Affairs, John Howard.
In his speech in March 1977 to the House of Representatives, Mr
Howard summarised the four basic elements of the cooperative scheme
of the Formal Agreement as:

* the establishment of a ministerial council made up of the Attorney
  General of each State and the federal Minister for Business and
  Consumer Affairs;
* the establishment of a full-time National Companies and Securities
  Commission;
* continuation of existing State and Territory corporate affairs
  commissions;
* the adoption of uniform legislation which does not require any

surrender of State power.

Abbrev.: **NCSC**.

national debt   a country's government debt to both foreigners and residents. The external side of national debt has been in the news in the past few years as several countries found that they had more than they could handle. See **external debt**.

National Economic Development Council   a body created by the UK Conservative government in 1962 which brings economists, business people, trade unionists and politicians together to consider economic issues and make plans for the future. Various industries have spawned their own 'little Neddies' designed to improve communications with the government. The value and contribution made by Neddy and the little Neddies is still a subject of debate. *Abbrev.*: **Neddy**.

National Economic Summit Conference   Held in April 1983, the conference was called to promote the climate of consensus between the federal (Hawke) government, Australian industry and the unions. The conference was held to assess the economy and industrial relations, to find a consensus among participants which would set the framework for recovery strategy. It established the Economic Planning Advisory Committee and discussed government policies on prices and incomes. See **Economic Planning Advisory Committee, Statement of Accord**.

national income   a measure of the health of the economy; it means the money value of the total flow of goods and services produced within the country, including what is spent in the country and income earned by residents abroad. Economists calculate national income in three ways, for the purposes of comparison:

- the value of the output of all goods and services in the country, net of indirect taxes and subsidies and adjusted to avoid double-counting;
- all household incomes and the retained profits of companies;
- all that is spent on consumer and investment goods, government expenditure and what foreigners spend on exports less domestic spending on imports.

In principle, these should come to the same value, but in practice there is usually a divergence because of deficiencies in the statistics. The Australian national accounts do not include a measure based on the value of production. National income is similar to gross domestic product at factor cost—which is now the trendier term. See **gross domestic product, gross national product**.

national income forecasting model   the econometric model constructed by Treasury and the Australian Bureau of Statistics in the early 1970s.

It has gone through a number of versions. It provides numerical forecasts which contribute to the official forecasts used in framing the annual budget. It has also been used to simulate the effects of alternative policies. *Abbrev.*: **NIF Model**. See **RB II**.

nationalisation   This occurs where privately owned and controlled industries and services are taken over by the State or government. The opposite process is privatisation. See **privatisation**.

nationalised industries   The UK ranks high in the nationalised industry stakes; the US is low on the list. Countries vary in the degree to which industries and services are owned and run by the government or by the private sector. Discussions over which industries and services should be nationalised, i.e. owned and controlled by the government, tend to become heated. Experience has shown that the least efficient industries are those most likely to be nationalised.

National Mortgage Market Corporation   incorporated in September 1984 by the State Government of Victoria, the corporation first issued mortgage-backed securities, called Aussie Macs, in April 1985. See **Aussie Mac**.

NBFI   *abbrev.* **non-bank financial institution.**

NCSC   *abbrev.* **National Companies and Securities Commission.**

near money   an asset that can quickly be turned into cash, such as call deposits or very short-dated government securities. See **short-dated**.

Neddy   *abbrev.* **National Economic Development Council.**

negative carry   what results when the cost of borrowed money is higher than the return earned on investments. For example money borrowed at 16 per cent to fund a bank bill yielding 14 per cent would result in a negative carry—though the deal could be profitable on an after-tax basis. Also **negative spread**. See **positive carry**.

negative gearing   This would not impress your bank manager. It would mean that the cost of borrowings is not covered by the returns generated by using the borrowed funds; your borrowing costs temporarily exceed cash flow. For example, you have borrowed money from a bank to buy a house for investment and the income from the rent on that investment is not enough to cover the interest and repayments on the loan. People do choose to put up with that, though, to get a tax deduction, which helps cash flow, and eventually to win a capital gain. See **gearing**.

negative interest   an interest rate gap not in your favour; it means earning a lower rate than you pay on deposits. There is little commercial sense in a money market trader paying 10 per cent per annum for deposit funds if money out on loan is earning only 8 per cent—that gives a **negative spread of 2 per cent. Also negative spread. See spread.**

negative pledge   A borrower who gives a negative pledge agrees with a lender under a loan agreement that he or she will not create security in favour of a subsequent creditor without the approval of the lender, or without extending the benefit of the security also to the first creditor.

negative spread   see **negative interest.**

negative straddle   see **straddle.**

negative yield curve   see **yield curve.**

negotiable instrument   a piece of paper representing ownership of debts and obligations; such ownership is passed on with the delivery, or endorsement and delivery, of the pieces of paper. Negotiable instruments are traded in the money market. Bills of exchange, promissory notes and certificates of deposit are negotiable instruments, being written orders promising to pay a specified sum of money at a predetermined time to the order of a specified person or to bearer.

negotiable order of withdrawal   the broad equivalent of a cheque in a particular kind of US interest-bearing current account. The account has the legal status of a savings account but withdrawals are made using a negotiable order of withdrawal. *Abbrev.*: **NOW.**

Nellie Mae   see **New England Education Loan Marketing Corporation.**

neo-classical economics   a system of economic theory built on some of the foundations provided by the classical economists. Neo-classical economists have provided a very elaborate and esoteric defence of Adam Smith's idea of the 'invisible hand'. This rests on a series of heroic assumptions which critics such as Galbraith have argued are too far removed from the realities of modern economics. From the 1870s emphasis has been placed on the notion that in a competitive market economy, made up of innumerable producers and consumers, the free operation of the market would produce the best outcome given the initial distribution of resources. Producers would combine the various inputs to maximise efficiency and consumers would receive the best possible basket of consumer goods. Government intervention should thus be kept to a minimum. Critics of this school of economics maintain that assumptions such as perfect knowledge and rationality on behalf of all the economic actors (and the alleged absence of a logical theory of distribution) raise serious doubts about the policy prescriptions which are drawn from this body of theory. Modern neo-classicists are reluctant to define the term—others try. The late Joan Robinson of Cambridge University is reported once to have said that the only real-world situation to which this kind of economics could be applied honestly was a concentration camp. See **classical economics, economists.**

net   after all necessary deductions have been made. Net income is what you take home after paying tax. 'Income net of tax' means income after tax. See **gross.**

net book value   see **book value.**

net investment   an economic term to describe total investment less the cost of replacing existing assets that have worn out. For example a company with assets worth $100 makes a new investment of $10 but loses $5 through depreciation of existing equipment. The net investment is therefore $5 (gross investment is $10) and assets have increased to $105.

net profit   gross profit less all expenses such as cost of goods sold, selling expenses, tax and interest on borrowings. See **bottom line, gross, profit.**

net realisable value   a measure of the worth of an inventory of goods or other assets that shows its market price less the costs of sale.

netting out   offsetting amounts in a transaction, to avoid exchange of cheques. For example, Company A is repaying Company B $1 million plus interest of $100 000, but Company B is relending Company A $1 million, so A pays B the $100 000—one cheque instead of an exchange of cheques.

net yield   the after-tax return on an investment.

never-never   see **hire purchase.**

New Deal   the policies of President Franklin D. Roosevelt of the US, introduced in 1933 to cope with the Great Depression. These were similar to Keynes's remedies but were independently formulated (some would say without the benefit of an underlying theory). The deficit was increased, the national debt almost doubled, trade unions were encouraged and farm prices raised. It is still debated whether the New Deal was solely responsible for the recovery: some claim recovery was already underway when the New Deal was introduced, others say that real recovery did not happen until after World War II. The New Deal did reduce unemployment but it had its drawbacks and many of its provisions were declared unconstitutional by the US Supreme Court in 1935-36.

New England Education Loan Marketing Corporation   a private non-profit organisation in Massachusetts, established to buy student loan notes under the federal *Higher Education Act* (1965). The Corporation sells tax-exempt bonds (Nellie Maes) to the public and the funds raised are used to buy loans for education. A Nellie Mae is a high school version of a Sallie Mae. See **Student Loan Marketing Association**.

new issue   This term encompasses all forms of security issues to raise more money. New share issues are offered outside existing shareholders as well as to them—these are different from rights and entitlement issues which are offered only to existing shareholders. New issues are often underwritten (for a fee) by merchant banks or stockbrokers and generally sold to the public through a prospectus. Recently issued shares are quoted as 'new' when they do not yet rank equally with existing shares in respect of dividend payments. See **entitlement issue, prospectus, rights issue**.

newly industrialised countries   countries which have progressed beyond being poor but are not yet rich. Candidates for the label are South Korea, Spain, Mexico or the Philippines. *Abbrev.*: **NICs**.

new money   the amount by which a replacement issue of securities exceeds the original issue (more money is raised for the borrower). People also talk somewhat snootily of those who have what is called 'new money' (the *nouveaux riches*)—those who have got rich quick but lack the pedigree that is so often considered to go hand in glove with old, inherited money. Conveniently it is often forgotten how that was come by.

NSW Treasury Corporation   see **central borrowing authority**.

New York Futures Exchange   Established in April 1979, this exchange opened for business in 1980 and is the US's youngest commodity exchange. It has been known primarily in recent years for its activity in the New York stock (share price) index futures contract. The New York Futures Exchange is a subsidiary of the New York Stock Exchange. *Abbrev.*: **NYFE**.

New York Stock Exchange   the oldest and largest stock exchange in the US. The New York Stock Exchange was established in 1792, and stands in Wall Street. It is also known as the **Big Board**. Shares traded on the New York Stock Exchange make up about two-thirds of all trading on US exchanges. *Abbrev.*: **NYSE**.

New Zealand Futures Exchange   The New Zealand Futures Exchange was established in January 1985 and has its head office in Auckland. Unlike most of its counterparts in other countries the New Zealand exchange does not operate by open outcry on a trading floor with a number of pits but trades electronically, with brokers communicating by screen. The exchange is one of the few in the world that operate the Automated Trading System. *Abbrev.*: **NZFE**. See **Automated Trading System**.

niche what every bank seeks — a (profitable) specialist slot. Niche or boutique banking is the opposite of operating as a financial supermarket. See **boutique, financial supermarket.**

NICs *abbrev.* **newly industrialised countries.**

NID *abbrev.* **Note Issue Department** (of the Reserve Bank).

Niemeyer statement the monthly statement of commonwealth financial transactions showing movements in government accounts, often called the Niemeyer statement after the person who devised it, Sir Otto Niemeyer (1883-1971). Sir Otto was an adviser to the Bank of England, who visited Australia in July 1930 at the invitation of the Prime Minister, James Scullin, to confer with the commonwealth government on the financial problems of the economic depression. He recommended a single solution: wage cuts. Jack Lang, then Premier of New South Wales thus nicknamed him 'Sir Rotter'—the *bete noire* of the 1930s.

NIF *abbrev.* **note issuance facility.**

NIF model *abbrev.* **national income forecasting model.**

Nikkei-Dow Jones index Japan's equivalent of the Australian all-ordinaries index, the US Dow Jones index, and the UK Financial Times index.

NL *abbrev.* **no liability.**

Nobel Prize Nobel Prizes are awarded each year for outstanding achievements in the fields of chemistry, physics, medicine, literature, the promotion of peace—and economics. The first Nobel Prize for economics was awarded in 1969, the Swedish National Bank having agreed to finance the prize (the sixth Nobel Prize). For economists, the Nobel Prize is the equivalent of the journalists' Pulitzer Prize. There is strong support for the idea that the Nobel Prize for economics be awarded less frequently (some would argue not at all). It is a more controversial award than, say, physics: it is a more complex task to reach agreement on who is the 'best' economist (economists would *never* agree on that point). The awards are supposed to be for a single contribution. It is hard to judge in economics whether a popular theory is a 'contribution' or just a fashion. The Nobel Prizes are the legacy of a Swedish chemist, Alfred Bernhard Nobel (1833-96) who invented dynamite (1867) among other explosives; this plus the exploitation of the Baku oilfields left him a wealthy man and the bulk of this wealth was left in trust for the Nobel Prizes. The following are Nobel Prize winners in economics since it was first awarded in 1969:

1969 Ragnar Frisch (Norway) and Jan Tinbergen (Netherlands)
1970 Paul Samuelson (US)

1971   Simon Kuznets (US)
1972   Kenneth Arrow (US) and Sir John Hicks (UK)
1973   Wassily Leontief (US)
1974   Gunnar Myrdal (Sweden), Friedrich von Hayek (Austria)
1975   Leonid Kantorovich (USSR), Tjalling C. Koopmans (Dutch/US)
1976   Milton Friedman (US)
1977   James E. Meade (UK), Bertil Ohlin (Sweden)
1978   Herbert Simon (US)
1979   Sir Arthur Lewis (US), Theodore Schultz (US)
1980   Lawrence Klein (US)
1981   James Tobin (US)
1982   George Stigler (US)
1983   Gerard Debreu (born France, naturalised US citizen 1975)
1984   Richard Stone (UK)

no liability   a category of companies where the shareholders with partly paid shares are not bound to pay calls for the unpaid capital, though non-payment of these calls means they forfeit their shares. The Australian Companies Code makes special provision for these companies, which are subject to the same code as other companies but which have been formed to provide a corporate vehicle for the development of relatively new ventures. Investors get the chance at various stages of the fundraising to review their investments and get out if they feel their money is going down the drain. The investor can lose the initial investment if the shares are forfeited but at least is not liable beyond that; and if the proceeds of a forfeited share sale total more than the cost of the shares, the excess is returned to the shareholder. *Abbrev.*: **NL**. See **company**.

no-liability company   see **company**.

nominal value   the stated (face) value of an asset as against its market price. See **face value**.

nominee   a name put forward as a surrogate, an agent acting on behalf of a principal, often used when buying/selling shares or securities and the purchaser/seller wants to keep his or her identity undisclosed or wants someone else to administer the portfolio, for example bank nominees for overseas shareholders.

nominee company   a company whose sole function is to hold shares or securities on behalf of someone else.

non-bank bill   a bill of exchange which does not carry the name of a bank, either as acceptor, drawer or endorser. Also known as commercial bills or commercial paper. See **commercial bills**.

non-bank financial institution   a term that has been around for years but which arrived in popular use recently, after the Campbell Report was released in 1981. Non-bank financial institutions are 'fringe' banking institutions such as merchant banks, finance companies, building societies, credit unions and life offices—any institutions, in fact, that are not banks but which are involved in finance. These institutions are still, at the time of writing (November 1984) on the 'fringe' of banking; with banks freer in their activities and non-banks keen to hook into the payments system, however, the distinctions between banking and non-bank functions are becoming increasingly blurred. Legislatively, there is still a difference. Many non-bank financial institutions are owned or controlled by domestic and/or overseas banks. Also **non-bank financial intermediary**. *Abbrev.*: **NBFI**. See **Campbell Report**.

non-competitive bid   bids lodged in a bond tender by those prepared to buy the stock at the average rates established by the competitive bidders. Non-competitive bids are restricted to smaller amounts (less than $100 000). The big-time buyers bid competitively, setting the rates, and the smaller investors pick up the bonds at the resulting average rates. See **tender**.

non-farm product   total industrial output; the part of gross domestic product which stems from production in industries rather than agriculture and services to agriculture.

non-performance loans   loans where the borrower has failed to pay on time or in the full amount but might be considered not to have defaulted but merely not to have performed—i.e. not met the legal terms of a contract. Non-performance loans spell trouble for banks and since anything is preferable to having funds not working for you, banks have turned to rescheduling. See **default, rescheduling**.

non-rebatable bonds   No tax rebate applies to these Commonwealth bonds, which are the most common type now traded. Rebatable bonds have not been issued since 1968.

nostro account   An Australian bank with an account in New York will call the record in its own books of its New York account a 'nostro account'—the same account in the New York bank's books would be a 'vostro account' (from the Latin, 'ours' and 'yours'). See **vostro account**.

note   A note can refer to paper money or to a type of security, issued by borrowers, bought by lenders and frequently traded in the money market. Examples of notes are Treasury Notes, which are issued by the federal government, and promissory notes, which are issued by semi-government authorities and private sector borrowers such as companies. See **promissory note, Treasury Note**.

note issuance facility   a founding member of the RUF family, this is now used as a blanket description of all underwritten euronote facilities. The note issuance facility has in the last few years overtaken syndicated lending as the most popular method of raising funds in international markets, largely because the notes provide cheaper and more flexible finance, and a tradeable security. *Abbrev.*: **NIF**. See **revolving underwriting facility, short-term note issuance facility.**

Note Issue Department   a statutory department of the Reserve Bank. The bank is the sole issuing authority of Australian currency notes and under the *Reserve Bank Act* the Note Issue Department has responsibility for the issue, reissue and cancellation of these notes. All Australian notes are printed at the bank's note-printing branch at Craigieburn, Victoria; notes are distributed from this branch to the different branches of the Reserve Bank. *Abbrev.*: **NID**.

notes to the accounts   a series of notes at the end of a company's financial statements, explaining details of selected items in the balance sheet and profit and loss statement. The notes make important reading for financial analysts as they flesh out much of the story behind the declared numbers.

not negotiable   A cheque which has been crossed and marked 'not negotiable' cannot be cashed over the counter (at a bank) but must be deposited into a cheque or savings account.

novation   a futures market term to describe the clearing house process by which one party's open position obligation to another is switched to a new entrant as one of the initial (two) parties to the contract withdraws. See **open position.**

NOW   *abbrev.* **negotiable order of withdrawal.**

number cruncher   a colloquialism referring to the 'faith in numbers' people (econometricians) who believe that by analysing data and crunching numbers, adequate policy will follow. More narrowly, 'number cruncher' is an Australian money market term for an economist, actuary or research and planning officer. Chartists are a breed of number cruncher. See **econometrics.**

numbered account   a bank account that is identified by a number rather than the accountholder's name. Numbered accounts are traditionally associated with Switzerland, though several other countries offer the facility. The common misnomer for such accounts is 'anonymous accounts', but they are not anonymous as the identity of such accountholders is known to the bank's top executives. Switzerland has a reputation as a safe haven for funds and a tradition of secrecy (the Swiss call it discretion) in banking that dates back seven centuries.

NX   Stock is listed NX from the time it is issued until the first interest payment; the first interest payment is paid to the original subscriber and therefore is discounted off the price. The letters 'NX' stand for 'new (stock) ex-interest'.

NYFE   *abbrev.* **New York Futures Exchange.**

NYSE   *abbrev.* **New York Stock Exchange.**

NZFE   *abbrev.* **New Zealand Futures Exchange.**

O

OBU *abbrev.* **offshore banking unit.** Earlier this century, OBU would have been taken to mean One Big Union, a concept that had a large following in Australia—and some would say is still around in the coordinating body known as the ACTU. See **offshore.**

odd lot a parcel of securities that does not conform to the conventional round numbers of 100 and multiples of it on the Stock Exchange. These are often handled by specialist 'odd lot' brokers.

OECD *abbrev.* **Organisation for Economic Cooperation and Development.**

off-balance-sheet financing methods of raising funds which are not reflected in a company's balance sheet. Examples of this are sale and leaseback and leasing, where the company leases rather than buys assets so that its reported gearing (indebtedness) remains unaffected because leased assets and corresponding lease liabilities are not shown in the balance sheet. Only the revenue account is affected since the lessee pays rental instalments (as expense). It is well understood, though, in the commercial world that on final payment of the residual value, the lessee will get title to the asset, so in effect the lessee is buying the asset and financing that purchase through a lease. Changes to accounting standards to be released shortly are likely to alter leasing to a balance sheet item. Joint ventures provide another form of off-balance-sheet financing as the liabilities associated with the joint venture are a separate entity from the companies who formed it. These companies have a contingent liability through the joint ventures as they would be liable for its debts should it fail, but this contingent liability is all that is shown on their balance sheet. See **leasing, sale and leaseback.**

off change away from the stock exchange floor. It can refer to any transactions for which a formal exchange exists, but which are carried out elsewhere. In Australia, the term usually denotes trading in fixed-interest securities not executed on the trading floor of a stock exchange but carried out by phone between brokers and other traders. Generally these transactions are for parcels of more than $100 000. Sometimes they are also called 'over the counter'. See **on change, over the counter.**

offeree the company which is the object of a takeover bid; the bid is made to the shareholders of this company. See **takeover.**

173

offeror   the aggressor, the party making the bid in a takeover. See **takeover**.

official dealers   a common alternative term used to describe the authorised dealers in the short-term money market. At the time of writing (November 1984) they total nine. The tag 'official' stems from the Reserve Bank's involvement with that sector of the money market. The dealers have certain privileges and responsibilities arising from their 'official' status. See **authorised dealer, daylight overdraft, exchange settlement account, lender-of-last-resort, repurchase agreement**.

offshore   Offshore transactions are trades in other than domestic currency, usually with non-residents. There are variations which involve residents (with or without restrictions).

OBUs (**offshore banking units**) are the financial institutions carrying out such trades; they may or may not be integrated with local activity. Offshore banking has been regarded as an alternative to opening up a local market to foreign banks; many offshore banking centres offer tax concessions to foreign companies operating within their perimeters. At the time of writing (November 1984) Sydney and Melbourne are interested in becoming offshore banking centres to attract more foreign exchange business. Offshore banking has come to mean banking or foreign exchange dealing free of regulations of the host country. The Euromarket was the first; others include Singapore, Hong Kong, Luxembourg, Bahrain. 'Offshore' has become an alternative word for 'overseas', as in 'funds from offshore'. See **OBU**.

off the run   a term used to describe stock that is infrequently traded. See **on the run**.

Old Lady of Threadneedle Street   an affectionate term for the Bank of England, the UK's central bank, which is located in Threadneedle Street, London.

Old System title   the original system of title to land where a purchaser receives a title that is only as good as that which the vendor has to sell. Old System transactions require examination of a series of deeds and documents relating to all dealings in the land back to what is recognised in law as 'good root of title' (for example, a conveyance for value more than 30 years ago). In Australia, title to Old System land theoretically dates back to an original Crown grant. Old System titles require considerable time-consuming research to establish satisfactory title and necessitate the storage of bundles of documents. Torrens title has simplified the procedures needed to prove title to land. Old System and Torrens co-exist today, though the proportion of land under Old System titles is rapidly diminishing. See **Torrens title**.

oligopoly   a situation in which an industry is dominated by a few companies. Oligopoly has similar effects to monopoly, in that control is not widespread. It is characterised by the interdependence of the small number of firms in the industry; the concentration of power and influence in the hands of a few can lead to cartels and collusion, particularly price collusion, which ultimately means no price competition. See **monopoly, oligopsony**.

oligopsony   a type of market characterised by a few buyers who are able to influence prices. See **monopoly, monopsony, oligopoly**.

on a covered basis   a phrase which implies that a form of insurance or protection has been taken out. It would typically be used in the context of borrowing or lending overseas, where the borrower or lender use a currency hedge contract or the forward market in foreign exchange to minimise the risk of loss due to exchange rate movements. The borrower or lender would then be described as 'covered'.

on change   Transactions conducted on the floor of the stock exchange are described as 'on change'. They are usually for parcels of less than $100 000. See **off change**.

one-name paper   see **promissory note**.

one-sided market   circumstances where the majority of market participants would hold the same view (or would have underlying business largely in the same direction on a day, for example exporters), so that there is a heavy leaning towards all sellers or all buyers and few are willing to take an opposite position.

onlend   to lend funds that have been borrowed from one party, to another party, often within a short space of time.

on-market   on the stock exchange trading floor, as in 'on-market offer'. See **takeover**.

onsell   to sell securities or other assets which have just been bought; as with 'onlend' it implies rapid turnover of the assets.

on the run   a term used to describe stock that is actively traded. See **off the run**.

ontrade   similar to 'onsell'; a dealer in the money market trades in securities and assets which have recently been bought, often only minutes earlier.

OPEC   *abbrev.* **Organisation of Petroleum Exporting Countries.**

open cheque   a cheque which has not been crossed and therefore can be cashed at the bank on which it is drawn and does not have to be paid into an account.

open economy   The term is used loosely, but essentially should refer to an economy where goods, services and funds are free to flow in and out of the country, i.e. there are no import quotas or export restrictions or exchange controls standing in the way of financial transactions.

opening call   a trading session conducted on the futures exchange at the beginning of each day's trading. The call chairman appointed by the exchange opens each traded contract by calling for offers and bids at the beginning of the day's trading; as each month is consecutively called and traded the opening markets are set out and the dealers move to the relevant pits where normal open-outcry trading takes place. See **futures, Sydney Futures Exchange**.

open interest   the number of open (unmatched) contracts in a futures market or in a particular class of options. Traders should note that markets outside Australia show one side only of transactions. The Australian convention is to show all unmatched bought contracts and all unmatched sold contracts.

open market operations   the activities of central banks in the market. In Australia this refers to the Reserve Bank's activity in foreign exchange and the purchases and sales of commonwealth government securities by the Reserve Bank, through the reporting bond dealers. By its transactions, the Reserve Bank affects conditions in financial markets, influencing in particular interest rates, day-to-day cash in the system and the rate of monetary growth. See **central bank intervention**.

open outcry   a trading method where dealers shout their bids and offers on the trading floor and prices vary accordingly; the system is used in share markets and futures trading.

open position   In foreign exchange, a trader who has an open position is one left exposed to exchange rate movements—assets denominated in a particular currency are not matched (as to amounts or maturity) by liabilities in that currency. Trading banks usually set internal limits on their open positions in foreign exchange; central banks may (often do) impose open-position limits on trading banks. In Australia, limits are imposed on the trading banks and other foreign exchange dealers by the Reserve Bank. In futures trading, the term 'open position' describes a futures contract which has been bought or sold and not subsequently offset by an opposite position in the same delivery month.

operating lease   a lease under which the lessor (the owner) effectively retains most of the risks and benefits that go with ownership of the leased property. See **finance lease**.

operating profit/loss   The after-tax profit/loss made by a business from its ordinary revenue-producing activities. Profits/losses derived from activities outside the ordinary operations of a business are called 'extraordinary items' and are added/deducted from operating profit to arrive at 'net profit/loss after extraordinaries'. See **extraordinary items, profit.**

opportunity cost   one of the most useful concepts developed by economists which has become a favourite with economists and accountants. Every action has a potential opportunity cost, because if you had not spent time on course A you would have been occupied with course B which may or may not have provided a better return. More dramatically, it means the value of a benefit sacrificed in favour of an alternative course of action. Pressure groups refuse to acknowledge its existence.

optimality   the best or most desirable situation; one which makes the most of some objective function, for example the pattern of inputs and outputs which gives maximum profit to the entrepreneur. See **Pareto optimality.**

options   contracts which give the holder the right to buy or sell a commodity or security during a given period of time. Option trading is used in the futures market and in the share market. Financial futures options were introduced on the Sydney Futures Exchange in March 1982 and were the first such options in the world. Futures options offer a useful method of limiting risk: if the option is not exercised the option taker (buyer) is limited in outlay to the cost of the premium on the option, plus brokerage. An option trader pays the grantor (seller) for an option to buy or sell a futures contract or parcel of shares on a certain day at a certain price. There are three kinds of options:
- **call options** give the trader the right to buy from the grantor of the option at the strike price, any time between the purchase of the option and its expiry date;
- **put options** give the trader the right to sell to the grantor of the option at the strike price, any time between the purchase of the option and its expiry date;
- **double options** combine the features of the other two: the trader has the chance to make more money no matter which way the market moves—provided that the profit is sufficient to offset the cost of the double premium.

See **exchange-traded options, financial futures, futures, over-the-counter options, strike price, Sydney Futures Exchange.**

option spread   a strategy used by a futures trader hoping to gain from the widening (bear spread) or narrowing (bull spread) of the gap between different options. The options bought and sold are in the same class (call or put) and are simultaneously bought and sold. There are several types of option spread:

- **calendar** or **horizontal spread**   the simultaneous buying and selling of the same class of options, at the same price but with different expiry dates. A calendar spread is a type of time spread.
- **diagonal spread**   a combination of vertical and calendar spreads; the trader buys and sells the same class of options at different strike prices and with different expiry dates. This is another type of time spread.
- **vertical spread**   the simultaneous buying and selling of the same class of options, at different strike prices but with the same expiry date.

See **bear spread, bull spread, interdelivery spread.**

order with discretion   an order which gives a futures trader a degree of latitude which would be defined as, for example, five or ten points around a specified price level. See **at best order.**

ordinary shares   fully paid shares. They rank after debentures and preference shares for dividend payments, and dividends can fluctuate with the company's fortunes. Ordinary shareholders have voting rights. If the company is wound up, they rank as unsecured creditors, behind secured creditors such as debenture holders.

Organisation for Economic Cooperation and Development   This organisation began in 1961 and aims to encourage economic growth, high employment and financial stability among member countries to contribute to the economic development of less advanced members and non-member countries; it also gives the industrialised countries an opportunity to discuss international monetary problems. The OECD has 24 member countries; its secretariat is in Paris. It was set up as part of the Marshall Plan for Europe's post-World War II recovery. It is an important discussion centre, putting out regular studies, producing valuable economic surveys and forecasts. Australia joined the Organisation for Economic Cooperation and Development in 1971. *Abbrev.*: **OECD.**
Member countries are:

Australia	Japan
Austria	Luxembourg
Belgium	Netherlands
Canada	New Zealand
Denmark	Norway
Federal Republic of Germany	Portugal
Finland	Spain
France	Sweden
Greece	Switzerland
Iceland	Turkey
Ireland	United Kingdom

Italy   United States of America.
(+ Yugoslavia as an associate member)

Organisation of Petroleum Exporting Countries   a formal grouping of major producers and exporters of crude oil, a forum for discussion and agreement on prices for crude oil exports. It also determines the level of aid granted by its members to developing countries. The organisation was established in 1960 but achieved a wider audience after the 1974 oil price rise. *Abbrev.*: **OPEC.**

ostensible authority   an elementary legal concept meaning that authority is implied, though a lawyer would point out the subtle distinction between ostensible and implied authority. Ostensible authority is the basis for most dealings in financial markets, fundamental to the telephone/telex dealing process. Two people putting together a transaction by phone or telex each rely on the other's ostensible or apparent or implied authority to deal on behalf of his or her company.

out of the money   a term used to describe an option that cannot be exercised at a profit. An out-of-the-money option is a call option whose strike price is higher than the current market level, or a put option whose strike price is below market. A call option on December bonds at 100 would be out of the money if December bonds are at 99 or less; a put option would be out of the money if they were at 101 or more. See **at the money, in the money**.

outside lag   see **leads and lags.**

outside the fees   Once an issue of securities trades outside the fees the underwriter loses money. The underwriter's fees are reduced to allow a corresponding boost to the return for the buyer, to encourage buyers into the issue. See **inside the fees.**

overbanked   A nation is described as overbanked when there are too many banks (in the banks' view) to be able to generate good returns.

overbought   A commodity which has been overbought is one whose prices have been pushed up to a level that some believe is unrealistically high and cannot be sustained. A trader who has overbought in a commodity would be described as having a 'long position' in that commodity. See **long position, oversold.**

overcapitalise   You buy an old property in a slum area with no views, surrounded by factories, under a flight-path, near a railway line and a freeway and you install a backyard pool, landscape the yard, build into the roof and construct a raised patio—you have overcapitalised, i.e. you have spent more money than you are likely to get back out of that investment.

overdraft   what you need before you can even contemplate over-capitalising. Banks allow selected customers who ask for it to spend more money than is in their current account by permitting them to write cheques in excess of the account balance, i.e. to overdraw. Overdrafts are arranged up to limits which vary with the customer's credit standing with the bank and the bank manager's humour. Overdrafts allow flexibility in the amount spent and equally allow flexibility in repayments (though technically a bank can demand repayment of an overdraft within 24 hours). In that respect overdrafts are unlike personal loans, which are structured with regular repayments. Interest on overdrafts is charged on the fluctuating daily balance; the bank can charge a fee for unused overdrafts to compensate for the funds not being usefully employed, from the bank's point of view.

overheads   costs incurred whether you make a profit or not, such as salaries, rent, buying the coffee, fringe benefits to employees; they are unavoidable and often expensive.

overheated economy   This sounds more exciting but is really similar to inflation, which is far from exciting. An overheated economy is often the result of a high level of activity (which is good) but which can put pressure on existing productive capacity, can run out of control and send interest rates rising and feed inflation.

overnight   This can mean dealing today for tomorrow, or it can refer to the shortest short-date swap and the most commonly used. This would involve a simultaneous purchase and sale (of currencies), of which the first transaction is settled today and the reverse transaction settled tomorrow. See **short-date swap, spot/next, tom/next.**

overnight money   the shortest period, except through daylight overdraft from a bank, for which money can be lent out and earn interest. Funds placed out overnight are recallable/repayable/re-negotiable by 11am the following morning.

oversold   the opposite of overbought. A commodity which has been oversold is one whose prices have been pushed down to a level that some believe is unrealistically low, unsustainable and therefore could herald an upward reaction. A trader who has oversold a commodity would be said to hold a 'short position' in that commodity. See **overbought, short position.**

oversubscribed   An issue is termed oversubscribed when the value of applications for stock (such as shares, debentures or any type of security) exceeds the amount to be allocated. Finance companies and (more recently) semi-government authorities are allowed to take oversubscriptions up to a given amount through their prospectuses.

over the counter   a method of trading shares of companies which for one reason or another (such as inadequate capital or insufficient spread of shareholders) do not meet the requirements for trading on the main stock exchange board, but are bought and sold in a secondary market (over the counter).

over-the-counter options   options that can be tailored to individual clients' needs. The client arranges the option with his or her bank or merchant bank, instead of buying an 'off-the-peg' model such as an exchange-traded option, so that details such as amount, maturity and price are arranged between client and bank. Over-the-counter options cannot be traded but they can be sold back to the bank or merchant bank which initiated the product. These options are a useful hedging device and like exchange-traded options they involve the cost of a premium. See **exchange traded options, options.**

overvalued currency   a currency whose quoted or traded rate is above what the market believes to be its correct level, given its country's balance of payments position and other relevant factors. Traders and speculators would be reluctant to buy a currency they believed to be overvalued as that suggests it should fall. If the domestic currency is considered overvalued, exporters would delay bringing in foreign currency payments, while importers would benefit from advancing payments. See **leads and lags, undervalued currency.**

P

paid-up capital   the proportion of a company's issued capital that has been paid for by its shareholders. Details of paid-up capital should show the different classes of shares issued, the number of shares issued in each class, the amount paid on each and what has been called and not yet paid.

paper   Traders talk of 'paper' when referring to securities (which are pieces of paper) such as government bonds or bank bills of exchange. Also **government paper, bank paper**.

paper profits   unrealised profits that would be crystallised if the owner were to act; for example land or securities might have improved in market value compared to their purchase price but the owner's profit remains on paper unless the land or securities are sold then; if the owner waits too long the paper profits could fade.

par   equal; used in foreign exchange to describe a currency whose forward rate is the same as its spot rate. See **par value**.

parallel loans   These offer a method of raising capital in a foreign country to finance assets there without going through cross-border capital moves. For example a $US loan would be made to an Australian company to finance its factory in the US; at the same time the US party who made the loan would borrow $A in Australia from the Australian company's parent to finance its project in Australia. Parallel loans are generally in different currencies. They had their heyday in the 1970s in the UK, when they were frequently used to get around the strict exchange controls then in existence; they have been described as the earliest form of swap transaction. See **back-to-back, swap**.

parcel   a bundle; the word refers to a collection of bills of exchange, bonds, Treasury Notes or shares whose details, such as maturity date and issuer, are identical.

parent company   a company that has a subsidiary or subsidiary companies. Parent company accounts are presented to show the parent's own financial situation, as well as that of the group (consolidated accounts). See **consolidated accounts**.

Pareto optimality (Pareto's law)   a concept of optimality, recognised as Pareto's law, which essentially means a situation in which nobody could be made better off without someone else being made worse off. It was the result of early work by the Italian economist and sociologist Vilfredo Pareto (1848–1932). See **optimality**.

pari passu   Latin for 'with equal progress'. This phrase is used to indicate simultaneous and equal change or to describe similar ranking of securities or lenders; for example when a new issue of shares is made, they could be said to rank *pari passu*, i.e. equally with existing shares for the purposes of dividend payments. A common agreement between joint lenders is a *pari passu* clause, under which, in the event of a shortfall, they agree to share equally whatever is available.

Paris Club   an informal grouping of government officials who meet about once a month to oversee government-to-government loans which get into difficulties. The Paris Club has been operating since 1956 more or less voluntarily and includes about fifteen or sixteen countries, depending on who needs to attend. It is located in Avenue Kleber, Paris, and is run by the French Treasury.

parity   equality; in financial terms, equality in value. The word has come to be used in the sense of 'one to one' in foreign exchange, so that when the $A fell to 99.60 US cents, it was described as 'falling below parity'. See **fixed parity**.

Part A (Part B, Part C, Part D)   see **takeover**.

partial equilibrium theory   see **general equilibrium theory**.

participation certificate   a pass-through security representing an interest in a pool of instruments such as mortgage-backed securities. *Abbrev.*: **PC**. See **Federal Home Loan Mortgage Corporation**.

partly paid shares   see **contributing shares**.

partnership   two or more individuals who have joined together to carry on a business, with a view to profits, sharing in risks and profits. As partnerships are not incorporated, each of the parties shares equally in these risks and rewards and is liable for all the partnership's debts. Creditors of a partnership can claim on the partners personally; there is no limited liability for the partners as is available to shareholders of a limited liability company. See **company, corporation, incorporated, limited liability**.

par value   If a security such as a Commonwealth bond is trading at $102 and it was issued at $100 then it is trading 'above par', i.e. at a premium. Conversely if the bond were sold for $98 and had been issued at $100 then it would be at a discount or 'below par'. Australian Savings Bonds are sold 'at par', i.e. at their face value, and are redeemable (cashable) at par on 30 days' notice, which means you pay the full face value when buying them and you get that same amount back when they are cashed in. The par value of a share is set by the issuing company and often is quite different from the share's market price. Also **face value**, **nominal value**.

pass a dividend   not declare (pay) a dividend. A company would choose not to pay a dividend if it had made no profit, if it had made a loss, or possibly because it was in the process of restructuring.

pass-through security   a security, such as a bond or certificate, that represents an interest in a pool of mortgages. All payments from the mortgagors on the loans in the pool pass through to the certificate holders to pay interest and principal. Mortgage-backed securities are the most common type of pass-through security; these operate in two ways, as direct issues of pass-through securities or as issues using an off-balance-sheet trust or company vehicle. With direct issues the originator of the mortgage issues pass-through securities to investors, giving them beneficial ownership of the underlying mortgage. The structure with an off-balance-sheet trust or company interposes a third party which can be an additional safeguard; in this case beneficial ownership of the mortgage passes to the trust or company vehicle which in turn issues pass-through securities which represent interests in the underlying mortgage. The securities are marketed by the party originating the mortgage. See **mortgage-backed certificate**.

patent   the right to exclusive use of a new invention. The law is codified in Commonwealth Patents Acts.

pay-back period   the length of time needed before an investment makes enough money to recoup the initial outlay of cash. This method ignores the time value of money.

PAYE   *abbrev.* **pay as you earn tax** see **taxation**.

payee   The person to whom a cheque or a bill of exchange is made payable. See **bill of exchange**.

paying bank   the bank on which a cheque is drawn (the bank whose name is printed on the cheque) and which pays the amount for which the cheque is written and debits that sum from the customer's account.

payola   a gift or remuneration to someone who has the potential to use his or her influence in your favour. It is often used of payments to, say, disc jockeys for air space to particular songs.

payout ratio   a measure of the proportion of profit that is distributed through dividends to ordinary shareholders. The ratio is calculated by dividing the dividends by the amount earned in profit.

payroll tax   see **taxation**.

PC   *abbrev.* **participation certificate**.

P/E   *abbrev*. **price earnings ratio.**

pegged   tied to. The value of the $A used to be constant in terms of sterling so that its exchange rate with other currencies moved in line with those of sterling; then in 1971 the $A changed to become linked to the $US and its moves against other currencies reflected the $US's moves against those currencies. The $A operated under a 'flexible peg' to a trade-weighted basket of currencies for a number of years before being floated in December 1983. See **exchange rate, float.**

penny dreadfuls   low-priced, highly speculative shares, an extension of the original meaning of cheap, sensational novels.

pension funds   superannuation funds which pay out the benefits in the form of a pension (i.e. in instalments) on retirement. In Australia all government (public service) funds are pension funds; most private companies operate superannuation funds which make lump-sum payouts.

percentile   The 'top percentile' is the same as the top one per cent. Percentile is a common breakdown on a scale of numbers. It appears 99 times in the scale of 1 to 100. The percentile of a set of numbers is that number below which a certain per cent of the numbers fall, for example in a range of 1 to 10, 5 is the fortieth percentile as 40 per cent of the numbers are below it. The fiftieth percentile is in the middle.

perfect competition   a theoretical device, found mostly in economic textbooks. Perfect competition assumes that buyers and sellers of a product are equally matched so that neither side can determine prices, the economy is free from barriers or restrictions and all participants have perfect knowledge and act in a rational manner. Despite the absence of perfect competition in the real world (except perhaps at the racetrack) the concept provides a necessary starting point for the analysis of forms of competition which are not perfect (and is an important influence on trade practices legislation).

performance-indexed commercial paper   commercial paper whose redemption value is linked to movements in a specified currency. They are similar to ICONs though issued for a shorter term. Created by Salomon Brothers. *Abbrev*.: **PIPS.**

perks   short for perquisites, which means, the additional or fringe benefits (which are tax-beneficial since they are the equivalent of income which is not taxed) provided by an employer to an employee over and above the employee's salary. These can be in the form of travel, cheap housing finance, paying children's school fees, even a generous expense account. See **expense account, Lunch.**

perpetual bond   a bond that is issued with no maturity date. The bondholder earns income on the bond through the coupon stream; a buyer has to be found in the market if the holder wishes to sell as the bond has no redemption date at which the issuer pays out the face value of the bond.

perpetual floating-rate note   a note with the same characteristics as the perpetual bond, i.e. no maturity date and even interest payments. Such notes were launched in 1984 and have been issued by many of the world's big banks because they represent a fairly inexpensive method of raising primary capital. The perpetuals were issued in volume, particularly in the second half of 1986. The underlying concept of the securities and the differences among the issues from different countries were not always widely understood by the buyers. These factors contributed to the perpetuals' becoming one of the market disasters of late 1986 and early 1987. Greater understanding of perpetual debt and of the differences among the issues should improve the market for these securities. See **primary capital**.

personal identification number   a number issued by banks to their customers as a personal code to be used in conjunction with a plastic card to gain access to automatic teller machines. *Abbrev.*: **PIN**.

personal loan   a type of loan available from trading banks, finance companies and credit unions. Funds are advanced (lent) to the customer for a fixed period, at a fixed rate with repayments calculated at the outset on (usually) the basis of monthly instalments. The interest rate is often expressed as a 'flat' rate and this can be misleading—8 per cent flat is not the same as 8 per cent per annum, because in the case of the 'flat' rate the principal sum is not being reduced during the loan. Eight per cent flat is about 15 per cent per annum. See **flat rate of interest**.

petrocurrency   the currency of a country with oil to export, for example riyals of Saudi Arabia. Sterling is now termed a petrocurrency, because of North Sea oil.

petrodollars   see **petrocurrency**.

Phillips curve   In 1958 A.W. Phillips examined the relationship in the UK between wage increase and unemployment, to show that periods of high unemployment were associated with small increases in wages and prices. This suggests that a government could make a choice between unemployment and inflation, which might be politically difficult. The theory is illustrated in the Phillips curve. Phillips reportedly said in later years at the Australian National University in Canberra that if 'he had known what they'd do with his graph he would never have drawn it'. Phillips was not as dogmatic in his causal relationship as the popular version of his theory suggests.

phone jockey   a non-decision-making money market or foreign exchange dealer.

PIBA   *abbrev*. **Primary Industry Bank of Australia.**

piggy-back option   the issue of a share option which when converted to a share automatically creates another option.

piggy-bank money   a wholesale money market term for retail-size deposits, i.e. deposits of less than $100 000 taken by the money market desk of a merchant bank.

pig on pork   a UK term to describe a bill of exchange (usually a less-than-top-name bill) where the drawer and the drawee (acceptor) are the same family, for example where a subsidiary company draws a bill on its parent.

PIN   *abbrev*. **personal identification number.**

pip   see **point**.

PIPS   *abbrev*. **performance-indexed commercial paper.**

pit   the area on the trading floor of the Sydney Futures Exchange (and other futures exchanges) where the traders gather for action. Each commodity traded on the exchange has its own pit and only traders are allowed into the pits.

plain vanilla (currency swap)   a transaction in which two counterparties exchange specific amounts of two different currencies at the beginning of the deal and reexchange the same amounts at the end of the deal. Over the life of the transaction the counterparties make payments to each other, reflecting the interest rate differentials between the two currencies. See **swaps**.

plateau indexation   see **wage indexation**.

plough back   to reinvest profits in a business rather than distribute them to the owners (shareholders). See **undistributed profits**.

PN   *abbrev*. **promissory note.**

point   This refers to the last decimal place in a foreign exchange quote. If the $A were to rise from 89.10 US cents to 89.40 US cents then it would have gained 30 points. Also **pip**.

poison pill   defensive action against a takeover. A company that is under threat of takeover takes action to make itself appear a less attractive target.

policy lag   see **leads and lags**.

portfolio   A person who holds a number of shares in different companies and a reasonable range of fixed-interest securities and money market instruments can be said to be 'running a portfolio'. People talk of 'portfolio investments' rather grandly when they own a couple of shares. A good portfolio will show a spread of investment to minimise risk —your broker or investment adviser will tell you 'not to put all your eggs in one basket'.

portfolio balance   trying to achieve the best blend of investments in your portfolio, taking into account interest rates, inflation, what else you might do with your money, whether you have invested in politically sensitive areas, etc.

portfolio insurance   a form of portfolio protection developed in the late 1970s by the California-based firm Leland O'Brien Rubinstein Associates Inc. At its simplest, portfolio insurance is an investment strategy designed to manage exposure to a risk asset (usually shares) to limit or control losses. The concept was tested in the October 1987 sharemarket crash. Supporters of the theory concede that such strategies may not achieve their targets if financial markets gap (record large, one-off movements in price) as severely as happened during the crash.

portfolio investment   the acquisition of bonds (of more than twelve months of maturity) or of shares in a company, domestic or foreign, for investing purposes only. Portfolio investment carries a share in profits and dividends but stops short of bringing a say in how the business is run. See **direct investment**.

portfolio management   managing a large single portfolio or being employed by its owner to do so. Portfolio managers have the expertise and skill which encourages people to put their investment decisions in the hands of these professionals (for a fee).

position   Money market, futures, foreign exchange and share market traders talk of 'taking a position' when they mean they are taking a stand, executing a deal when perhaps others are hanging back; 'position' can also refer to a trader's cash/securities/currencies balance, whether he or she is short of cash, has money to lend, is overbought or oversold in $US, etc.

position paper   This sounds rather more awe-inspiring than 'report' but it means the same.

positive carry   With a positive carry the cost of borrowed funds is lower than the return earned on investments. For example borrowed funds cost 12 per cent per annum whereas an investment in bank bills yields 14 per cent. Also **positive spread**. See **negative carry**.

possessory lien   see **lien**.

posting   transferring details of financial transactions to ledger accounts.

post trading   the system used in Australian share trading where the bid and ask prices of shares and securities are recorded on boards.

power of attorney   If you grant someone else power of attorney, shown by an appropriate document, you are giving that person power to do in your name and, legally speaking, as if it were your act, whatever is done within the limits set out in the power. Specific powers of attorney are often granted to a person such as a solicitor or executive to sign named documents on behalf of a person or company.

PPS   *abbrev.* **prescribed payments system.**

PR   *abbrev.* **public relations.**

preferential trading   a style of futures trading that allows floor traders to deal with anyone they choose. The rules were introduced on the Sydney Futures Exchange in 1987 and were modelled on Chicago's Board of Trade and Mercantile Exchange. Under the new system buyers and sellers are free to choose the party with whom they trade; for example if there is one buyer and five sellers, the buyer can chose one seller or any combination of sellers. Previously if a seller had one contract for sale and there were five buyers the buyers had to toss. Now they say 'right' and the seller chooses the buyer, for whatever reasons appeal.

preference shares   shares which rank ahead of ordinary shares for the purposes of claiming dividend payments or any assets of the company should it be wound up. Preference shares rank behind debentures.

Premiers' Plan   Adopted in June 1931, by the Scullin government, the Premiers' Plan proposed reduced interest rates and a 20 per cent cutback in government expenditure, including a reduction in public sector wages. The objective was to reduce Australia's huge budget deficit problems. Australia had to get its books in order if the country was to continue to get overseas finance; devaluation had already been forced and increased tariffs tried. The rationale behind the Premiers' Plan was to revive business confidence. The plan was welcomed in the 1930s as an example of creative economic planning; Douglas Copland claimed it was 'a judicious mixture of inflation and deflation'. Later it was criticised as overly deflationary. See **Copland, Douglas** in **economists.**

premium   A commodity that stands at a premium is one that is valuable, for example when tomato stakes are described as at a premium it means they are too useful and costly to throw away when the tomato plants die. Shares or securities bought at a premium are bought for more

189

than their par or face value. In foreign exchange a currency trading at a premium is worth more in the forward market than in the spot market. In insurance, the premium is the regular (usually monthly) instalment paid by a policyholder to the insurance company to maintain an insurance policy. Premium is the opposite of discount. See **discount, insurance, par value**

premium raid   see **dawn raid**.

prepayment   paying a bill or debt before it is due. Some loan agreements carry penalties for very early prepayments, reflecting the lender's expectations of when and how much interest was due under the original contract. Sometimes exporters will hasten payments if they believe that their own currency is about to appreciate or be revalued.

prescribed payments system   see **withholding tax**.

preshipment finance   This covers an exporter's costs before goods are sent overseas.

presold issue   stock that has been placed with subscribers before the issue officially opens and before all details of rates, terms and conditions have been released.

price discrimination   see **price maintenance**.

price-earnings ratio   Generally this is considered a good yardstick for measuring the value of a company's shares; it shows the relationship between the market price of a company's shares and the earnings per share. Divide the annual earnings per share of, say, $2, into the market value of say $12 and the P/E ratio is 6. *Abbrev.*: **P/E**. See **earnings per share**.

price fixing   see **price maintenance**.

price maintenance   collusion among manufacturers to maintain an artificially high level of prices for their products; such concerted action is now illegal, under Section 45 of the *Trade Practices Act*. Dealing with customers on differing terms can be a normal aspect of business in any market but in certain cases is outlawed by the *Trade Practices Act*. Also **price discrimination, price fixing**. See **Trade Practices Commission**.

price takers/makers   In perfect competition, all producers are price takers as they have to accept what the market says is the appropriate price and they cannot do anything to shift that price; in a pure monopoly, though, one firm is the price maker and the rest of the market has to take that price. Real-world markets are mostly oligopolistic, with a handful of producers able to make prices which price takers often have to accept.

primary capital   a concept used in the US and adopted elsewhere as

190

part of a move to ensure that banks have sufficient capital to support their activities. The definition of primary capital varies between countries but broadly usually covers items such as the initial investment by shareholders, retained earnings and capital reserves. Subordinated notes, debentures and so on are ranked as secondary capital by the US Federal Regulatory Agencies. Regulators add primary and secondary capital together when assessing a bank's overall capital adequacy.

primary dealer   a US bank or investment house that is authorised to buy and sell government securities directly with the Federal Reserve Bank as part of the central bank's open market operations. Broadly the US equivalent of Australia's official dealer and the UK discount house.

primary industry   agricultural and pastoral activities, once the backbone of Australia, and still important, especially as an export, though it tends to hit the headlines only in times of drought, flood and falling prices.

Primary Industry Bank of Australia   a bank established in 1978 to help provide long-term funds to farmers. It is jointly owned by the commonwealth government and the major Australian banks. *Abbrev.*: **PIBA**.

primary market   the new issue market. Bonds and Treasury Notes sold by the Reserve Bank in regular tenders are primary market stock; once they are sold into traders' hands they are in the secondary market. See **secondary market**.

prime rate   the benchmark rate charged by banks on large overdrafts (more than $100 000 in Australia) to their best (prime) customers. Most of the banks' customers pay the prime rate plus a margin. It is often abbreviated to just 'prime'. See **benchmark rate**.

prime underwriting facility   a form of RUF, in which the maximum margin is set against the US prime rate. *Abbrev.*: **PUF**. See **revolving underwriting facility**.

principal   the face value amount of a loan, on which interest is calculated. See **rule of 78**.

prior charge   a charge that ranks ahead of another. For example, a specific mortgage will usually rank ahead of a floating charge. See **charge**.

private company   see **company**.

private enterprise   business that is owned and controlled by individuals as against those owned and run by the state.

private placement   a method of fundraising, where the borrower obtains cash by selling securities—bonds or promissory notes—direct to a group of investors. There is no advertising of the issue; no prospectus has to be circulated as the stock is not on offer to the public, and the fundraising is often only publicly recorded after the event in a 'tombstone'. See **tombstone**.

private sector the opposite of public sector. The private sector encompasses all companies and activities that are operated by and undertaken by private individuals, and companies and owned by private individuals, rather than by government. See **public sector**.

private sector foreign exchange transactions the amounts by which the cash base of a country's financial system changes because of foreign exchange transactions carried out by individuals and businesses. They represent the changes in the Reserve Bank's holdings of foreign exchange, due to central bank transactions with the private sector, corrected for valuation effects. Since it is a private sector measure, commonwealth government activities are excluded. PSFET had more relevance before the December 1983 switch to a floating $A. Before the float, ebbs and flows across the exchanges had a direct impact on domestic liquidity; under the float, domestic liquidity is affected through Reserve Bank market operations. *Abbrev.*: **PSFET**. See **cash base, central bank intervention, open market operations**.

private sector liquidity money and short-dated government securities in the hands of the private sector, i.e. companies and private individuals. See **liquidity, money supply, private sector**.

privatisation a word that has become popular in the UK in the last couple of years to illustrate the Thatcher government's declared intention of moving some of the more efficient government-owned services back into private hands. The concept has been espoused to a degree by the Liberal–National Country Parties in Australia. See **nationalisation, nationalised industries**.

probate the hearing and determining of any queries arising from a will about who is entitled to what. The executor of a will has to obtain the probate document (certificate) from the court to enable him or her to act. A deceased person's estate or wealth can be described as 'subject to probate', which means it is frozen pending the probate certificate which confirms that the will is valid and can be executed. Probate comes from the Latin *probatus* meaning 'proved' and is the executor's authority from the court to administer the estate.

product Once clearly understood to mean something tangible, which resulted from a creative effort and usually involved physical energy and machinery, the word has taken on a new colouration in the language of business. Now it means anything that can be sold, bartered, taken advantage of or just talked about. When an advertising man talks of a product he may mean his strategy for selling an item, rather than the item itself. A financial dealer may call an interest rate a product, as if he had made it with his own hands. 'I'd like your conceptual input on an innovative product' means 'What do you think of this idea?'.

profit   a synonym for 'income' in accounting; what you have left (you hope) from earnings after all expenses have been provided for. Profit can be gross, which is the difference between sales and the costs of those goods sold; or operating, which is the difference between gross profit and operating expenses, including income tax expenses. The term 'net profit' can be used to refer to 'operating profit' or 'operating profit after extraordinary items'. See **bottom line, gross, net profit, operating profit.**

profit and loss account   an account showing a company's earnings and expenses over a period, what it has done with its profits, how much is being paid out in dividends and how much is retained for the company. It shows the results of activities during a period, whereas the balance sheet shows the company's assets and liabilities position at a point in time (balance date). At the end of the accounting period all income and expense accounts are closed and the balances transferred to the P & L account. After calculating profit and determining dividends, the balance of retained earnings is transferred to owners' equity in the balance sheet. The new year's income and expense account begins with a clean sheet, at a zero balance. *Abbrev.:* **P & L.** See **balance sheet.**

profit maximisation   doing what achieves the largest profit. This is reached when marginal revenue equals marginal cost. Economists debate whether it is the most important motivator for managers; some companies, for example, shoot for market share. See **market share.**

profit-taking   cashing in on paper profits while the going looks good; if traders or speculators believe a commodity has reached its peak or near it after a good run, they will take their profits by selling, which can have the effect of pushing the commodity's price down again.

pro forma   A balance sheet or profit and loss statement is described as *pro forma* if it is drawn up using various stated assumptions or if some of the details disclosed could change, for example a proposed deal (fundraising or merger) is shown but has not yet been concluded. From the Latin 'as a matter of form'.

program trading   a highly computerised method of trading and arbitraging between physical, futures and options markets. It is used in the US, to a lesser extent in the UK and Australia. See **triple witching hour.**

project finance   This refers to financing arrangements where the funds

193

are made available for a specific purpose (the project), with the loan repayments geared to the project's cash flow. Project finance is used in connection with raising large amounts of money for big-ticket, energy-related facilities. The term has come to be loosely applied to various forms of financing; a strict definition (from *Project Financing* by Peter K. Nevitt) sums it up thus: 'A financing of a particular economic unit in which a lender is satisfied to look initially to the cash flows and earnings of that economic unit as the source of funds from which a loan will be repaid and to the assets of the economic unit as collateral for the loan.' Project financing *can* be—though is not always—off-balance-sheet. See **big ticket, off-balance-sheet financing**.

promissory note   an IOU issued by a borrower, whose name appears on the front of the note and who undertakes to pay the amount stated on the note to the noteholder, at a specified date. PNs can be issued at a discount from face value, representing the interest (yield/return) on the funds for the lender and the cost for the borrower. PNs are actively traded in the money market. In the US they are referred to as **commercial paper**; in Australia they are also known as **one-name paper**, as distinct from bills of exchange where two names appear on the front of the bill. PNs are covered by the *Bills of Exchange Act* 1909-73 and hold the same legal status as bills of exchange. *Abbrev.:* **PN**. See **bill of exchange**.

property trust   a type of unit trust which pools its unitholders' funds into real estate investments. See **unit trust**.

proprietary limited company   see **company**.

prospectus   a brochure that has to be issued by any company or authority, such as a finance company, unit trust or semi-government borrower, seeking to raise money from the general public through the issue of shares or other securities. The prospectus sets out details of the investments offered, spelling out what interest rates are offered, what different investment maturities are available, and other terms. It must be registered with the relevant Corporate Affairs Commission.

protectionism   Protectionism favours high tariffs and import re-strictions to give domestic industry an advantage over imported goods. Protectionist moves by governments or industry groups would include duties and restrictions on imports, heavy subsidies to exporters. In extremes, this is the opposite of free trade. Non-tariff forms of protectionism exist, such as the US health regulations on the import of Australian beef. See **tariff**.

provisional liquidator   see **liquidator**.

provisional tax   see **taxation**.

provisions   the allowance that companies make as a charge against profits in order to account for expenses which have been incurred but for which the amount and time of payment can only be estimated—for example provisions for long-service leave or provision for bad debts. Sometimes provisions are used to manipulate reported profits. Overprovision in good years can create 'hidden reserves'. These overprovisions can be reversed in bad years to avoid a fall in profits.

proxy   one person acting on another's behalf, usually these days in the context of company meetings. A shareholder in a company can give another person the authority to represent him or her at a company meeting (and is usually required to notify the company of the appointment). See **annual general meeting**.

PSBR   *abbrev.* **public sector borrowing requirement.**

PSFET   *abbrev.* **private sector foreign exchange transactions.**

Pty Ltd   *abbrev.* **proprietary limited company.**

public listed company   a company listed on the stock exchange, whose shares can be bought and sold by members of the public. See **company, going public**.

public loan   A company or authority such as a semi-government authority can raise funds through a public loan, which means that the securities for sale can be bought by members of the public. When raising funds through a public (as opposed to private placement) loan, the borrower has to draft a prospectus and have that approved and registered with the relevant Corporate Affairs Commission. Public loans can be underwritten by a group of financial institutions who would also market the stock. See **private placement**.

public policy   Certain acts or contracts are said to be against public policy when the law refuses to support or enforce them as they are seen to be against the public interest.

public relations   Let's not be coy: Goebbels and the Chinese have been content to call it propaganda, and that is the most honest description of the art of the public relations person. The finest definition that can be put on public relations is that it is the craft of disguising reality in a web of words that make the person (or company or product) paying for the service smell like a rose. The man credited with the conception of public relations was an American newspaperman named Ivy Lee who, in 1906, convinced the US coalmining industry that its image would improve if the public knew more about what the industry did. He opened the closets of the industry—one which the American populace distrusted—and the mining companies were delighted to find that the public began to believe and accept them. Ivy Lee went on to serve the American railroad companies, which had also suffered from a tarnished image, and started an industry which continues today in a much refined form. PR (the universally recognised acronym) is essential to businesses today. Highly skilled specialists, often with degrees in this nouveau-science, command high salaries because they use words cleverly enough to soften potential conflict between industry and consumer, or government and citizen.

PR and advertising have been equated on the ground that they both use information to persuade the consumer. This may be too harsh a comparison; the PR consultant is often the one person, because of training in communication science, who can make sure that accurate and clear information can reach its intended audience. It is true that a cynical PR can sell latherless soap, but just as true that an honest one can right wrongs. Ivy Lee, it should be noted, was the man who made America love John D. Rockefeller. *Abbrev.*: **PR**.

public sector   the part of the economy which is not privately owned and is controlled by the State or commonwealth government. Examples of public sector participants are Telecom, a commonwealth authority, and State instrumentalities such as an electricity commission or water board. Nationalised industries fall within the ambit of public sector. The public sector has become a large part of western industrialised economies, accounting for more than 20 per cent of gross domestic product in the US, UK and most European countries—the public sector often has an excess of expenditure over receipts and this has led to a large and continuing public sector borrowing requirement

public sector borrowing requirement   the expected or actual shortfall between government revenues and expenditure plus the requirements of all other public sector entities such as local and semi-government authorities. Many Western countries have run big deficits since World War II. PSBR can be financed by increasing notes and coins in circulation (printing more money), by selling more government securities or by borrowing overseas. In the Australian context, PSBR has increased dramatically since the late 1970s, and since it includes the federal government's borrowings plus borrowings by local and semi-government bodies it encompasses more than the budget deficit. *Abbrev.:* **PSBR**.

public securities trust   a form of unit trust that invests in government and semi-government securities, and selected short-term money market instruments. Public securities trusts engage in long-term investments on behalf of unitholders. See **unit trust**.

public utility   a grand name for services such as water and electricity boards, gas companies, etc.

PUF   *abbrev.* **prime underwriting facility**.

pulling an issue   withdrawing an issue of bonds or notes after it has been announced — embarrassing for an investment banker (underwriter) as it implies misreading legislation or misinterpreting a technicality which means the issue cannot go ahead as planned.

pump priming an alternative expression for deficit financing. See **deficit financing**.

punter in gentleman's language, someone who invests money in a chancey game or business in the expectation of making a profit. Most gentlemen punt on horses, which run races at a predictable pace and have an assessable chance of winning. Some punters chance their intuition in the share market or more esoteric branches of the investment field. The odds in favour of winning are roughly the same. A punter's results are as good as his information. In the financial markets the successful punter is the well-informed one.

purchase tax an ad valorem duty imposed on consumer goods, i.e. what we all buy; purchase tax is calculated on the wholesale price and is paid by the wholesaler who passes the cost on to the retailer, who in turn recoups from the customer. Value-added tax replaced purchase tax in the UK in 1973. Australia does not have a specific form of purchase tax. See **sales tax, value-added tax**.

pyramiding This has a number of meanings in the business world:

- a new form of corporate structure, based on a chain of units, where the level of ownership held by the initial holding company is progressively watered down as subsidiary companies acquire further subsidiaries. The holding company has control but significantly less ownership in the subsidiaries further along the chain.
- expanding a business by making heavy use of borrowings to build up the corporate structure.
- in the context of investments, using unrealised profits from, say, futures trading, as security to borrow funds to buy more investments, such as additional positions in the futures market.

These techniques have quite different meanings from pyramid selling, which refers to a sales scheme where the person initiating the sales (at the top of the pyramid) sells agencies to others, who in turn sell them to others so that goods are sold only by those at the foot of the pyramid and the rest sell agencies. There is a strong moral opposition to pyramid selling on the grounds that it disadvantages the last-in investors.

Q

QANGOS   *abbrev.* **quasi autonomous non-government organisations.**

quality stock   a blue-chip stock. See **blue-chip.**

quantity theory of money   a very influential (some say tautological) notion which asserts that there is a relationship between the quantity of money in an economy and the level of prices (basic monetarist principle). The tautological nature can be illustrated by the following: any student of economics, set the question 'Describe the manner in which the price level is determined on an island in which the currency consists of shells picked up on the beach', would glibly reply, 'The price level on this island is determined by the number of shells and their velocity of circulation'. Only the brightest and cheekiest would add that it is equally true to say that the number of shells in circulation is determined by the price level.
The oldest form is $MV = PT$

$$\text{where } M = \text{money supply}$$
$$V = \text{velocity of circulation, i.e. how often the same money changes hands;}$$
$$P = \text{price level}$$
$$T = \text{volume of transactions in goods and services.}$$

The concept was a favourite among classical economists. The quantity theory of money originated in the seventeenth century and was revamped into twentieth-century form notably by the Chicago economists Irving Fisher and Milton Friedman. The formal theory has been criticised empirically because V and T are not constant, particularly V which depends on the consumer/business person's investment and spending whims. Monetarists say that if there is a change in the money supply, either the price level will adjust or the supply of goods will alter; assuming full employment, the price level will be affected by a change in the money supply. The modern form to express the quantity theory of money is $M = \frac{Y}{V} P$ where M, V and P are defined as above, and Y is a measure of the flow of goods and services. See **economists, monetarist.**

quants   *Abbrev.* **quantitative analysts.** See **rocket scientists.**

quasi autonomous non-government organisations   organisations established by the government and required under their charters to function as self-supporting, though not necessarily as profit-making entities. They have frequently been under fire as in many cases they compete with private enterprise but with the security of government sponsorship. *Abbrev.:* **QANGOS**.

query In stock exchange language, this means questioning a company about its shares or some aspect of its performance. For example, an erratic price movement in a company's shares would prompt a stock exchange query to the company, requesting an explanation. It is a process that generally halts trading in the shares of the company concerned.

Quesnay, Francois see **economists**.

quick test see **liquid ratio**.

quorum the minimum number of people who must attend a business meeting to allow it to proceed—the number is stipulated in a company's articles of association.

quotas a form of trade protectionism which takes no account of price, demand or quality but stipulates a given quantity (quota) of say, cars, that can be imported from one country by another in a given year. Quotas do not produce revenue for the government but can raise the price of an imported category of goods if supply is restricted, thereby (it is thought) giving equivalent domestic goods a head start. Quota systems can operate domestically, to protect a particular domestic industry; the quotas on margarine that were designed to protect the dairy industry were fiercely debated twenty years ago.

quote a price offered or asked. Financial markets traders talk of a quote when they mean an interest rate or exchange rate at which they are prepared to deal. For example, the question 'did you get a quote on these 180-day bank bills?' means 'what interest rate were you offered on these bills?'

quoted securities the shares and securities of companies listed on the stock exchange. The companies are described as 'listed'; their shares are 'quoted' and available for trading to the general public.

R

Radcliffe Committee   Lord Radcliffe's committee was set up in the UK in 1957 to examine the country's monetary system. Its report, published in 1959, concluded that monetary policy, when implemented through changes in the bank rate, had little effect on money supply and inflation. The Radcliffe Report remained influential till 1971 when UK monetary policy began to depart from the Keynesian influences of the report. See **Campbell Report, Martin Committee**.

Rae Committee   a committee established in the early 1970s in Australia, following the collapse of the mining boom, which had focused concern on the need to regulate the securities industry, to protect investors, and to lay down ground rules on trading practices. The committee's full title was the Select Committee on Securities and Exchange, known as the Rae Committee after its chairman, Senator Rae. It tabled a five-volume report in July 1974, which was the forerunner of the national companies and securities legislation. See **National Companies and Securities Commission**.

raid   rapid, active buying of a large quantity of shares in one company by another company, often signifying the intention of seizing control or at least taking a major shareholding position. Also **market raid**.

raider (corporate)   the twentieth-century stock market pirate. A corporate raider buys into a target company with the intention of securing a controlling interest and managing the company.

rally   an upswing; a brisk improvement in activity and prices after a downturn.

ramping   a practice that can be used in any market to create an impression of generalised market activity that forces prices higher, so that advantage can be taken of the higher prices to sell out at a quick profit.

R & D   *abbrev.* **research and development**.

random walk hypothesis   a theory that explains movements in share prices as independent of previous changes. Each new change is explained by new information.

RANs   *abbrev.* **revenue-anticipated notes**.

range forward contract a currency exposure management tool designed to provide downside protection and share in upside potential. It contains a put and a call option and is designed so that the user does not incur the cost of a premium. Created by Salomon Brothers.

rate of return profit earned in relation to capital invested; what you get back as a reward for risking your money. It sounds a simple concept but the statistics used in the various methods of measuring the rate of return make a nightmare of the exercise. To be accurate, you have to consider inflation, human resources employed, cost-benefit analyses, to name but three factors.

ratio analysis an examination of a company's ratios — gearing, liquidity and so on — to determine its financial worth.

rational expectations Economists who subscribe to the 'rational expectations' theory believe that people are not systematically wrong, i.e. they are not continuously surprised by outcomes because they revise their expectations. This makes it harder for governments to implement policies aimed at giving 'short, sharp shocks' to the private sector. People anticipate government action and so are prepared for its effects.

rationalisation pruning and reorganising a business or sector of the market to improve efficiency and cut costs.

RATS *abbrev.* **Reform of the Australian Tax System**.

RBA *abbrev.* **Reserve Bank of Australia**.

RB II The Reserve Bank's equivalent of the National Income Forecasting Model. RB II was born in 1975, has been revamped a number of times since then. It is used for policy analysis and forecasting, with particular emphasis on monetary factors. See **National Income Forecasting Model**.

real estate land, houses, buildings; the term can be contrasted with personal property, which is what you put into or on the real estate, such as furniture. A car is personal property. People who deal in real estate see themselves in a different light from those who deal in cars.

real interest rates interest rates less the rate of inflation. If inflation is 10 per cent and the interest rate is 10 per cent the real rate of return is zero. To illustrate: $100 invested at 10 per cent per annum would yield $10 at the end of one year—but if inflation is running at 10 per cent, that $110 buys the same amount of goods as $100 would have bought a year earlier. **Negative real interest rates** occur when interest rates are lower than the inflation rate—for example the return on funds invested is 10 per cent but inflation is running at 15 per cent.

real unit labour costs see **unit labour costs**.

real value   In contrast to nominal value, real value takes inflation into account when calculating worth. It is easier to set a nominal present value on a business, house or investment, harder to judge its continuing or future real value because inflation is an unguessable variable. See **real interest rates.**

real wages   what you earn, expressed in terms of how much you can buy with it. If prices are rising faster than your pay, then your real wages are falling. Trade unions watch this closely and will sometimes mount militant campaigns to make up any loss.

real world   Economists talk of the 'real world' when they mean the actual or existing world as against a theoretical world often used to demonstrate economists' concepts.

rebatable bonds   a type of Commonwealth bond last issued in 1968; a rebate of tax was paid equivalent to 10 per cent of the coupon (interest) rate.

receivables   debts owed to you; money that should be coming your way.

receiver   a neutral administrator appointed to take charge of the affairs and property of a person or company until debts are paid or a court matter settled. A receiver can be appointed by a secured creditor or by a court. When a company goes into receivership, the powers of the receiver are set out either by the court order or by the terms of the creditor's security and the document appointing the receiver. The receiver's responsibility where he is appointed by a creditor is to realise the belongings of the person or company and try to pay off the debts of the security holder. The appointment of a receiver need not stop the company's normal business, but to ensure trading activity continues a **manager** has to be appointed, who undertakes to maintain the company as a going concern, to try to help in an effort to have the person/company trade out of difficulties. To achieve this, it is usual to appoint a **receiver/manager** who has the powers of both.

recession   too often used as an alternative to depression, though only by pessimists with historical myopia. A recession means that an economy has slowed down considerably, but not to the depths of an economic trough. The Americans, who are good at making precise definitions, officially apply the term to a situation where gross national product has fallen in two consecutive quarters. A recession would be indicated by a slowing of a nation's production, rising unemployment and falling interest rates usually following a decline in the demand for money. A popular distinction between recession and depression is attributed to Ronald Reagan, in his presidential campaign speech, October 1980: 'Recession is when your neighbour loses his job; depression is when you lose yours.'

reciprocal rate   the price of one currency in terms of another when the official quote gives the second currency in terms of the first. For example, the usual $A/$US quote gives the $A in terms of US cents; the reciprocal would show the $US in terms of the $A: if the $A is worth 90 US cents, the reciprocal quote of the $US is $A1.1110.

reciprocity   You scratch my back and I'll scratch yours. A concept revitalised in the recent debate surrounding Australia's banking system and how it should be opened to foreigners, which foreigners should be allowed to participate and how many. Reciprocity is also a ploy in international trade, where one country will make tariff concessions to another in return for similar favours.

recourse   In financial terms, if you have recourse to someone, you can claim payment of a debt or obligation even if that person is not primarily liable. If you are the guarantor of a defaulted debt, you may be a recourse target. There is also non-recourse financing, popular in leveraged leasing and mineral exploration, where the borrower has no liability to repay the debt except from the proceeds of the venture in which the funds are used. In the case of mining, this means that someone lends money to an exploration company in the knowledge that if there is nothing at the bottom of the hole, there will be no return on the funds. Non-recourse lenders are usually confident that something will come up.

recycling   an environmental term popularly adopted by economists during the oil price crisis of 1973-74 when analysts talked of 'recycling petrodollars', meaning using the currency surpluses of the oil-exporting countries to ease the deficit burdens of the oil-importing countries. It was a bandaid solution; the deficit countries fell further and further into debts they could not afford.

red   'You're in the red' means you are in debt, you owe money; debits used to be written in red ink in bank statements. See **black**.

redeemable   usually, exchangeable for cash. If, as an impecunious student, you pawn your clarinet, you could redeem it by paying back the pittance you borrowed against it. Aussie Bonds are 'redeemable at par' which means when you take your Aussie Bonds to your bank, stockbroker or the Reserve Bank you can exchange them for the cash equivalent of their face value, i.e. for $100 worth of Aussie Bonds you get $100. Redeemable preference shares are those which, on a stated maturity date, the issuing company will buy back for face value plus dividend.

redemption   paying off or cancelling a debt. Commonwealth bonds are redeemable at face value on maturity, that is, the commonwealth government pays you, the lender, your money and redeems its debt. If you hold your Commonwealth bonds until they mature, the yield you earn is called **redemption yield**. With some lending institutions early redemption of a debt carries a penalty; if you find you do not need the personal loan you have borrowed you might decide to pay it off ahead of schedule, but it would be worth checking if any penalty is involved. See **prepayment**.

redemption yield   see **yield to redemption**.

rediscount   ·resale or resell. The word is used in the context of selling a security such as a bill of exchange or Treasury Note which has already been discounted (i.e. sold for less than face value). The Reserve Bank offers rediscount facilities in Treasury Notes which holders can use to generate cash by selling (rediscounting) the Notes to the central bank. See **discount window**.

refinancing   extending existing loans or replacing existing funds with alternative borrowings, which may be at different interest rates or for longer or shorter terms. See **rescheduling**.

reflation   Economists and politicians talk grandly of 'reflating the economy' which simply means they adopt measures which they hope will improve productivity and demand while they try to lower, or at least control, the inflation rate and reduce unemployment. Common tactics have been tax cuts and increased government spending, perhaps leading to lower interest rates and more generous money supply growth. This can lead to rising inflation. Ideally, demand should rise without pushing up interest rates or inflation. But existing economies are never ideal.

Reform of the Australian Tax System   The Australian government has implemented a wide range of reforms to the country's tax system, known as the RATS package. The main moves include the introduction of dividend imputation, a capital gains tax, a foreign tax credit system, a change in the treatment of deferred interest and discount securities, a tax on fringe benefits, an increase in domestic corporate tax and a progressive decrease in personal income tax. *Abbrev.*: **RATS**.

regression analysis   a technique used in statistics to measure the relationship between a dependent variable and one or more independent variables. For example, a company producing camping equipment would be interested to identify the relationship between sales of camping gear and the growth rate of employment, on the assumption that if employment rises, more people have more money to spend on leisure gear.

Regulation Q   An almost extinct edict, handed down by the United States Federal Reserve (US central bank) which placed ceilings on interest rates charged by banks and savings-and-loan associations. Regulation Q began to look out of place when interest rates shot up, leading to the development of money market funds which offered investors better returns than were available from banks and savings-and-loan associations. The Fed capitulated in 1980 and agreed that Regulation Q would be phased out over five years. See **Fed.**

reinsurance   the insurance companies' insurance, which enables them to spread their risk by paying premiums to other insurers. On the racetrack, it is called 'laying-off'.

reintermediation   a reversal of the process of disintermediation; for example it occurs when regulations which created disintermediation (i.e. which caused transactions to revert to direct financing) are removed and business flows back to financial intermediaries. See **disintermediation, intermediation.**

reneg   see **renegotiation.**

renegotiation   Rates in the money market are subject to 'reneg' either by 11am or by 4pm depending on whether the funds are 11am call or 24 hours' notice of call. *Abbrev.*: **reneg.**

rent   payment made to the owner of an asset for the use of that asset, as in paying a fee to occupy someone else's house. In English the word originally meant income from property. Its economic use, as in 'resources rent', reflects that meaning. See **economic rent, resources rent tax.**

rentier   someone whose income comes from sources other than wages, who makes money from investments.

reorganisation and divestment   getting rid of the dead wood; selling off the loss-maker; sacking the manager.

repos   see **repurchase agreements.**

repurchase agreements   deals between the Reserve Bank of Australia and the authorised short-term money market dealers, by which the dealers' commonwealth government securities are transferred to the RBA in exchange for cash, on the basis that the deal will be reversed at a predetermined date and at an agreed rate. This gives the central bank an additional mechanism for managing liquidity.
  Reverse repos are the opposite. The Reserve Bank sells securities to the dealers, thereby draining funds from the financial system, and buys them back on predetermined conditions when the system tightens up again. The rate at which repurchase agreements are carried out is watched with interest, as an indication of the level at which the central bank is prepared to deal. 'Repos' are a well-established liquidity-management mechanism in overseas markets. *Abbrev.*: **repos.** See **lender-of-last-resort.**

resale price maintenance a practice involving a supplier or manufacturer influencing or requesting a wholesale or retail seller to stick to a particular price or minimum price level when reselling goods. In many Western economies a supplier or manufacturer can only *recommend* a resale price, and in the approved way.

rescheduling a euphemism for postponing payment of money owed. The word has become popular in recent years since the controversy which arose over the foreign debt financing of a number of countries such as Poland, Mexico and Brazil, which took on more debt than they could handle. Traditional lenders such as multinational banks have been reluctant to lend more to countries with balance of payments problems caused by a surfeit of short-term borrowings (themselves a consequence of reluctance on the lenders' part to lend long-term). Impoverished nations have found that a world recession makes it virtually impossible to trade themselves out of debt; the answer is to rewrite the debt so that interest and principal payments become less of a burden. Lenders quite like rescheduling: it means that interest payments keep rolling in, even if the principal drifts further away. After all, they can't repossess the country which owes them a few billion. Consider this maxim: if you owe a bank five dollars, you are in its power; if you owe it five million, you call the shots. See **refinancing**.

research and development a handy way to divert sums of money, which might otherwise go to the tax collector, into the creation of new products, which may, at the extremes of possibility, be useful. R & D sometimes results in valuable additions to the comforts of life, such as the wine cask and the ballpoint pen. It is a very trendy occupation. *Abbrev.*: **R & D**. See **patent, product, taxation**.

Reserve Bank of Australia As the country's central bank, the Reserve Bank combines the roles of financial system supervisor, banker and federal government adviser. The bank was created by an Act of Parliament in 1911 as the Commonwealth Bank of Australia, and was renamed and reconstituted as the Reserve Bank of Australia in 1959. It began operations in 1960. As central bank, it does not compete with the commercial banks; its duties are overseeing the activities of Australia's financial markets, with particular responsibilities for and controls over the banking system. The commercial banking business of the Commonwealth Bank was separated from its central banking functions in 1959 legislation which established the central bank under the new name Reserve Bank of Australia, with its own board, governor and staff. The Reserve Bank's activities, powers and responsibilities are spelled out in three pieces of legislation: the *Reserve Bank Act* 1959, the *Banking Act* 1959 and the *Financial Corporations Act* 1974.
Under the *Reserve Bank Act* the central bank has the responsibility of ensuring that its monetary and banking policies contribute to

the stability of the Australian economy and to the welfare of its people. Under the *Banking Act*, the Reserve Bank has a duty to protect the deposits of the Australian banks, and has the power to regulate bank lending and interest rates and to influence banks' asset holdings. The *Financial Corporations Act* provides the means for the government—through the Reserve Bank—to monitor and, if necessary, control the activities of non-bank financial institutions registered under the Act.

The Reserve Bank acts as banker and financial agent for the federal government, as banker to the banking system and the authorised money market dealers. Together with the Department of Federal Treasury, the Reserve Bank is responsible for managing the federal government's annual borrowing programme; as agent for the commonwealth, it sells government securities (Aussie Bonds, Treasury Bonds and Treasury Notes). Through its Note Issue Department the Reserve Bank prints and distributes paper currency in Australia. Reserve Bank publications, such as its annual report, monthly bulletin, information booklets and occasional papers are regular sources of information on Australia's economic and financial conditions.

Governors of the Reserve Bank have been:

Dr H. C. Coombs 1949-1968 (1949-1959 Governor of the Commonwealth Bank of Australia)
Sir John G. Phillips 1968-1975
Sir Harold Knight 1975-1982
R. A. Johnston 1982-

reserve currency   Central banks hold a significant proportion of their country's reserves in reserve currencies (the rest is in gold) and international debts can be paid using these currencies. Qualifications for being a reserve currency are stability and belonging to a country which features prominently in world trade. Sterling was a dominant reserve currency in the heady days of the British Empire; in recent decades the $US has been a traditional reserve currency and many central banks including the Reserve Bank of Australia hold their foreign exchange reserves mostly in $US.

reserves   Companies may retain a proportion of their profits as reserves. They are created from accumulated profits which have not been distributed to shareholders through dividend payments. Issued capital and reserves are called shareholders' funds, being the company's capital base. (Reserves are not set aside for known but unquantifiable liabilities; these are provisions.) Countries also hold reserves, which are usually held by central banks and are generally made up of gold and foreign exchange. Trading banks are also required to lodge reserves, which are a proportion of their assets, with the central bank, as a liquidity control. See **provisions, reserve currency, statutory reserve**

deposit.

residual value   the value of a leased property such as a car or photocopier at the end of the lease term, as agreed at the beginning of the lease period. If the lessee decides to buy the property at that stage, then the residual value is what would usually be accepted as the price by the owner of the property, the lessor. See **leasing**.

resistance level   theoretically, the price level at which buyers and sellers lose interest and at which the price should stabilise or move back. Chartists use the term to analyse share and futures prices, as well as interest and exchange rates. 'Resistance level' is used to explain why a currency or commodity will shoot up then stop, or tumble then steady—chartists will tell you it hit its resistance level. If you are unsure what resistance level means, ask yourself whether a transaction is worth doing at that prevailing price. See **chartists**.

resources boom   At the end of a yellow brick road, or at the end of a rainbow, there is Arcadia, or paradise or a pot of gold, a field of buttercups, or a boom. A resources boom is a rapid expansion of an economy, based on mineral produce. It happened in the 1850s gold rush in Australia, then at the turn of the century and again in the late 1960s. The predictions of the early 1980s did not materialise to the extent of previous booms. Booms are forecast because from time to time a belief emerges that if a country has oil, or iron or gold in its ground then it will become wealthy. The promotion of this belief is good politics because it makes people feel comfortable; however, it is not necessarily good economics. The value of these resources depends on the appetite of the importing countries. Australia was poised for a resources boom, to be fed by the stuff in the ground, at the beginning of this decade, but was lowered into a recession instead as demand for her exports fell. See **boom**.

resources rent tax   the tax levied on profits over a level (theoretically) defined as an 'adequate' return from a resource project. It is therefore a profits-related tax and as recently finalised (July 1984) will apply to new Australian offshore oil projects. The threshold level of return on a project at which the tax would start to apply has been set at 15 per cent above the long-term Commonwealth bond rate. Once applied, it will be levied at a rate of 40 per cent. Resources rent tax has two advantages—though the benefits of these are estimated to be far outweighed by disadvantages in the eyes of the companies concerned. These advantages are:

- federal government royalties would cease;
- investors are allowed recoupment of capital expenditure before the tax is applied.

Because RRT will be levied on new, as against existing projects, it could be some time before the federal government receives much revenue from this source. Those who justify RRT claim that to tax so-called 'super' profits should not scare away investment and would provide a fair share of the benefits of resource development to the host country. Those who oppose RRT believe it will deter exploration investment. Oil exploration is a high-risk activity and could well use incentives (such as those afforded to the new technology and the film industries), to increase the present exploration level which would ultimately lead to more discoveries. This in turn must benefit the country. *Abbrev.*: **RRT**. See **rent, economic rent**.

restrictive trade practices   market activities which manipulate supply and/or demand to create an unfair collusive or monopoly-based profit—for example cartels fixing prices, market-sharing deals, some mergers and a number of resale and discriminatory pricing practices. Steps were taken to minimise the possibilities for exploitative arrangements in Australia with the *Trade Practices Act* 1974. The Act encourages price competition by working against monopolies and against conduct which is likely to lessen competition substantially in a market. The official watchdog is the Trade Practices Commission. The will of the federal government to enforce legislation is a key variable. Australia tends to have a heavy incidence of restrictive trade practices which is a product of her small domestic market, limited opportunities for exploiting the economies of scale and the volume of imports. See **Trade Practices Commission**.

retail banking   the type of banking catering for you and me as distinct from large corporations. Retail banking is the provision of services to the individual and small businesses, offering deposit facilities, lending money, transferring funds, being prepared to deal in small amounts in contrast to wholesale banking which deals in millions of dollars, or at least hundreds of thousands. See **wholesale banking**.

retail price index   the UK equivalent of what in Australia and the US is called the consumer price index. It is used to measure inflation and movements in the cost of living. See **consumer price index, index**.

retained earnings   the proportion of profit that is held in a business after dividends have been paid. Also **accumulated profits, unappropriated profits, undistributed profits**.

retire a bill   to pay a bill of exchange before it falls due. A company which has issued bills of exchange or promissory notes as a method of raising short-term finance can retire the paper by buying it back before its maturity date. See **bill of exchange**.

return   the amount earned on an investment or made on a transaction.

revaluation   The word has wandered from its literal and general meaning of a change in value to denote specifically an upward movement in the worth of, for example, a currency. See **devaluation**.

revenue   earnings; what a company makes in monetary terms from its activities.

revenue-anticipated notes   US securities, issued by States and cities to finance current account expenses in anticipation of later income. An example would be the financing of a local concert hall through RANs on the basis that the hall would generate income to pay off the note. *Abbrev.*: **RANs**.

reverse repos   see **repurchase agreements**.

reverse takeover   purchase of the controlling interest in a company by one of its subsidiaries.

revolving credit   As with Bankcard, a borrower can repay part of the funds on loan and immediately borrow it again. It is a convenience for the borrower, and a generator of continuing interest payments to the lender.

revolving underwriting facility   a type of note issuance facility involving a medium-term commitment by a group of underwriters (usually banks) to purchase one, three or six-month euronotes at a fixed margin that is set against LIBOR, in the event that a single agent fails to place the notes with investors at, or under, that margin. *Abbrev.*: **RUF**. See **prime underwriting facility**.

Ricardo, David   see **economists**.

rigged market   A market is said to have been rigged if prices have been manipulated so that buyers or sellers have been attracted to come in, crystallising profits for those who initiated the manipulation. See **daisy chain**.

right-hand side   see **trading on the right-hand side**.

rights issue   an offer of additional shares to existing shareholders, in proportion to their holdings, to raise money for the company. Unlike a bonus issue, a rights issue is not free. The shareholder is not obliged to take up a rights issue—the offer can be allowed to lapse—but rights issues are renounceable, which means the shareholder can sell or transfer his or her right to the shares. See **bonus issue, entitlement issue**.

risk-averse   Most sensible people try to avoid high risks when investing or, if they knowingly incur a higher-than-average risk, they ask a higher return as compensation. The term risk-averse has come to be used not only to describe the unadventurous investor but is a tag

210

often attached to conservative bankers to distinguish them from their (allegedly) more aggressive and entrepreneurial investment/merchant banking counterparts.

risk capital   similar to venture capital, money invested in a business or project which offers a lower than usual probability of profit, but if successful, a big return. See **venture capital**.

risk management   A grand description for the age-old concept of making sure you do not lose any more than necessary. Good risk managers cut down the odds of losing but should be able to spot a worthwhile opportunity.

Robinson, Joan   see **economists**.

rocket scientist   one of Wall Street's wunderkinder, the geniuses of investment banking who invent the new financial products, devise the money-spinning techniques based on options, futures and swaps that give birth to the acronyms and to programmed equity trading. Also **quants**.

rollover   the renewal of a loan facility or continuation of a deposit at each maturity date, usually including a revision of the interest rates. (Rollover periods are often written into financing arrangements, as against refinancing or rescheduling, which suggest continuing a debt that should have been paid off.) Rollovers allow long-term funds to be provided with flexibility in the interest rate charged. For example, a merchant bank lends a client $5 million for five years but on condition that the funds are rolled over every six months, i.e. that the interest rate can be adjusted. You can place funds in a fixed deposit and when that deposit matures you can choose to roll the funds over (probably at a different interest rate) for a further term, or you can withdraw the money. See **cash and conversion loan**.

The rollover, in the sense of a conversion, became a feature of the investment scene in 1983, following the Australian federal government's changes to superannuation. Those changes were introduced to encourage people to provide income for their retirement rather than rely on receiving a lump sum to spend as they chose, and then apply for an age pension. The government legislated for increased tax to be levied on lump-sum benefits but offset this by providing tax relief on lump sums 'rolled over' (converted) into specified forms of investment which would either maintain the lump sum until retirement age or convert it to an annuity or pension. Lump sums accrued before 30 June 1983 attract the earlier tax rate, i.e. 5 per cent of the lump sum is taxable as income at the marginal personal tax rate of the person receiving the funds. Lump sums or parts of them accrued since then attract tax rates starting at 30 per cent of the first $55 000 if the person receiving the funds is under 55, 15 per cent if 55 and over and increasing with larger amounts (plus the Medicare levy). See **annuity**.

round robin   a circular transaction that shifts funds from one account to another but has no effect on the overall level as cash — taking from Peter to pay Paul. Peter uses funds from his unused overdraft to lend Paul overnight money, which Paul then onlends to another. They help each other but the improvement in the appearance of account balances is more apparent than real. See **handkerchief transaction, round-tripping**.

round-tripping   moving funds around to take advantage of interest rate differentials between, say, the bank overdraft rate and bank bill rate. A typical example would be drawing down funds available under a bank overdraft facility and using the cash to invest in bank bills of exchange or bank certificates of deposit at interest rates that offer a higher return than the cost of the overdraft funds. Round-tripping arose out of ceilings on bank interest rates which at times prevented them from matching market rates.

Royal Australian Mint   see **mint**.

Royal Commission into Money and Banking   The report of this commission (1935-37) published in August 1937, gave serious consideration to the banking system in Australia; it stimulated thinking about the role and responsibilities of the banking system, particularly the function of a central bank. A major recommendation of the report was the establishment of special deposits by the private banks with the Commonwealth Bank; the private banks opposed this, and special deposits were not introduced until World War II was underway. The bill drafted as a sequel to the commission's report never reached Parliament; war interrupted consideration of the report and it was not until the 1945 *Banking Act* that special deposits were legitimised. That Act also confirmed the increased powers of the Commonwealth Bank and divided the bank into central banking and commercial banking functions, paving the way for the later (1959) separation of central banking functions into the Reserve Bank of Australia. The royal commission is widely regarded as the forerunner of the Campbell Report. See **Campbell Report, Reserve Bank of Australia**.

royalties   what authors hope to earn when they write, inventors when they invent, governments and landowners when oil is found on their property. Royalties are payments, funded by those who benefit from the use of the product of inventiveness, authorship or ownership.

RRT   *abbrev.* **resources rent tax**.

RUF   *abbrev.* **revolving underwriting facility**.

rule of 78   the usual method of calculating how much interest has been earned by a lender at any stage during the repayment of a loan on which the interest rate has been agreed in advance. The rule is applied to consumer finance where loans are repaid in instalments. Its effect is distorted in the longer-term consumer loans common today; the '78' refers to the twelve parts of a one-year loan—the sum of those parts is 78 (12 + 11 + 10 + 9 etc.). The lender earns 12/78ths of total interest in the first month, 11/78ths in the second month, and so on. People who decide to pay out a loan early in its course are often surprised to discover how little impression their instalment payments have made on the principal—the rule of 78 helps explain why this is so.

run   a rapid rise in a share price or, in a different context, a rush to withdraw deposits from an institution, as in 'panic caused a run in deposits from XYZ bank or building society'.

runner   in futures trading the person who connects between the booth moll and the floor trader, passing on and taking orders and fetching coffee. See **booth moll, floor trader**.

running yield   the interest rate on an investment expressed as a percentage of the capital invested. This takes no account of the capital accrual—it is the actual cash flow related to the price paid for the investment.

Rural Credits Department   This department of the Reserve Bank of Australia provides short-term finance to eligible government authorities and cooperative rural marketing bodies to fund primary producers who are awaiting payment on sales of their produce. The Campbell and Martin Reports both recommended that the Rural Credits Department be phased out.

S

sale and leaseback a form of off-balance-sheet financing in which instead of borrowing on the security of, say, its property, a company sells its property to a lending institution (often an insurance company) and at the same time takes out a long-term lease on the property from the lending institution. This frees money for alternative uses and does not affect the company's gearing as the lease (loan) is 'off-balance-sheet', i.e. neither the asset nor the liability will appear on the company's balance sheet. The property then ceases to be an asset and the rent payment is an expenditure in the profit and loss account, but not a liability in the balance sheet. Gearing may even improve if the property is sold for more than book value. See **off-balance-sheet financing**.

sales tax a form of 'indirect taxation', levied by the federal government since 1930 on the wholesale value of a commodity. Sales tax is imposed as an ad valorem tax, i.e. it is expressed as a percentage of the value of the goods taxed. The wholesale customer pays the tax when goods are bought and passes it on as part of the retail price so that its effect is similar to that of a purchase tax for the ultimate buyer. Sales tax applies to a range of items, including whitegoods and motor vehicles; many commodities, including foodstuffs, are exempt from sales tax. See **ad valorem, purchase tax, value-added tax**.

Sallie Mae see **Student Loan Marketing Association**.

same-day cash see **11am call money, exchange settlement account**.

Samuelson, Paul see **economists**.

Samurai bonds yen-denominated bonds issued in Japan by a foreign borrower. These are appealing when the yen is strengthening, but a weakening yen would frighten off foreigners because of the exchange rate risk.

savings-and-loan association a US financial institution which mainly lends funds for home buyers—similar to the UK and Australian building societies. The savings-and-loan associations began in the 1850s, are large deposit-taking institutions for small savers, borrowing short to lend long. They had to raise their rates during the 1970s, to attract deposits, and margins were squeezed as mortgages were at fixed rates. They were also constrained by Regulation Q which enforced interest rate ceilings. The result was that the associations lost funds to the more competitive money market funds and some associations went to the wall. See **money market mutual funds, Regulation Q**.

savings banks   Savings banks were established in Australia in the 1950s and 1960s; the oldest is the Commonwealth Savings Bank, with the major private trading banks following. The main function of savings banks has been to gather deposits from the public, to provide funds to be lent to home buyers. Savings banks operate under the Banking (Savings Bank) Regulations, which give them the security of Reserve Bank protection as set out in the *Banking Act*. Over the years the competitive position of the savings banks had been eroded by the freer, non-bank institutions such as building societies and credit unions; these institutions operate free of federal government regulation and therefore without Reserve Bank backup (though subject to varying degrees of State government control). To allow them to compete more effectively for the household dollar, savings bank regulations have been substantially altered, allowing the savings banks to offer more attractive rates while retaining the security of operating under the *Banking Act*. The most significant changes were effected in August 1982 and included:

- replacement of the previous detailed asset structure with a 15 per cent minimum liquidity ratio, i.e. savings banks have to hold a minimum of 15 per cent of deposits in cash, deposits with the Reserve Bank and commonwealth government securities;
- ability to accept deposits from profit-making organisations up to $100 000 from any one such entity;
- freedom to invest up to 6 per cent of deposits in 'other assets' besides those prescribed by the regulations.

From 1 August 1984, savings banks have been allowed to offer cheque account facilities.

Say's law   the embodiment of the ideas of the French economist Jean-Baptiste Say (1767–1832), whose thoughts have been popularised into a law which asserts that 'supply creates its own demand'.

scalping   speculative buying and quickly selling shares or securities to make a swift profit. The commercial practice has extended to theatre queues and football matches: those who get in early buy tickets and sell them at a profit to those who are keen but who have arrived later.

scarcity value   Hen's teeth, rocking horse manure—any item that is hard to find and whose supply is hard to increase will become more in demand and greater in value—it's human nature.

scheme of arrangement   This refers to a rearrangement of a company's capital structure or its debts, which is binding on all creditors and shareholders. There are two types of schemes, a creditors' scheme and a members' or shareholders' scheme.

- A **creditors' scheme** is used by companies in financial difficulties. Creditors may agree to defer payments in the hope that they will receive a greater total payment as a result of the scheme than would be received were the company liquidated.
- A **members' scheme** is used to effect corporate reorganisations, including mergers, although it cannot be used to avoid the provisions of the takeover code.

A scheme of arrangement is carried out in three steps:

1 the court is approached to order a meeting of creditors or shareholders directly affected;
2 the scheme must be approved by a vote of a majority of the creditors or members present and voting who represent 75 per cent of the total debts or nominal value of shares of those present and voting at the meeting;
3 the scheme is referred back to the court for confirmation.

Schumpeter, Joseph   see **economists**.

SCOUTS   *abbrev.* **shared currency options under tender**.

screw rule   a useful method for remembering that in a foreign exchange transaction, you always get the smaller amount and give up the larger. For example, in a two-way $A/$US quote of 84.04/11, an exporter would give away 84.11 US cents to generate $A1, whereas an importer would receive 84.04 US cents for each $A. When travelling overseas and changing foreign currency at a bank, the same applies—you would get 84.04 US cents for each $A, but give away 84.11 US cents to get one $A back.

scrip   a document showing entitlement to a parcel of shares; an abbreviation for 'subscriptions'. A scrip certificate used to be a provisional certificate issued against payment for shares but now has become synonymous with share certificate. See **share certificate**.

scrip issue   a bonus issue of shares to existing shareholders, made in proportion to their shareholdings. See **bonus issue**.

scrubber   odd lots of securities such as bills of exchange or promissory notes—the money market equivalent of a 'broken' parcel of shares. Not a nice round figure.

SDRs   *abbrev.* **special drawing rights**.

SEAQ   *abbrev.* **Stock Exchange Automated Quotations**.

seasonally adjusted   Numbers (statistics) which are affected by regular seasonal fluctuations each year can be adjusted to remove such fluctuations. A simple form of seasonal adjustment which is widely used is to compare the value for this month with the value for the same corresponding month last year. Seasonally adjusted statistics are used to help identify movements in economic variables which are due to cyclical or trend influences. Some important series with much seasonal variation are employment, the money supply and retail sales.

seat Membership of a stock exchange used to be referred to as a 'seat' now it is just called membership. This changed with the new stock exchange rules and the abolition of the distinction between 'members' and 'non-members' in broking firms. Companies and individuals now become stock exchange members when they buy into a broking firm.

SEATS *abbrev.* **Stock Exchange Automated Trading System.**

SEC *abbrev.* **Securities and Exchange Commission.**

second mortgage This is a second security over, say, a house that already has a mortgage on it. The interest rate on a second mortgage will be higher than on the first because the lender of the funds in the second has less security; the claim of the first mortgagee ranks ahead. (Mortgages can be for purposes other than house purchases, though they are most commonly associated with home finance.)

secondary market a market where existing securities are traded, as against the primary market, which is where they are issued. See **primary market**.

second board the stock exchange board in Australia through which smaller companies raise capital and on which their shares are listed. Listing requirements are less onerous than for the larger companies listed on the main board. See **main board**.

second rank shares of industrial companies which fall short of being tagged 'blue-chip' but which are nevertheless regarded as financially sound companies.

secured creditor someone who has rights not only against the debtor personally but against specific assets of the debtor which the security might entitle the creditor to sell if that should be necessary to recover the amount of the debt.

securities In the context of financial markets, 'securities' (an abbreviation for 'marketable securities') are written undertakings securing repayment of money. They are typically documents such as bonds, bills of exchange, promissory notes or share certificates, which establish ownership and payment rights between parties. The word 'securities' has come to mean any interest-bearing piece of paper traded in financial markets. 'Securities' in the sense of 'marketable securities' may be unsecured (that is, simply debt obligations) and so a holder may not have 'security' in the generally accepted sense. See **security**.

Securities and Exchange Commission   the US watchdog over the country's securities industry, established in 1934. *Abbrev.*: **SEC**.

Securities Industry Act 1980   This Act sets down the basis of conduct and practice in trading securities and is expressed in the Securities Industries Codes of each State. These codes came into force in July 1981. The law regulating securities industries and companies codes has been streamlined to be nationally uniform, following the establishment of the National Companies and Securities Commission which is the national policymaker.

Legislation on the securities industry was first introduced in Australia in 1970 and by 1971 had been adopted in New South Wales, Queensland, Victoria and Western Australia. The regulation of the industry had become a subject of concern after the collapse of the mining boom; this prompted the appointment of a Select Committee on Securities and Exchanges, later known as the Rae Committee after its chairman. The first securities legislation to apply more or less uniformly throughout Australia was the *State Securities Industry Act* 1975 which superseded the 1970-71 State Acts. The basis for the 1980 *Securities Industry Act* and the State Securities Industry Codes was in the Formal Agreement of December 1978 between the commonwealth and the six States; this agreement also laid down the groundwork for the establishment of the NCSC. See **Corporate Affairs Commission, National Companies and Securities Commission, Rae Committee**.

Securities Institute of Australia   Formally incorporated in 1966, the institute was established to improve education in the securities industries (share, bond and money markets) by providing recognised courses in all aspects of securities markets. The institute added a further dimension when it merged in 1975 with the Australian Society of Security Analysts. The institute lists its aims as follows:

- to improve and develop the standards of the securities industry, including educational qualifications;
- to secure professional standing for members of the Institute;
- to conduct courses, conferences and meetings of members;
- to represent the members' views in matters relating to the securities industry;
- to disseminate information relating to the securities industry by circulating the *Journal of the Australian Society of Security Analysts (JASSA)* and other appropriate publications.

Abbrev.: **SIA**.

securitisation   This rather ungainly word refers to a trend in the world's capital markets that became dominant in the 1980s. At its simplest, it means making things marketable. The process involves the packaging of an income stream by the party entitled to it, and the subsequent sale of such income stream to investors. For example, a bank or merchant bank or other category of lender converts an asset such as a loan into a marketable commodity by turning it into securities. A bank securitises a parcel of loans when it gathers a number of different loans together and sells them. Bills of exchange and promissory notes were early forms of securitisation. The process has been developed so that parcels of, say, mortgages can be put together and sold in the market, thus enabling the lender to reliquefy the asset. Any asset that generates an income stream can be securitised, for example mortgages, car loans, credit card receivables and so on.

security In the legal sense, someone holding security has rights against a particular asset belonging to another, for example a lender holding bills of exchange belonging to a borrower as security on a loan between the two parties. A creditor without security has rights only against the debtor, not against any specific asset. See **collateral, lien, mortgage, securities**.

seed money money that is provided to start up a new business or enterprise, often associated with venture capital financing, either in the form of a loan or an equity investment in the infant operation.

sellers' market where demand outpaces supply so that there are more buyers than there are goods for sale. Anyone selling is therefore in a better position to demand the best price. See **buyers' market**.

sellers over what occurs in the futures market when a trade has taken place at a given price but there are still sellers left in the market. See **buyers over**.

semi-government securities stock issued by a State government authority such as an electricity authority or a water board, offering a rate of return that is generally at a margin above what is available from a Commonwealth government bond of a similar amount and maturity. Semi-government securities raise funds through public loans and through private placements of securities. *Abbrev.*: **semis**.

Sep futures market shorthand for September.

separate trading of registered interest and principal of securities paper issued directly by the US Treasury, selling the interest and principal payments separately on selected government securities. *Abbrev.*: **STRIP**.

series of options a group of options with the same exercise date but different underlying securities or contracts.

settlement date A transaction can be organised today but will not be executed till tomorrow (or next week) so tomorrow (or next week) is settlement date, when money and securities change hands.

shakeout   a sudden shift in activity or prices which forces speculators to sell their holdings and forces less successful participants in an industry out of business. This sorts out the wheat from the chaff.

share   A person who buys a portion of a company's capital becomes a shareholder in that company's assets and as such receives a share of the company's profits in the form of an annual dividend; if lucky or astute the shareholders will also reap a capital gain on the sale of the shares.
Shares come in different forms:

- **ordinary shares**   No special rights (except voting rights) are attached to these, and the bulk of a company's capital is issued this way.
- **preference shares**   These have priority over ordinary shares: preference shareholders have a prior claim over ordinary shareholders to dividend payments and to the assets of a company if it is wound up.
- **cumulative preference shares**   The holder of these shares is entitled to a fixed annual dividend, and if this is not produced one year, the amount due is carried forward and paid the following year and ranks ahead of ordinary shareholders' dividends. (Sometimes these are redeemable, in which case they are similar to loan securities.)
- **participating preference shares**   The holder receives a stated dividend each year and is entitled to share in any profits that are left after ordinary shareholders have had their bite.

sharebroker   see **stockbroker**.

share capital   the capital of a company contributed by shareholders; the authorised capital of a company as regulated its memorandum of association. The issued capital is the proportion which has been subscribed (paid for) by the shareholders of the company. See **authorised capital, issued capital**.

share certificate   the document issued by a company to its shareholders showing the number of shares that are held, the amount paid and the name in which the shares are registered. See **scrip**.

shared currency options under tender   Designed and marketed by the UK's Midland Bank, these are used to help cover the foreign exchange risk associated with bidding on tenders for contracts involving different currencies. The awarder of the contract buys a currency option, and the cost of the premium is allocated among the tenderers in the same currency. When the tender is awarded the successful bidder receives the benefits of the option but each tenderer has paid a proportion of the cost. *Abbrev.*: **SCOUTS**.

shareholders' funds   what belongs to the shareholders of a company: issued capital, retained profits. Such money is not generally paid to the shareholders, unless the business is wound up; then they have to fight it out with other creditors and get what is left according to where they rank, i.e. ordinary or preference shareholders etc.

shareholders' interest   the net amount of a company's funds that belong to its shareholders. The shareholders' ratio is calculated by dividing shareholders' funds by total assets of the company.

shareholders' scheme   see **scheme of arrangement**.

share price indexed together with fixed-interest returns   a short-term (maximum maturity of twelve months) certificate of deposit which allows the investor to fine-tune sharemarket investments while receiving an income stream similar to that available in the money market. Designed by Bankers Trust Australia. *Abbrev.*: **SPITFIRE**.

share price index futures   see **futures market, Sydney Futures Exchange**.

share register   the record of a company's shareholders, showing their holdings.

shelf company   a company which has been created but has never traded. Its memorandum and articles can be bought 'off the shelf'.

shipping conference   an association of shipowners who have grouped together to coordinate freight charges.

shogun bonds   a bond issue made in Japan, not denominated in yen. The first such issue was made in September 1985 by the World Bank. The bonds could be denominated in, say, $US or other foreign currencies, but would be distributed in Japan to raise funds for a foreign company.

short   short term. In financial markets, 'short' can refer to an excess of liabilities over assets, where a trader has sold more of a commodity than has been bought. 'I've gone short $US' means 'I have sold $US'. See **long, short covering, short position, short term**.

short covering   buying securities such as bills or a commodity such as foreign exchange to cover a 'short' (sold) position in those securities or that commodity.

short-dated   Securities such as bonds, bills or notes which are described as 'short-dated' generally have less than one year to maturity, though the definition is fairly arbitrary.

short-date (swaps)   swaps, usually of one currency for another, which span periods of less than one week. See **overnight, spot/next, swap, tom/next**.

shortfall   the difference between the expected amount and the amount achieved. For example, a borrower might issue securities to the market, hoping to raise $1 million, but sells enough to raise only $900 000, which leaves a shortfall of $100 000.

short position   To have a short position is to be oversold. In foreign exchange this means that a trader has an excess of sales over purchases (a net liability position and the opposite of long position). Similarly, in the futures market a trader with a short position has more contracts sold than bought. In the money market a trader can be said to have a short position, which would imply that the securities held, such as bills of exchange, have a relatively brief maturity, for example less than six months—which could be described as 'having gone long on shorts'. See **long position, overbought, oversold**.

short selling   selling a security or commodity (bond, bill of exchange) that you do not yet own, but believe will fall in price so that it can be bought back later at a lower price (and higher yield).

short term   The NSW financial institutions duty legislation defines short term as not exceeding 185 days. The phrase is used fairly loosely but generally would describe a loan, deposit or security that had less than six months and certainly less than one year to run. See **short-term money market**.

short-term money market   the sector of the financial market which caters for the borrowing and lending of funds for short periods of time, usually less than six months, and nearly always less than twelve months (though longer-term finance can be accommodated): short-dated securities are also traded. The short-term money market includes the cash market (overnight and seven-day money), trading in 90- and 180-day bills of exchange, negotiable certificates of deposit, promissory notes and Treasury Notes and the fixed-interest market which focuses on government and semi-government bonds. Players in the short-term money market include the authorised dealers, banks and merchant banks, finance companies, stockbrokers and a range of financial institutions. *Abbrev.*: **STMM**.

short-term note issuance facility   This technique followed the RUF, providing for notes to be placed by a tender panel instead of by a sole agent as with the RUF. *Abbrev.*: **SNIF**. See **revolving underwriting facility**.

short-term underwriting facility   The short-term version of a RUF, whereby members of an underwriting syndicate have a short-term (less than one year) commitment to underwrite eurodollar securities on behalf of an issuer. *Abbrev.*: **STUF**.

SIA   *abbrev.* **Securities Institute of Australia**.

SIBOR   *abbrev.* **Singapore Inter Bank Offered Rate**.

sideways   markets, prices and interest rates are said to have moved sideways if they have shifted within a narrow range.

Silver Thursday   the Thursday in March 1980 when the Hunt Brothers were unable to meet a margin call on their silver futures contracts. The Hunt brothers, Nelson Bunker and his younger brother Herbert, were two of the fourteen children of the Texas oil magnate, H.L. Hunt, who was the richest man in the US when he died in 1974. Bunker and Herbert began investing in silver as a hedge against inflation and by 1980 it was estimated they held one-third of the world's supply of silver. When silver prices slid the Hunt brothers failed to meet huge margin calls on their silver futures contracts, which sparked a panic on commodity and futures exchanges. A consortium of US banks provided a $US 1.1 billion line of credit to enable the Hunt brothers to pay their debts. The brothers lost several hundreds of millions of dollars through their speculation in silver but the Hunt family fortunes were sufficient to withstand the setback.

SIMEX   *abbrev.* **Singapore International Monetary Exchange**.

simple interest   interest calculated on the principal amount only of a loan for each period on which interest is paid, as against compound interest where interest is added back to the original balance so that the subsequent interest calculation is made on principal plus interest. For example, $10 000 invested at 10 per cent per annum would earn $82 in a 30-day month; interest is not cumulatively added to capital through the year, but is calculated each month on $10 000. With compound interest, the second month's interest would be calculated on $10 082 and so on. See **compound interest, flat rate of interest, principal**.

simulated deposits/loans   An Australian financial institution will provide these facilities to clients who want an asset or liability in a foreign currency to offset an existing position. The bank or merchant bank provides a foreign currency deposit facility to give a client an asset in the same currency as an existing liability so that on maturity there is an offset. One advantage of this method is that it effectively avoids the need to pay withholding tax as no non-resident lender is involved, but the client still gets a foreign currency borrowing.

Singapore Inter Bank Offered Rate   This serves the same purpose in Asian markets as LIBOR in the euromarkets and is useful when European markets are closed because of the time difference. It is the rate charged among banks in the Singapore interbank market; funds are onlent to customers at a margin relative to (usually above) SIBOR. The rate is relevant for a number of Australian transactions funded out of Singapore. *Abbrev.*: **SIBOR**. See **London Inter Bank Offered Rate**.

Singapore International Monetary Exchange   This exchange was established in 1984 as a commodity futures exchange, trading initially in gold and eurodollars. *Abbrev.*: **SIMEX**.

sinking fund   A fund established to reduce a debt with the fund maintained by regular payments or contributions which will eventually pay off the amounts owed. The first sinking fund was set up by Sir Robert Walpole in the UK in 1716 to pay off the national debt; the fund was mismanaged and the concept of a sinking fund lost much of its credibility. Sinking funds have since been resurrected and regained status as a useful method of making provisions to pay off a large (especially) public debt. Their successful operation depends on two main factors: the regular investment of a given amount of money which reduces the debt and the accumulated interest which also contributes to that purpose. A sinking fund is an important component in leveraged leasing as the fund is notionally accumulated and invested to pay deferred tax.

skinned   cheated, screwed, as in 'I've been skinned a few points'.

sleeper   an attractive share whose appeal has yet to be recognised. Recognition of its potential pushes up its price.

slump   This word is more or less interchangeable with depression: it is an extreme form of recession, the worst in history being in the 1930s, characterised by a sharp and worldwide decline in economic activity. See **depression, recession**.

Slutzkin   a tax scheme where shareholders in a company which has undistributed profits have no further use for the company, and sell its shares to a tax promoter for full value less a discount, thus avoiding personal tax on the distribution of profits. Slutzkin schemes are so named after a High Court decision and are sometimes confused with bottom-of-the-harbour schemes. For further details, for example the difference between wet and dry Slutzkins, you will need to consult a tax lawyer. See **bottom-of-the-harbour, tax promoter**.

Smith, Adam   see **economists**.

Smithsonian Agreement   In December 1971 the Group of Ten countries met at the Smithsonian Institute in Washington, to agree on a realignment of currencies; it was becoming clear that the Bretton Woods system of fixed exchange rates was not coping effectively. The Smithsonian Agreement produced a decision to devalue the $US against gold and against most other currencies, but these were only bandaid improvements and within a matter of months a number of major currencies decided to abandon fixed exchange rates in favour of floating. Sterling floated in 1972, the $A took considerably longer to follow the trend and was launched into a float in December 1983. See **Bretton Woods, float, Group of Ten**.

Smokestack America   the industrial mid-west of the US, encompassing established heavy industries such as steel and car production. These industries were hardest hit during the recent recession.

snake   The matrix of rates under the European Joint Float was often called the 'snake'. The system existed from April 1972 until the creation of the European Monetary System in 1978. Members of the snake were West Germany, the Netherlands, Belgium, Luxembourg, Denmark and Norway. See **European Monetary System**.

SNIF   *abbrev.* **short-term note issuance facility**.

soc   *abbrev.* **stop-on-close order**.

Society for Worldwide Interbank Financial Telecommunications   a consortium of more than 1000 member banks, based in Brussels but operating a worldwide system for the rapid transfer of money and messages. The system is owned and directed by the member banks. *Abbrev.*: **SWIFT**.

socioeconomic stratum   Socioeconomic refers to the social as well as the economic aspects of life. Your socioeconomic stratum would identify which side of the tracks you hail from.

soft currency   A soft currency is traditionally one which would not be used as a 'reserve currency' and would not be in demand in world markets. Examples at present are the Philippines peso, the Mexican peso, the Hong Kong dollar. Such currencies are not in demand in the way that big-league currencies are such as the deutschmark, $US, Swiss franc and so on. See **hard currency**.

soft loan   money on loan at favourable terms which the same borrower would probably not be able to get in the commercial market. The lender could be the government or a government organisation making a subsidised loan to encourage a particular activity. Merchant bankers could be said to get soft loans from their employers as their salary packages include low-cost home finance.

solicitors' funds   fixed-interest money, made available by solicitors (acting as brokers, not intermediaries) from investment funds supplied by clients. The funds are lent out usually for fairly short periods such as one to three years, during which time the borrower pays interest only on the money; the principal amount of the debt is not reduced. The borrower would use this type of financing perhaps as bridging finance pending a building society or bank loan; during the term of the solicitors' funds loan the borrower would be looking to organise refinancing from one of these sources of longer-term funds. Solicitors' funds are often regarded as emergency money but are a convenient alternative to bank or building society finance if for some reason the borrower does not qualify for a loan from these institutions. Solicitors' funds are a handy source of finance in a booming real estate market where house prices are rising; you can grab a bargain and rely on making a capital gain on the property which will more than offset the cost of the borrowed funds. Solicitors' funds are different from solicitors' trust accounts, which hold funds in trust for clients. See **trust fund**.

South Sea Bubble   The South Sea Company was founded in 1711 in the UK and launched into some ambitious plans for developing trade with South America and the Pacific; its schemes included paying off the UK's national debt—even the British King and Parliament got involved in the South Sea Company at one stage. Shares in the company zoomed in price then suddenly collapsed. The bubble burst and left a legacy of caution about forming new companies that lasted about a century in the UK.

sovereign risk   the extra dimension of risk involved in international, as distinct from domestic, transactions. Sovereign risk is the aspect of the credit proposal which is outside the individual borrower's control; it can override the borrower's willingness and ability to repay financial obligations, even though the borrower may be a government. Sovereign risk involves risk additional to the usual commercial risks such as credit, foreign exchange and transport risks. It implies the possibility that conditions will develop in a country which inhibit repayment of funds due from that country (such as exchange controls, strikes or declaration of war). An international lender should (but does not always) compensate for perceived sovereign risk by adjusting the interest rate charged. International banks operate with lending limits on individual countries, though that is not foolproof. Also **country risk**. See **rescheduling**.

special drawing rights   Established in 1969 by the IMF countries, special drawing rights are used in international trade, as international reserve assets to settle transactions between countries and to help balance international liquidity. They are an important feature of the international monetary system; they are regulated by the IMF and allocations to each country are distributed according to the IMF quotas. *Abbrev.*: **SDR**. See **International Monetary Fund**.

specie   gold and silver used to back paper money, or money in the form of precious metal (usually gold or silver) which was considered superior to coins in base metal or paper money. The end of the gold standard meant an end to a formal link between money supply and specie. See

gold standard.

speculator   a trader in any market who uses the market purely to make a profit, who may not have any direct interest or connection with the commodity traded. The speculator often takes a risk (punts) but does so deliberately, in the hope of reaping a handsome gain.

SPIN   *abbrev.* **Standard & Poor's 500 Index-Subordinated Notes.**

SPITFIRE   *abbrev.* **share price indexed together with fixed interest returns.**

split rating   what happens when two major ratings agencies, such as Moody's and Standard & Poor's, attach different ratings to the same country or security. One agency might downgrade a country from AAA to AA+ while the other maintains the AAA rating—as occurred for some time in the case of Australia in 1986.

split trust   a **unit trust** offering a combination of units that produce income and units producing capital growth, with investors usually able to switch between the two.

spot   a foreign exchange market term meaning 'now' or 'immediate' (when distinguishing a prevailing rate from a forward rate). As with secondhand car dealers who advertise 'spot cash', it is presumably derived from 'on the spot'.

spot-against-forward   foreign exchange shorthand for a trader's spot position (i.e. present position) against his or her forward position. The phrase refers to the purchase of a currency or other commodity to meet future commitments. Banks use this method if their forward purchases or sales do not match (companies can do this too) so that they can offset an imbalance in their forward books by holding a corresponding amount of the foreign currency involved. See **spot, spot market, spot/next, spot price/rate.**

spot market   the part of the market calling for spot settlement of transactions. The precise meaning of 'spot' will depend on local custom for a commodity, security or currency. In Australia, the UK and US foreign exchange markets, 'spot' means delivery within two working days. See **forward market.**

spot month   the closest listed contract in futures trading.

spot/next   a term that describes a currency transaction for spot value against that of the next working day (i.e. three working days hence, assuming 'spot' is two-day value).

spot price/rate   the price or rate for spot settlement of a transaction.

spread   the difference between the buying and selling rates (also the margin above a benchmark rate such as LIBOR); banks quote a spread on their buying and selling rates, which means that when you buy your yen for a trip to Japan you find you get a different number of yen for your $A than is achieved on the way back when you are selling yen for $A, even if the exchange rate was unchanged in the meantime. Spreads in rates can widen if dealers are uncertain about currency movements or if a money changer (*bureau de change*) is out to make a large profit. Investors hoping to profit from the narrowing or widening of the spread between different options use one or more of the various option spread strategies. See **combination, negative interest, option spread, screw rule.**

spread order   an order to buy or sell a series of options, in a specified spread. The order is only carried out if the floor trader can secure the spread that has been requested.

spreadsheet   an electronic worksheet consisting of columns and rows used extensively in financial modelling. Useful in analysing 'what-if' strategies as variables can be changed and the computer automatically recalculates the results. Spreadsheets do not replace ledgers; they are used more as an analytical and modelling tool rather than for showing details of a company's financial position.

square   A trader is square if purchases and sales, borrowings and loans all match—the trader has no 'open' position or mismatched maturity, no need to deal further; he or she is balanced.

squawk box   loudspeaker system used in foreign exchange and fixed-interest trading between brokers and dealers.

squeeze   A general market term to indicate pressure, it has come to be most commonly used in futures, to describe a situation where the deliverable supply is insufficient to cover open futures positions—with the result that holders of sold futures contracts must bid up the price of futures to close out their contracts. This is a **bull squeeze**, where supply is not enough to cover open positions; the opposite would be a **bear squeeze**, where sellers want to deliver, which pushes prices down (rare).

SRD   *abbrev.* **statutory reserve deposit.**

stag   someone who aims to make a quick killing in the stock market by subscribing to new issues and selling on the first day of trading.

stagflation   a state of the economy, characterised by high or rising inflation and static or declining output and employment, for example as it was world wide in the 1970s. The word is a combination of 'stagnation' and 'inflation'.

STAGS   *abbrev.* **sterling transferable accruing securities.**

stale bull   a disgruntled stock market animal; an optimist who has run out of steam, become disenchanted with his or her investment and so turns to sell instead of holding out longer in the hope of more profit. This very action can push prices down, justifying the stale bull's drop in optimism.

stamp duty   A duty imposed at State (not federal) level on certain legal instruments and a number of commercial and financial transactions. The application of stamp duties varies from State to State; the recent thrust in New South Wales, Queensland and Victoria has been to abolish stamp duty on corporate debt instruments, such as debentures and notes, and on mortgage-backed certificates, to encourage trading in these securities.

Standard & Poor's   a highly regarded US corporate credit ratings bureau. See **Australian Ratings, Moody's Investor Services, Standard & Poor's Index**.

Standard & Poor's Index   a US share market measure, based on the performance of 500 widely held shares, calculated by Standard & Poor's.

Standard & Poor's 500 Index-Subordinated Notes   Created by Salomon Brothers Inc and traded on the New York Stock Exchange these notes incorporate the features of debt, equity and options. They offer the investor the chance to make a four-year loan to Salomons, with no payments until the loan matures but with repayment of principal on maturity plus interest that is tied to the performance of the Standard & Poor's 500-stock index. *Abbrev.*: **SPIN**.

Starr Bowkett building society   see **building societies**.

statement   There are three main types of statement:

- a **financial statement**, such as a profit and loss account, a balance sheet;
- a **bank statement**, showing transactions in the customer's account and the debit/credit balance;
- a **statement of account**, such as from a department store, itemising what has been spent and giving the balance due.

See **statement of affairs**.

Statement of Accord   The Statement of Accord between the Australian Labor Party and the Australian Council of Trade Unions on economic policy was issued in February 1983 and outlined the ALP (now Labor government) policy on prices and incomes. It called for continuous consultation between government and the trade union movement on prices and incomes policies. The accord laid the basis for the establishment of the Economic Planning Advisory Council and was included in discussions at the National Economic Summit Conference held in April 1983. See **Economic Planning Advisory Council, National Economic Summit Conference**.

statement of affairs   The list of assets and liabilities, similar to a balance sheet, of an insolvent company or individual, whose affairs may be wound up. The statement of affairs would be prepared for the benefit of creditors who want to know exactly what the score is or might be, bearing in mind that the statement of affairs shows only the estimated value of the company or individual in question.

statistics   the collection, analysing and interpretation of figures; the word can also mean the figures themselves. Australia's official statistics (stats) collector is the Australian Bureau of Statistics, in Canberra. Benjamin Disraeli expressed the feelings of many when he said:'There are three kinds of lies: lies, damned lies and statistics.' Or even more colourfully, Andrew Lang said on the same subject:'He uses statistics as a drunken man uses lamp-posts—for support rather than illumination.'

statutory lien   see **lien**.

statutory reserve deposit   Australian banks (at the time of writing, November 1984) are required to lodge a variable percentage of their deposits (based on the previous month's deposits) with the Reserve Bank. The accounts are kept in line by adjustments on the second Wednesday of each month. Changes in the percentage required can be made by the Reserve Bank for the purposes of monetary policy: releases from statutory reserve deposits add cash to the system, a call-up of more funds to these deposits tightens liquidity, and by reducing the banks' volume of free money (in the sense of being available for lending) the central bank also reduces their capacity to lend. The banks receive a below-market rate of interest on the funds lodged in these accounts—5 per cent at the time of writing. It has been foreshadowed that these accounts are likely to be replaced by a liquidity ratio for the trading banks. *Abbrev.*: **SRD**.

step-down floater   a security that is designed to provide a generous spread over LIBOR during the initial years of its life, with the spread decreasing over the life of the security. This suits investors who want high current income and lower income later.

sterling CP   *abbrev.* **sterling commercial paper**.

sterling transferable accruing securities   A UK copy of the US's TIGRs and CATS, these are euro-sterling zero-coupon securities backed by gilts. *Abbrev.*: **STAGS**. See **ZEBRAS**.

STMM   *abbrev.* **short-term money market**.

stock   interchangeable with equities, shares and bonds. It can also mean a company's inventory of goods.

stockbroker   A person whose business is the buying and selling of shares and securities on behalf of others (clients), earning a commission (brokerage) on the trades. Stockbrokers advise clients which shares best suit their investment requirements, and most today operate extensive research departments which produce useful analyses of company performances and market trends.

April 1984 changes to stock exchange regulations in Australia changed the nature of stockbroking: negotiated commissions were introduced and broking firms were given freedom to become incorporated. A number of banks and merchant banks took advantage of the new rules to team up with broking firms and form limited companies. Also **sharebroker**. See **incorporated, partnership**.

stock exchange   the market place for trading equities (shares), government bonds and other fixed-interest securities. Stock exchanges are also known as bourses. The exchanges date back to seventeenth-century Europe, to the coffee houses of London where traders met. Modern stock exchanges evolved from those original meeting places. Stock exchange activity began in Australia in 1828; the gold rush of the 1850s gave the market a boost, with stock exchanges established in Bendigo and Ballarat. By the end of the nineteenth century exchanges had been set up in Sydney, Melbourne, Hobart, Brisbane, Adelaide and Perth. Each exchange elects a committee from its members and this committee functions much as a board of directors. Stock exchange activity is governed by a number of legislative provisions. See **bourse**, *Companies Act*, **National Companies and Securities Commission, Securities Industry Act 1980**.

Stock Exchange Automated Quotations   the London stock exchange's price information system for international securities — the stock exchange's version of NASDAQ. *Abbrev.*: **SEAQ**.

Stock Exchange Automated Trading System   the computer-assisted trading system being developed by the Australian Stock Exchange, similar to **CATS**. *Abbrev.*: **SEATS**.

stop-loss order   an instruction left by a client with his or her broker to sell if the stock reaches a particular level—which is normally a below-market level. A sharp fall in prices can trigger stop-loss orders and exaggerate an embryonic trend. Stop-loss orders are used more in Australian futures and options trading than in the share market. They are common in the US, especially in the context of margin accounts.

stop-on-close order   This type of futures market order is left resting in the market and, if the stop-loss is activated within the last five minutes of trading the order is executed at market. *Abbrev.*: **soc**.

stop order   see **stop-loss order**.

straddle   a type of speculation in futures trading which involves the simultaneous purchase in one delivery month and selling in another to take advantage of an expected change in price differentials between the two. A **negative straddle** is the opposite: the trader sells in the near month and buys in the distant month. (These can be used to advantage from a tax point of view.)

strangle   see **combination**.

strapper   an inexperienced money market dealer, whose duties would be restricted to keeping a record of transactions and helping with settlements. In racing terminology it is a stable boy, in money market terms a trainee dealer.

strike price   a futures term to describe the price at which an option on a particular contract may be exercised. The strike price is set when a trader enters into an option contract and it must be the prevailing price of the commodity in the futures delivery month to which the option relates. Also **exercise price**. See **option trading**.

STRIP   *abbrev.* **separate trading of registered interest and principal of securities**.

stripped bond   a bond whose coupon has been separated from the bond certificate. See **zero coupon bonds**.

structural deficit   see **deficit**.

Student Loan Marketing Association   a US organisation established in 1972 to boost the supply of loans for college and university education. The association buys loans from financial institutions and provides funds for state-based student loan agencies. It has also raised finance by issuing its own short- and medium-term notes called Sallie Maes. See **New England Education Loan Marketing Corporation**.

STUF   *abbrev.* **short-term underwriting facility**.

suasion   see **moral suasion**.

subordinated loan   a type of loan which ranks behind other debts should a company be wound up. Typical providers of subordinated loans are major shareholders or a parent company. An outside party providing funds through a subordinated loan would want compensation for the loan's status, for example through a higher interest rate. (A loan's status, whether subordinated, secured or unsecured, is spelled out in the contract between borrower and lender.) Merchant banks and finance companies in Australia have used subordinated loans to boost their potential borrowing base, to demonstrate parent company back-up or to lift their credit rating. From the recipient's point of view a subordinated loan offers advantages similar to increased capital, but with greater flexibility in that the subordinated loan can be repaid fairly easily. The Reserve Bank regards subordinated loans as liabilities which will require payment at some future date, and does not include them as part of the trading banks' capital—some banks disagree with this interpretation.

subpoena   an instruction issued by a court to a person to appear in court or before an examiner or referee as a witness, either to give evidence or to present documents specified in the subpoena and give evidence about these documents.

subscriber   someone who agrees to buy shares or other securities such as bonds.

subscription   payment for shares, bonds, debentures and so on.

subscription warrant   see **warrant**.

subsidiary   a company under the control or parentage of another company which owns all or most of it. Unlike a branch, a subsidiary company is its own entity, and pays its own tax.

subsidy   government or other support of an industry, or section of the community or company or individual, theoretically to encourage productivity. A subsidy can result in consumers paying marginally less for a product than it cost to produce—it can also help local industry remain competitive vis-a-vis imported goods, or can help exporters. It is something all producers want.

substantial shareholder   a shareholder whose shares total more than 10 per cent of a company's issued capital. Substantial shareholders must advise the stock exchange of any purchase or sale that changes their holding.

summit   see **National Economic Summit Conference**.

sunrise industries   the new high-technology manufacturing industries featuring automated and computerised processes. (On these industries, it is said, the economic sun is rising.)

sunset clause   a provision, inserted in a set of regulations, for the expiry of specified arrangements should certain conditions prevail.

superannuation   Superannuation operates rather like a bank account-cum-special type of life insurance; it incorporates payments to the insured person on retirement (or if he or she dies before retiring, the funds would be paid to the nominated beneficiary or beneficiaries according to the deceased person's will). Many life offices provide superannuation schemes and most companies offer superannuation to employees. (Employees often have no choice but to join a fund if they work for such a company). In public and private sector superannuation schemes, both the employer and the employee contribute; the employer usually pays the larger amount but the contributions are tax-advantageous for both sides. Superannuation payments are deducted from employees' salaries; in the case of self-employed people they can take out their own policies with a life office or set up their own recognised fund.

superannuation bonds   similar to life insurance bonds in concept but with a different tax structure and subject to superannuation rules. In the case of personal superannuation bonds, if the purchaser has no company superannuation cover, the single premium for a superannuation bond is tax-deductible up to $1500. This type of bond differs from the ordinary bond in that the benefit payable is locked into the investment until the pre-set retirement ages specified under Section 23(ja) (for self-employed) or 23FB (for employees). Superannuation bonds have a higher earnings rate than ordinary life bonds, because the investment manager does not have to pay tax on the income or dividends received. When the bond pays out the individual is taxed, at the superannuation lump-sum tax rate on collection, i.e. 30 per cent plus the Medicare levy of the amount paid out, unless the person is more than 55 years old, in which case tax on the first $55 000 is levied at the rate of 15 cents in the dollar plus the Medicare levy. Corporate superannuation bonds are similar to the personal bonds but the individual is locked in under Section 23F until he or she terminates employment. See **insurance bonds**.

supply and demand   The concept dates back to the ancient Greeks but was formalised over the last 200 years by economists who made a law—the law of supply and demand—out of the commonsense concept that the price of any item is determined by how much of it is available and how many people want it. Subsidies and taxes distort the straightforward effects of supply and demand but generally in a competitive economy, it is the rule that a scarce commodity will rise in price and a surplus of a commodity will push its price down.

supply-side economics   Supporters of this recently popular concept are in favour of tax cuts because these (they believe) will stimulate production, by increasing incentives. Increases in production will tend, over time, to reduce the budget deficit. Supporters of supply-side economics focus on the need to encourage supply instead of controlling demand; the concept challenges Keynes' 1930s position that the important objective is management of demand. Supply-side supporters say that government moves to boost private sector demand by deficit spending are a source of instability. In their more relaxed attitude to fiscal deficits, the supply-siders are more akin to Keynesians than to monetarists, who worry about the possibility of overheating—supply-siders would not like that comment as they dislike Keynesians. Supply-side ideas gained ground because they seemed an attractive answer to the problems of inflation. Critics of supply-siders say they exaggerate the incentives that might be produced by tax cuts—as do critics of the Laffer curve. See **Keynes, John Maynard** in **economists, Laffer curve, monetarist**.

surrender value   what the life office will pay if you choose to cash in your policy before its expiry date.

sushi bonds   bonds issued in the euromarkets by a Japanese company, aimed at Japanese investors, often insurance companies, who are under restrictions regarding their purchases of foreign bonds. They can claim a sushi bond is not a foreign bond as it is issued by a Japanese company.

suspended   Trading in a company's shares is described as suspended when it is temporarily stopped, either by the company or by the exchange, pending an announcement by the company or a decision by the exchange.

swap-driven   Traders talk of notes or bond issues being swap-driven when they mean that the securities are issued in conjunction with an accompanying swap rather than because the borrower (issuer) particularly wanted to sell the paper in the form in which it is issued.

swaps   The financing technique of the 1980s, swaps are the exchange of one entitlement for another. In financial markets, they can be interest rate swaps or currency swaps.

In **interest rate swaps**, two parties—banks, companies or individuals—may choose to swap their types of borrowings (with no exchange of principal amounts), because the interest rate structure of each suits the other better. For example, a borrower with a ten-year fixed-rate loan may choose to swap these funds with another borrower for that party's floating-rate finance. Interest rate swaps are the largest swap category; they can be used to achieve lower borrowing costs or to obtain access to fixed-rate finance for borrowers who otherwise would not be able to tap those markets.

Currency swaps are also increasing in popularity. They can be the simultaneous purchase and sale of a currency for different value dates, so that the underlying position of the foreign exchange trader does not alter but the value dates change. They can also involve the swap of one currency for another. The important number is the swap rate, i.e. the difference between the rate at which the currency is bought and the rate at which it is sold in the swap.

Central banks have carried out swaps (the first being handled in 1962), as part of their intervention/currency support tactics. See **fixed-rate loan, floating-rate finance**.

swaptions   see **interest rate swap options**.

sweep   the automatic shifting by a bank of surplus current account customer balances into an interest-bearing deposit or money market fund.

sweetener   a condition added to a share issue or offering of securities that enhances its appeal to investors, for example notes that are issued with the option of converting into equity at a later date.

SWIFT   *abbrev.* **Society for Worldwide Interbank Financial Telecommunications**.

swissy   foreign exchange dealers' shorthand for Swiss francs.

switching   simultaneous buying and selling of securities which differ in maturity or coupon or type, to improve the investment return.

Sydney Futures Exchange   The Sydney Futures Exchange began operating in 1960 as the Sydney Greasy Wool Futures Exchange. It changed its name in 1972 as part of a move to diversify from a focus on wool. The exchange now offers a range of futures contracts. It was the first futures exchange outside the US to offer financial futures—these began in 1979 with the introduction of the 90-day bank bill futures contract. The Sydney Futures Exchange first branched out from wool in 1975, with the introduction of the cattle futures contract; in April 1978 it added the first non-pastoral commodity, gold. Currency futures were introduced in 1980 and share price index futures in 1983. A ten-year Commonwealth bond futures contract was launched in December 1984. It introduced exchange-traded options in 1985, and eurodollar interest rate futures and US Treasury Bond futures in 1986 under a link with the London International Financial Futures Exchange. Also in 1986 a link was formed with Comex in New York to trade a new gold futures contract. At the time of writing (December 1987) the Sydney Futures Exchange has 29 full floor members. It is located a 13–15 O'Connell Street, Sydney, but plans to move to new premises in Grosvenor Place late in 1988.

The Sydney Futures Exchange has kept pace with other recent deregulatory moves in the Australian financial system and switched to negotiable rates of commission. A new class of membership, called locals, was introduced in June 1984. Clearing services for the Sydney Futures Exchange are provided by the International Commodities Clearing House. At the time of writing, the following contracts were available for trading on the Sydney Futures Exchange:

	date introduced	*contract based on*
wool	May 1960	greasy equivalent of 2500 kilograms of clean combing wool

live cattle	July 1975	10 000 kilograms live weight
90-day bank bills	Oct 1979	$A500 000 bank-accepted bills
share price index	Feb 1983	$A value of 100 times the all-ordinaries index
Treasury Bonds	Dec 1984	$A 100 000 of a ten-year 12 per cent coupon notional Treasury Bond
eurodollar interest rates	Oct 1986	$US1 million three-month time deposit
US Treasury Bonds	Oct 1986	$US100 000 of twenty-year 8 per cent notional US Treasury Bond
gold	Nov 1986	100 troy ounces
$A	—— 1988	$A100 000

Options are available on bank bills, ten-year Treasury Bonds and share price index futures, and will be available on $A futures when introduced.

See **futures contract, futures markets, International Commodities Clearing House, local, London International Financial Futures Exchange.**

syndication   This occurs when a group of financial institutions pool resources on a specific financing project to spread the risk. Individual return from the investment is proportionate to the degree of risk or amount of funds that each has underwritten or put up.

synthetic option   a product that is created using forwards and futures to allow a company to control its losses on, say, foreign exchange or interest rates, while still retaining the potential to make gains.

T

tail-gating   a broker placing an order on his or her own account on the tails of a customer's order, hoping to take advantage of the effect of the customer's transaction on the market.

take a bath   trade badly. Usually used to describe a severe loss that results from speculation.

takeover   the acquisition of a controlling interest in a company by another company through the purchase of its shares. The acquired company's identity is often submerged and merged into that of the company taking it over. Because of the predatory implications of the word 'takeover', those in the business often prefer to talk of 'mergers', which suggests a hungry company finds a willing partner with whom to join forces—though the result is not much different.

Takeovers can be effected through a formal takeover offer, an on-market offer or various other less common means. The **formal takeover offer** is the most common; before the offer is made the 'Part A Statement' has to be given to the company for whom the offer is being made, outlining necessary information; the company receiving the Part A Statement should then arrange for a 'Part B Statement', incorporating information on itself and the takeover offer, to be provided to its own shareholders and to the offeror company. The National Companies and Securities Commission supervises the contents of the Part A and B Statements and the offer documents.

An **on-market offer** involves a stockbroking firm undertaking to buy all shares offered in the market at a specified price (of the target company) for a period of at least one month on behalf of the offeror company. This involves 'Parts C and D Statements' similar to Parts A and B above, and would also involve NCSC supervision. Part C does not follow a Part A and B Statement; it is a different takeover technique. Nothing is sent out to the shareholders of the target company with Part C beyond notifying them of intention to buy. Part D is the response by the board of the offeree company to the Part C Statement. See **merger and acquisition, offeree, offeror, on-market**.

takeover bid   an offer made to shareholders of one company by another company or individual to buy their shares at a stated price to gain control of the company.

taking a view   forming an opinion on market trends such as interest rates or inflation and acting upon it.

tap stocks   A commodity which is 'on tap' is constantly available, usually at a known price. Before the introduction of the tender system for selling Commonwealth government bonds they were on tap, which meant they were available for purchase each day from the Reserve Bank, at a known price. Australian Savings Bonds are continuously available (on tap) from the Reserve Bank, banks, stockbrokers and post offices at a rate that is set by the federal government. Since July 1982 other Commonwealth bonds have been sold through periodic tenders; Treasury Notes have been sold using a tender system since December 1979. See **tender**.

tariff   a schedule of charges levied on imports, either to raise revenue or to protect local industry and supposedly increase employment. Tariffs interfere with the flows of international trade. GATT has, with some success, tried to reduce the use of tariffs in many countries. See **General Agreement on Tariffs and Trade**.

taxation   the compulsory transfer, usually of money, from the private sector to the government, for public purposes. Taxation is one of the three main sources of government revenue. The government raises the funds it needs to finance its expenses and payments through taxation, charges and borrowings. The notion that workers pay the government through their taxes is embalmed in the oft-heard indignant phrase 'a third of the time I'm working for the government'—a common observation among taxpayers. The amount the government extracts from your salary will depend on the amount you earn; tax is levied at rates which increase with income so that lower income earners pay a smaller proportion of their wages in taxes than do those on higher salaries. Governments would liken the tax system to the Robin Hood legend—'taking from the haves to provide for the have-nots'; most taxpayers regard the taxman more in the light of a Ned Kelly.
Tax on personal income in Australia dates back to 1884 when it was introduced in South Australia. Other States followed and the commonwealth started taxing in 1915. Between 1915 and 1942 income tax was levied by both State and federal governments; control of personal tax shifted to the commonwealth during World War II, and stayed there by agreement of the States which take their share by way of grants. Tax is collected by various methods. Tax levies are:

- **PAYE or pay-as-you-earn** tax, which is deducted in instalments at source by an employer from employees' wages and salaries. PAYE was introduced in Australia in 1942, in the US in 1943 and in the UK in 1944.
- **provisional tax** which is payable in April, on income for the current financial year, by self-employed people such as dentists and doctors and small business people who do not make PAYE instalment payments. A wage or salary earner can be liable for provisional tax

if he or she receives enough additional income through interest payments, investments, royalties or moonlighting.

- **payroll tax** is levied on business, in proportion to the number of people employed, and is imposed as a State tax in Australia. Payroll tax was introduced in 1941, initially as a way to fund child endowment payments, but this link was removed in the early 1950s. Payroll tax was transferred from federal to State control in 1971 and has become a major source of State revenue.

The classification **indirect tax** is still widely used to describe levies such as sales tax, purchase tax, customs and excise. See **indirect taxation**.

tax avoidance   As distinct from tax evasion, this is the lawful way of minimising your tax bill. In tax avoidance you employ legal means, exploit loopholes in tax legislation to reduce your liability to tax. This interprets the letter, rather than the spirit, of the law. See **tax evasion**.

tax-effect accounting   a method of bringing income tax expenses into account during the period in which the expenses are incurred rather than the period in which the income tax is payable.

tax evasion   illegal attempts to avoid paying tax, for example by not accurately reporting all income, overstating deductions or, in extreme cases, fleeing the country. See **tax avoidance**.

tax haven   This conjures up names such as Monaco, the Cayman Islands, the Bahamas, where enviably low tax rates apply. Companies like to have their 'brass plates' in such places even though their business is carried out elsewhere. Well-known European tax havens are Switzerland and the little principality of Liechtenstein. The cost of living in some of these idyllic spots would deter all but the wealthiest. Companies do not have to live there though—establishing a holding company in a tax haven would be enough for the transfer of money. (Non-haven countries impose restrictions on tax havens to stop loss of tax.) Tax havens have also been set up by governments keen to win foreign business and to develop a major financial centre in their country. In these cases, banks, including foreign banks, have been allowed to operate with more favourable tax rates, but often as 'offshore banking units' outside the domestic financial system. Also **tax shelter**. See **offshore**.

tax loss   A tax loss occurs when total expenses are more than total income for taxation purposes. People often try to create tax losses in an attempt to minimise their tax bill. A business can incur a loss for tax purposes but a profit for accounting purposes, hence a tax loss can be distinguished from an actual loss, for example, in the case of someone letting a house, making a tax loss but still doing well out of the exercise because of the capital gain. Tax loss schemes have been devised by nimble accountants for those who have accumulated too much taxable income.

tax-loss selling   trading securities from your portfolio at rates which deliberately create a loss which is useful for minimising tax. Also **tax-loss switching**. See **tax loss**.

tax minimisation   a more polite expression for the aim involved in tax avoidance or tax evasion. The goal remains to pay the federal government less in taxes than it would prefer or deem necessary according to your assessable income and getting away with it by arranging your business affairs legally. See **tax avoidance**, **tax evasion**.

tax promoter   someone who markets schemes for tax avoidance or tax evasion. See **Slutzkin**.

technical analysis   see **charting**.

technical correction   an interruption to the general trend, for example a brief fall in a bull market or a brief rise in a bear market. Usually a technical correction occurs when the general trend has moved too far too fast in one direction. See **technical rally**.

technical position   fundamentals which influence the market such as short-term interest rates, the amount of money around, trends in rates and inflation.

technical rally   a sudden improvement in prices after a lull or fall; a downward movement in interest rates after a period of rising rates. See **technical correction**.

teigaku certificate   the commonest form of savings instrument offered by Japan's postal banking service. It offers compound interest, paid semi-annually, to the small saver; compound interest is unusual in Japan so this is a popular investment. The minimum maturity is six months, then withdrawal can be made at any time; funds can be left for up to ten years.

telegraphic transfer   used to transfer funds for rapid settlement of a foreign exchange transaction. *Abbrev.*: **T/T**. See **SWIFT**.

tender   a type of auction with written bids sought for the sale of a commodity, often bonds or other securities such as promissory notes. Commonwealth government bonds have been sold through periodic tenders since July 1982, with those wishing to buy submitting their bids at the allotted date and time to the Reserve Bank. Treasury Notes have been sold through regular (usually weekly) tenders since December 1979.

term deposit   money placed for a fixed period at a stated rate of interest which will apply for the duration of the deposit. Also **time deposit**. See **fixed deposit**.

term insurance   a life policy under which the benefit is payable only if the life insured dies before the specified age or date. In most cases if the insured person outlives the term of the policy, he or she gets no payout, so term insurance can be said to be similar to taking out an insurance policy against burglary but not being robbed. It is the cheapest form of life insurance because it provides death cover only, has no investment content and does not attract bonuses.

term to maturity   the number of days, months or years until a loan, bill of exchange, bond, insurance policy or other security becomes due for repayment.

testator   a male person who has made a will.

testatrix   a female person who has made a will.

Texas hedge   an expression used in futures markets that describes a strategy that doubles the risk: what looked like a hedge (protection) turns out to increase the esposure instead of netting out the risk as expected.

thin market   a market characterised by low activity, lacking in depth or volume, so that large transactions cause large movements in price. A thin market for a particular security can indicate a lack of demand for or supply of that security; a generally thin market indicates holiday times, the silly season or dealers sitting on the sidelines because of uncertainty or lack of interest.

third currencies   Trading in third currencies involves transactions which do not include the local currency; for example in Australia this could involve trading $US for yen.

Third World   The term was first used in 1947 by the French geographer Renee Dumont, but many of the countries it originally described have since become industrialised, necessitating a fourth world category for those in real strife. **First World** countries are the advanced industrialised nations, **Second World** consists of the eastern European countries, **Third World** includes those who do not fit in either first or second, and **Fourth World** describes the problem areas such as Tanzania, Ethiopia. See **less developed country**.

30/20 Regulation   This referred to a tax concession to life insurance companies and superannuation funds, in return for their holding no less than 30 per cent of their assets in public securities, with at least 20 per cent of total assets in commonwealth securities. It enticed or forced loan funds into the public use by tax concessions. The Campbell Committee recommended abolition of 30/20 legislation, the Martin Review Group endorsed this view and the federal government announced its removal on 10 September 1984.

thrift institution   a US expression for a savings institution whose main function is attracting individuals' savings and lending those for housing finance. The two main categories of thrift institutions are the savings-and-loan associations and the mutual savings banks. Thrift institutions suffered when interest rates rocketed and money market funds could pay far higher rates than the thrifts could afford; this arose out of the tendency for mortgages to be provided on the basis of fixed rates.

TIBOR   *abbrev.* **Tokyo Inter Bank Offered Rate.** See **HIBOR, LIBOR.**

TIC   *abbrev.* **transferable investment certificate.**

tick movement   the smallest change in market price possible in each futures contract. For example, a bank bill price movement from 89.02 to 89.03 would be a 'one-tick movement'. It is the minimum price movement in a futures contract, as defined by each contract's regulations.

tight money   Cash is in short supply; interest rates will rise making money more expensive; money market dealers look tight-lipped. See **easy money.**

TIGR   *abbrev.* **Treasury investment growth receipt.**

Tijuana spread   a futures market strategy. A trader takes a huge position in the market and buys a ticket to Tijuana, and goes to Tijuana if the position proves a loser.

time deposit   see **term deposit.**

time spread   see **interdelivery spread, option spread.**

time-sharing   two or more individuals or companies sharing the use of, say, a computer or holiday home.

time value   in the context of options trading, this describes the difference between an option premium and the intrinsic value of an option, i.e. the amount by which the option is in the money. Time value reflects the value of the period remaining before the option expires. See **intrinsic value.**

title   the right to ownership of property, or the documents constituting evidence of that ownership.

TN   *abbrev.* **Treasury Note.**

Tokyo Stock Exchange   Japan's largest and oldest stock exchange, which began operating in 1949. The second largest exchange in Japan is in Osaka. Other exchanges are Kyoto, Hiroshima, Nagoya, Sapporo, Niigata and Fukuoka.

tom   foreign exchange dealers' shorthand for 'tomorrow'.

tom/next   Foreign exchange market shorthand for tomorrow/next day. It refers to a form of short-date swap, mainly used to try to maximise return on funds. For example, a trader with a surplus of, say, $US has a choice of lending the $US or selling them for $A, investing the $A and buying the $US back next day. If the $A interest rates are higher, it could be more profitable to swap the $US for $A and invest the $A than simply to lend the $US. Thus the trader would (today) sell the $US and buy the $A for settlement tomorrow (tom) and at the same time would buy back the $US and sell $A for settlement the next day (next). The tom/next swap is frequently used in the Australian currency hedge market to try to minimise exposures peculiar to the settlement process of that market. See **hedge market, hedge settlement rate, short-date swap, spot/next.**

tombstone   a colloquial but accepted expression used especially in the euromarket to describe an international advertisement recording details of a loan and listing all the participants in the financing. Tombstones appear after the event and are edged in black—hence the name.

toppy   traders' jargon to describe a market that has reached a level that equals either as previous or expected high, so that the next move forecast is downward—that is, the market is expected to 'top out' or decline. See **bottomish.**

top up   making up the difference between what you have and what you need. A building society or savings bank will lend you say, $40 000 for a $65 000 house; your deposit is $20 000 so you 'top up' with a $5000 personal loan from another source. The term was used in the context of financial institutions with ratio requirements such as 30/20 which 'topped up' their holdings of the required assets ahead of balance date or the end of the financial year. See **bridging finance, solicitors' funds, 30/20 Regulation, window dressing.**

Torrens title   the modern simplified system of showing title to land through one document registered at a central registry. The Torrens system was introduced in South Australia in 1858 by the State's first premier, Sir Robert Torrens. It has since been adopted throughout Australia and used widely overseas. The Torrens system contrasts with Old System. Torrens title eliminates the need to store piles of documents, so saves time and money. A duplicate certificate of title is held by the owner or registered proprietor (or the mortgagee) and the original remains in the register. In the absence of fraud, being registered as proprietor normally is conclusive evidence of title. See **Old System title**.

TPC *abbrev.* **Trade Practices Commission**.

trade bill (of exchange)   the traditional form of the bill of exchange, based on a specific transaction. Accommodation bills evolved out of trade bills. See **bill of exchange**.

trade deficit   a shortfall in the trading account of the balance of payments. See **balance of payments**.

trade finance   the term used to describe the credit terms provided to overseas buyers, also known as export finance. Such finance is available in two forms:

- **supplier credit,** under which an exporter allows credit terms to an overseas buyer and then arranges funds to cover these terms from a local financial institution;
- **buyer credit,** under which a local financial institution provides funds direct to an overseas buyer or other approved borrower so that an exporter can be paid immediately goods are shipped.

Trade Practices Act 1974   This Act outlines regulations on practices and consumer protection; practices such as collusion, monopolies, exclusive dealing and price discrimination have been declared illegal, as have false representation and misleading advertising. Specific exemptions from the Act are possible. See **restrictive trade practices, Trade Practices Commission**.

Trade Practices Commission   The body responsible for administering the *Trade Practices Act*, including the consumer protection provisions. The Trade Practices Commission has three main functions:

- investigating possible breaches of the Act and enforcing its provisions;
- authorising certain exemptions from the Act;
- keeping the public informed of the operations of the Act.

The TPC has wide powers for obtaining information about activities that could be contravening the Act; it can also grant approvals for restrictive practices under Part IV of the *Trade Practices Act* if it considers an action is not against the public interest but is likely to be of benefit. *Abbrev.*: **TPC**.

trade-weighted index   The Australian trade-weighted index is an index of the average value of the $A vis-a-vis currencies of Australia's major trading partners. The weight given to each currency reflects the level of trade between Australia and the country concerned. Before December 1983 and the decision to float the $A, the trade-weighted index of the $A was the basis for setting the exchange rate each day. The Reserve Bank of Australia still publishes the index, though less regularly and is merely measuring the average movement of the $A against the currencies of Australia's trading partners. Most other countries also publish an index of the average value of their currency. The most significant currencies in the $A basket are the $US, yen and sterling. *Abbrev.*: **TWI**.

trading banks Australian trading banks are financial institutions in the business of borrowing and lending, and providing a range of financial services to customers. These include cheque accounts (on which interest is now payable), fixed deposits and lending in the form of overdrafts, personal loans and bill lines. Australian banks operate under the *Banking Act*, which affords Reserve Bank protection to their depositors and leaves the banks subject to a (diminishing) number of regulations on interest rates and assets.

Relaxation of federal government controls has allowed the trading banks to extend their activities, for example to pay interest on overnight deposits, take equity in sharebroking firms, hold wholly owned merchant bank subsidiaries.

At the time of writing (November 1984) the trading banks are subject to interest rate ceilings on housing finance and the small (under $100 000) overdraft rate. Bank liquidity is regulated through the statutory reserve deposit and liquid assets and government securities convention; these are likely to be replaced in the near future by a trading bank liquidity ratio. See **liquid assets and government securities convention**, **Reserve Bank of Australia**, **savings banks**, **statutory reserve deposit**.

trading on the right-hand side a foreign exchange term to indicate that the market sees a currency, for example the $A, higher than an officially determined midrate; in the case of a floating exchange rate, it describes a currency under buying pressure, and likely to rise. The opposite is 'trading on the left-hand side'. See **left-hand side**.

tranche a French word meaning 'slice', this has come to be used in eurocurrency and other markets to mean a 'portion' of a loan drawn down at a particular time, as in 'the first tranche of the $1 million facility will be issued at par'.

transferable investment certificate Launched in October 1985 by the Australian Bank, this investment is in the form of a transferable certificate which offers a good return, solid security and a choice of maturity dates. The certificate represents investments in bank-, government- or semi-government-guaranteed securities. Investment terms range from one day to three years. Each certificate owns a specifically identified group of securities, chosen by the investor. Interest is payable in arrears. The certificate allows the issuing bank to securitise investment management services. *Abbrev.*: **TIC**. See

securitisation.

transferable revolving underwriting facility a technique that evolves from a RUF and is an alternative to a syndicated bank loan. Banks underwrite the credit but they do not hold the underwriting commitment which is transferable. *Abbrev*.: **TRUF**. See **revolving underwriting facility**.

transfer payments government expenditure such as grants, social security payments, which are not payments in return for productive services.

transfer pricing a favourite pastime of many multinationals, so that their sales are made to their own subsidiary in another country at artificially low prices to minimise their profits in a country with high tax rates. It is now specifically dealt with under Australian tax laws.

Treasuries shorthand for US government securities. **Treasury bonds** are long-term securities issued for more than ten years and **Treasury notes** are medium-term securities issued for periods of more than one year but less than ten. The shorter-term US government securities are **Treasury bills**, known as **T-bills**, which are issued for one year or less.

treasury The treasury division of a company typically has responsibility for all aspects of fundraising, the terms for which funds are raised and the methods used, including foreign currency management, accounting and taxation. The functions of the treasury division and the corporate treasurer vary considerably from company to company.

The federal government department of Treasury, based in Canberra, is responsible for federal government revenue and expenditure, looks after commonwealth fundraising, domestically and overseas, and manages the government's outstanding debt. Treasury advises the federal Treasurer, and through him the government, on policies affecting the economy, monetary policy, financial and taxation matters, and prepares the annual budget.

The government department of Treasury was created at the time of Federation through the *Commonwealth of Australia Constitution Act* 1901; it is now divided into seven divisions:

- General Financial and Economic Policy Division, which assesses current and prospective domestic economic conditions and gives advice on budgetary and monetary policies.
- Overseas Economic Relations Division, which is concerned with Australia's external economic relations, including the balance of payments, international economic and monetary systems, Australia's membership of various international organisations and role in international financial affairs.
- Taxation and Industry Division, which looks after taxation and industry policies;

- Incomes Prices and Development Division, which oversees matters relating to incomes and prices, such as the Accord and wage cases, and monitors long-term development;
- Financial Institutions Division, concerned with the structure and functioning of the banking system and other financial institutions;
- Foreign Investment Division, which oversees foreign investment in Australia, provides executive services to the Foreign Investment Review Board;
- Revenue Loans and Investment Division, which deals with commonwealth loan raisings in Australia and overseas, monitors the operations of Loan Council, the provision of finance to the States, Northern Territory and local authorities.

Following a Fraser government decision in 1976, the Department of Finance was split off from the Treasury. This Department looks after the day-to-day outlays and expenditure—but still shares the Friday evening happy hour with Treasury.

Treasury Bills short-term commonwealth government securities issued by the federal government to the Reserve Bank. These are not available to the public, but are used only for funding within the government family. Treasury Bills in Australia were the forerunner of the present-day Treasury Notes. The US and UK have Treasury Bills which are equivalent to the Australian Treasury Notes, i.e. they are short-term government obligations. In the US, Treasury Notes are a longer-term security. See **Treasury Notes.**

Treasury Bonds These are available in two forms—Australian Savings Bonds (Aussie Bonds) and medium- to long-term securities issued through periodic tenders, at · yields determined by bidders (buyers). Also **Commonwealth bonds.** See **Australian Savings Bonds, bonds, tender.**

Treasury investment growth receipt a breed of zero coupon US Treasury bond devised by Merrill Lynch. These are also issued in New Zealand, as zero coupon New Zealand government bonds, marketed jointly by the Development Finance Corporation and Merrill Lynch. The New Zealand TIGRs were first issued in June 1986 and are based on the same philosophy as those in the US, i.e. separating the interest and principal payments of New Zealand government stock and selling each individually, as **Principal TIGRs** and **Interest** or **Coupon TIGRs.** *Abbrev.*: **TIGR.** See **zero coupon bond.**

Treasury Notes Commonwealth government short-term securities, issued through the Reserve Bank as agent for the commonwealth, for periods of thirteen and 26 weeks, at a discount from face value. The Treasury Notes are highly negotiable and are aimed at professional, short-term money market investors rather than the ordinary individual.

TN tenders are generally held weekly, on a Wednesday, with buyers lodging bids with the Reserve Bank by 12 noon and results announced later in the afternoon. The Reserve Bank advises details of TN tenders each Friday afternoon, for the following week. *Abbrev.*: **TN**.

Treaty of Rome   see **European Economic Community**.

trickle down   Economists who support the trickle down theory believe that a healthy and prosperous business sector is good for the economic growth of the wider community, on the grounds that business' well-being will spread (trickle) into the other sectors of the economy, giving them a boost. Also, at the level of the individual, incentives such as tax cuts which are introduced to encourage effort at the upper end of the scale will flow through to the lower end. See **multiplier**.

Triple A   see **AAA**.

triple bypass   a US loan facility where the borrower is given the option of pricing funds relative to bankers' acceptances, the US prime rate or the appropriate Eurodollar rate.

triple witching hour   US market jargon for the close of trading on the Friday at the end of every quarter when three key option and futures contracts mature: equity, index options and index option futures. Volume rises as traders and speculators close out their positions. See **program trading**.

truncation   Used in the context of truncation of cheques, this means reducing the length of time taken to process cheques. The cheques remain in the one clearing place and details are checked electronically.

TRUF   *abbrev.* **transferable revolving underwriting facility**.

trust   in the legal and commercial sense, money or property vested with an independent third party (the trustee) to administer on behalf of others (the beneficiaries of the trust). See **trust deed, trust fund, trustee, unit trust**.

trust account   the bank account that must be maintained by a sharebroker, into which the broker pays the funds received from clients for share purchases. Funds are held in the trust account until the broker has to pay out to a seller. The purpose of the trust account is to protect clients' funds against potential defalcation by the broker. See **defalcation**.

trust deed   a document conveying title to trust property to the trustee and setting out the purposes for which a trust has been formed, the rights and obligations of the trustee, of the trust's manager and of the trust's beneficiaries. The trust deed lays down the rules within which the trust must operate, dictates its investment guidelines and describes how benefits will accrue to the unitholders (beneficiaries) under the trust. See **trust, trustee, unit trust**.

trustee   All trusts have a trustee who monitors the trust's activities on behalf of the beneficiaries. It is the job of the trustee to ensure that the trust operates within the guidelines of its trust deed and complies with legal requirements. The trustee is also responsible for the trust's bank accounts and the safe custody of securities held by the trust. The trustee maintains ownership of the trust's assets on behalf of the beneficiaries (unitholders, in the case of a unit trust) and ensures that these assets are separately held and classified.

trustee status   a status conferred on qualified investments named under the various State Trustee Acts in Australia. Commonwealth, semi-government and local government securities are generally treated as acceptable trustee investments under the relevant State trustee legislation. Semi-government and local government securities are often trustee investments in some States but not in others.

trust fund   money held on behalf of investors or depositors, to be used at the discretion of the trustee in their interests. Legal requirements and the trust deed dictate how trust funds may be invested. Trust funds can also refer to the solicitors' funds which serve as a secure repository for clients' money in periods when the money is not accessible to the client, such as during the probate period on a will. Trust funds of this kind are generally secure, as the Law Society requires that lawyers take insurance against mishaps and also manages a fidelity fund to provide protection against defalcation (knocking off the money). See **defalcation, solicitors' funds, trust deed, trustee**.

TSE   *abbrev.* **Tokyo Stock Exchange**.

T/T   *abbrev.* **telegraphic transfer**.

turn   the difference—profit—that a dealer makes between buying and selling a parcel of securities or currencies. Traders talk of 'making a turn on the deal'.

turnover   The usual definitions are:
- total sales for a given period (for example annual turnover of $2 million);
- the changing of goods (stock) as they are sold and replaced.

In financial markets, turnover means the number of times something (usually assets such as trading stock) is replaced by assets of the same class as a result of the company's trading throughout the period. Money market traders have been heard to boast of 'turning over the whole book' in an active day's trading, meaning that securities on hand were sold and replaced with new stock; share and futures brokers talk of 'turnover on the exchange' when referring to the amount of shares or futures contracts that changed hands.

TV stocks   the series of bonds which appear on the trading screens (hence TV). These are the currently actively traded stocks.

24-hour call money   money for which 24 hours' notice must be given of any intention to repay the funds, recall the money or renegotiate the interest rate by either borrower or lender; after an initial seven-day period.

TWI   *abbrev.* **trade-weighted index.**

TWINS   securities whose redemption value is linked to two commodities, usually one currency, for example the $US spot exchange rate for a selected currency, and one interest rate commodity such as the ten-year Treasury Bond.

U

unappropriated profits   see **undistributed profits**.

unbundled   The services of a bank, broker or financial institution are described as unbundled when no single service is priced so cheaply that it is subsidised by another. Each service is marketed and priced on its own merit, to be independently viable. See **cross-subsidisation**.

uncleared funds   money in the banking system which represents cheques that have not yet been processed through the clearing house. Customers cannot draw cash against an 'uncleared cheque'—that is until the cheque has been accepted by the bank on whom it was drawn and the funds paid out against it. See **clearing house**.

undercapitalisation   a situation where not enough money is supplied by the owners to support the activities of a business. The shareholders would need to fork out more money if the business is to expand. Undercapitalisation is therefore a constraint on expansion and in extreme cases can mean not having enough resources to stay afloat.

undervalued currency   a currency which is quoted or traded below what is perceived to be its true market value, given its country's balance of payments position, economy, interest rates and so on. An undervalued currency will be in demand as traders and speculators believe it will rise and therefore will buy it to make a profit; enough of such buying, and expectations become self-fulfilling, as demand will push the currency higher. Exporters' and importers' views on currencies would influence how they manage their cash flows. An exporter would bring foreign exchange receipts into the country if the domestic currency were considered undervalued and therefore likely to rise; an importer would delay payments in the hope that the undervalued domestic currency would rise, thereby reducing the cost of imports.

underwriter   A broker or merchant bank, or more likely a group of brokers, merchant banks, banks and other financial institutions, will underwrite an issue of securities for a borrower. This means they arrange to sell the securities for the client to the public or to other institutions (for a fee) and the underwriters take up any securities not sold which allows the client (borrower) the guarantee of raising the full amount of money sought.

undigested securities   Traders talk of a market having 'indigestion'

252

when there are more securities around than buyers willing to take them at the price offered. The surplus paper is undigested, i.e. not in the hands of willing buyers or endholders.

undistributed profits   the proportion of a company's profits that is not handed out to shareholders in the form of dividends; instead it is retained for reinvestment in the company. Also **accumulated profits, retained earnings, unappropriated profits**. See **plough back**.

unfranked dividends   dividends paid out of company profits which have not been subject to full Australian tax, or which were derived before 1 July 1986. Such dividends are taxable in the hands of shareholders at their marginal rate. See **franked dividends, imputation of dividend**.

unit costs   This concept is calculated by dividing total costs by the quantity of production, to illustrate how much it costs to produce, for example, one car. Unit costs would typically be used in microeconomic studies of, say, business pricing and performance analysis.

unit labour costs   Economists arrive at the concept of unit labour costs by dividing average earnings by productivity (output per worker). This gives the cost of the labour necessary to produce one item (unit) of production—which is one factor influencing price levels. The concept of unit labour costs is used in macroeconometric modelling of the wage-price sector (for example in the national income forecasting model). **Real unit labour costs** are calculated by dividing unit labour costs by the price level, to give an indication of the real cost of labour per unit of output.

unit-priced demand-adjustable tax-exempt securities   US floating-rate, municipal securities devised and sold by Merrill Lynch. *Abbrev.*: **UPDATES**.

unit trust   A unit trust is structured to allow small investors to pool their money, which enables them to earn a greater return than if each investor had acted individually. The three components of a unit trust are:
- the trustee (custodian)
- the management company
- the unitholders

The success of a unit trust depends on the expertise and experience of the management company, which is responsible for the trust's investment strategy. Unit trusts operate under a trust deed between the management company and a trustee company which holds the trust's assets and distributes income to unitholders.

The most popular trusts in recent years have been **cash management trusts**, **equity trusts** and **property trusts**, depending on which market is booming and which is languishing. Beneficiaries of trusts are termed unitholders. See **cash management trust, equity trust, mutual fund, property trust, trustee, trust deed**.

unlimited company   see **company**.

unlisted security   a security that is not listed or traded on the stock exchange floor.

unsecured loan   money on loan to an individual or company where the borrower offers no security to the lender so that the lender is entirely dependent on the borrower's capacity and willingness to repay. The lender has a legal claim on any of the borrower's assets, but has to go through a legal process to recoup.

unsecured notes   These are issued regularly by finance companies, usually for periods ranging from three months to three years. The notes offer a higher rate of return than a debenture of the same maturity but do not carry the security of a debenture. See **debenture**.

UPDATES   *abbrev.*   **unit-priced demand-adjustable tax-exempt securities**.

upfront   at the beginning. Upfront fees are charges due to the lender by the borrower at the outset on, say, a loan.

upside potential   the amount by which a share or security might raise in value. The opposite of **downside risk**.

usury   Originally usury meant lending for profit (interest) but over the centuries the word has come to be used to describe unusually high rates of interest. In the early and medieval church canon law (church law) forbade, on biblical grounds (for example, Ex. 22:25, Lev. 25:36, Deut. 23:19), the practice of charging interest on money; in the Middle Ages in Europe, usury—in the sense of interest charged on loans—was wrong in the eyes of the law and the church. The rising tide of commercial activity from the sixteenth century gradually eroded the weight of church influence in favour of commercial expediency. Many ways were devised to evade the anti-usury laws: bills of exchange escaped the accusation of usury through the claim that the discount or interest represented payment for work done. As commercial activity increased, the usury debate switched focus from the principle involved to arguments about the legal rate. By the late eighteenth century, charging interest had been justified on commercial grounds and major European trading nations repealed their anti-usury laws.

utility   Economists use the word 'utility' as a synonym for 'satisfaction'. It is now agreed that it is impossible to measure the amount of utility obtained by a person consuming a good or service or to compare it with the satisfaction obtained by somebody else consuming the same good or service. Nevertheless, an individual can tell us which of two bundles of goods and services he or she prefers (which gives him or her greater satisfaction) and this is usually sufficient for economic analysis. See **marginal utility**.

V

value-added tax   This was first suggested in Germany, in 1918, was introduced in Argentina in 1935 and part-introduced in France in 1948. The European Economic Community adopted VAT in 1962 and this tax is now levied in all countries of the EEC as a broad indirect tax on consumers. It was introduced in the UK in 1973, when it replaced purchase tax and selective employment tax. VAT has generally been introduced as a substitute for forms of indirect tax, such as turnover tax, sales tax or excise. It is applied successively to the value added to products at every stage of manufacture and handling and the aggregate of all successive levies is eventually passed to the consumer. *Abbrev.*: **VAT**.

value date   the date on which payment is made to settle a transaction which was organised previously. A spot transaction organised on a Wednesday (in Australia) would typically have a value date of Friday. See **spot**.

vanilla product   a US and UK capital market term for straightforward eurobond issues; it describes standard fixed-interest products that do not include more sophisticated techniques such as options or swaps. Also **straight products**.

variable deposit requirement   A regulation introduced in Australia in 1972, for the purposes of monetary control, by which a proportion of funds borrowed from overseas had to be lodged in Australian dollars with the Reserve Bank as an interest-free deposit. The variable deposit requirement was changed several times between October 1973 and June 1977 when it was suspended. *Abbrev.*: **VDR**.

variable rate mortgage   A US home loan structured with an ·interest rate that varies in line with money market rates or a benchmark rate chosen by the lending institution. Such mortgages were popular when rates were high and rising but lost their appeal as the general level of interest rates came down and borrowers turned back to the more predictable fixed-rate mortgages. *Abbrev.*: **VRM**. Also **adjustable rate mortgage** or **ARM**.

VDR   *abbrev.* **variable deposit requirement**.

velocity of circulation   the speed with which the same money changes hands; regarded as an important economic measure, though it is only

256

observable after the event. If everyone hangs on to money, velocity of transactions slows down, indicating a decline in business activity. In the Great Depression in the 1930s, velocity of circulation fell as commercial activity dwindled. If people are spending rapidly velocity of circulation rises as a reflection of the increased activity. Velocity is influenced by people's enthusiasm for savings and investment, the total amount of money around plus new money, and interest rates. The formal monetarist argument assumes that it is constant in the short run. Some measures of velocity may be influenced by shifts of funds between bank and non-bank sectors. See **depression, quantity theory of money.**

venture capital   similar to risk capital, though more often associated with providing funds for new technology; it is essentially money invested in a comparatively risky and often new enterprise (in the hope of making a good return which will justify the risk). See **risk capital.**

Vernon Report (Committee of Economic Inquiry)   This report was published in 1965. It examined the postwar development of Australia and the means by which growth could be further encouraged. The chairman of the committee was Sir James Vernon, general manager of CSR Ltd. The main recommendation of the report—that an independent group of economic policy advisers be established—was summarily dismissed by the Prime Minister, Sir Robert Gordon Menzies. The Treasury mandarins had won yet another victory in their battle to remain the dominant force in policy analysis. The report remains a useful compendium of information about its era. The National Economic Summit and the Economic Planning Advisory Council have their origins in this report.

vertical spread   see **option spread.**

virgin bond   see **back bond.**

visible trade   the stuff you can see and touch, tangible exports and imports such as cars, wine, shoes, as against the 'invisibles' such as shipping and services.

volatility   an overworked word of the 1980s, meaning wild, inconsistent, freakish, fickle, skittish, prone to unpredictable fluctuations. Interest and exchange rates in recent years have at times deserved all of those epithets. Australian interest rates were particularly volatile in 1982 and 1983—that is, they were prone to sharp, unpredictable rises and falls—but have stabilised following the switch to floating the $A instead of a managed exchange rate. See **float.**

voluntary liquidation   a situation where shareholders agree to put a company into liquidation, as opposed to a situation where the creditors put the company into liquidation.

vostro account   the counterpart to nostro account; vostro (Latin, 'yours') describes the record of an account held by a bank as correspondent on behalf of an overseas bank. See **correspondent bank, nostro account**.

VRM   *abbrev.* **variable rate mortgage**.

W

wage drift   a situation where average earnings tend to exceed award wage rates because of shift loading, penalty rates, overtime and other above-award payments. In Australia the term is used to describe the difference between arbitration awards and the actual ordinary-time payments (i.e. net of overtime on the job). Under full wage indexation in the mid-1970s, wage drift fell, but partial indexation in 1976–78 was accompanied by a rise in wage drift. Because of the effect of the wage drift on people's capacity to save and spend, controlling wages alone is not enough if a government is trying to control inflation. Wage drift is an important factor for the Australian Conciliation and Arbitration Commission—which sets minimum wages—as it frustrates much of the commission's efforts. In many industries the 'take home pay' is well above the award level set by the commission. The size of the wage drift tends to fluctuate with the health of the economy.

wage indexation   This can be full or partial, or it can be **plateau indexation** where, for example, the bottom 20 per cent of wage earners are indexed and higher wage earners receive a fixed monetary increase. Plateau indexation is essentially a system in which percentage increases in wages are higher for lower income earners than for others. Full wage indexation means wages are fully adjusted to keep pace with inflation. Wage indexation has existed for decades, often under different names such as cost-of-living adjustments. It was introduced in a formal sense in Australia in 1975 (its history goes back much further), was reduced to partial indexation in 1976 and put to rest in 1981. The Hawke government revived the notion of wage indexation in 1983. The possible effects of wage indexation generate much heated debate but cannot be accurately forecast.

wage–price spiral   the notion that if prices are rising and employees demand higher wages, production costs rise and flow on into even higher prices, all of which leads to rising inflation (of the cost-push variety). See **inflation**.

wage rate   the basic minimum rate of payment for any employee, excluding bonuses, overtime etc., generally expressed as an amount per hour.

Wall Street   New York's financial centre in Manhattan and often the name used when talking of the New York stock market in general. The

New York Stock Exchange was founded in 1792. Wall Street is probably best known for the crash of 1929. See **depression**.

Walras, Marie Esprit Leon   see **economists**.

warehousing   taking on board a swap as principal until the right counterparty is found. In the sharemarket, warehousing can be part of organising a takeover. The aggressor has limits beyond which it is not possible to go publicly, but a friendly company can store stock on the aggressor's behalf, allowing build-up of a strategic position. In the money market, warehousing can mean holding stock on behalf of another.

warrant   an option issued in the form of a security, usually written for a longer term. A warrant has the same function as an option, i.e. it provides the right to buy the specific amount of the underlying shares or securities, but is itself tradeable. There are various types of warrant:

- **debt warrant**   a warrant that is exercisable into a debt security, such as a bond or note;
- **equity warrant**   a warrant that is exercisable into an equity (share);
- **killer warrant**   a warrant which, when exercised, automatically calls for the redemption of the security for which it was originally issued. This type of warrant is typically used with debt warrants;
- **naked warrant**   a debt warrant issued alone without a host (underlying) bond or security;
- **wedding warrant**   a structure of debt warrant attached to a host bond that protects the issuer from the potential doubling up of debt should the warrant be exercised. The warrants can only be exercised during the early part of their life into virgin bonds by tendering them along with the original callable host bond. Also **harmless warrant**.

Also **subscription warrant**. See **host bond**.

warranty   Generally, a term in a contract in which one party undertakes to the other that some aspect, for example the quality of goods sold, is as stated by the person giving the warranty. In a more narrow sense, it is an assurance of agreement regarding goods under a contract of sale. Breach of warranty gives the purchaser the right to claim damages but does not invalidate the contract. For example, a faulty distributor in a new motor car would give rise to a claim for breach of warranty, but not for a claim for breach of an essential term of the contract, so the buyer would not be entitled to cancel the contract. See **guarantee**.

washing deals   a foreign exchange term, used to describe a transaction where a lender is 'full' with a client (i.e. has commitments with that client up to the maximum permitted by his or her company's board) but the deal proposed is too good to turn away so the lender persuades his or her company's bank to 'wash' the deal through so that the credit risk is in reality with the bank as the bank takes the loan on its books. Companies in foreign exchange dealings have limits on their dealing capacity with individual clients, in the same way that money market companies have lists of 'approved' borrowers, each with individual limits imposed by the lending company's board. See **full**.

wealth tax   a tax on wealth. It is founded on the belief that once personal wealth grows beyond a specified level, it should be taxed. It is hard to apply in practice: special interest groups can find solid reasons for exemptions and wealth can easily be hidden from tax inspectors. No one ever believes that he or she is THAT well-off. Australia at present is one of the few countries that does not apply some form of wealth tax. See **capital gains tax, death duties**.

We'll run the numbers through and get back to you   traders' bluff—buying time to put off the inevitable moment of decision. They really mean they need three hours to work out figures—or they are not enthusiastic about the proposed transaction. It would most often by used by traders dealing by phone, in areas such as fixed interest and swaps.

white knight   market jargon for the saviour in a takeover. The white knight saves the target company from an unfriendly suitor by fending off the aggressor.

whole-of-life policy   Under this type of policy the life assurance company pays out the insured amount plus any bonuses under the contract when the policyholder dies. The beneficiaries named in the insurance policy or in the deceased's will receive the benefit of the policy.

wholesale banking   borrowing and lending in the big numbers—you and I are the small fry (retail banking) and the big corporations, banks, merchant banks and money market operators are the wholesalers in the financial world. See **retail banking**.

wholesale price index   This measures price changes in the wholesale market. See **consumer price index**.

widget   generic term to describe any manufactured item.

widow-and-orphan shares   shares in a stable company that offer an attractive dividend and are regarded as secure long-term investments.

will   a document which sets out how an individual wants his or her wealth and property to be distributed after death.

windfall profit   an unexpected benefit from a commercial activity often resulting from a development beyond the control of the recipient—similar to winning the lottery or pools.

window dressing   The process by which financial institutions organise their deposits, loans and portfolios to best advantage or to meet requirements on balance date for balance sheet purposes.

window guidance   see **moral suasion**.

window open   an Australian foreign exchange term indicating it is attractive to borrow or lend offshore on a covered basis, i.e. including the cost of taking out protection against exchange rate movements. It means there is an opportunity for arbitrage. See **arbitrage**.

withholding tax   a tax on dividends and interest sent abroad to non-residents. **Dividend withholding tax** was introduced in 1959 and **interest withholding tax** in 1968, both taxing earnings paid to foreign lenders or investors. Withholding tax is deducted when the payment is sent overseas. Until May 1983, companies classified as 'Australian entities' and the Australian Industry Development Corporation were exempt from interest withholding tax. The May 1983 mini-budget of the Hawke government abolished these exemptions (as recommended by the Campbell Committee). Unless overseas lenders are prepared to absorb the withholding tax, it is in reality an increased cost for Australian borrowers using overseas sources of funds. Borrowing overseas using widely distributed publicly issued bearer securities is one method which legitimately avoids withholding tax.
Employment within Australia has been subject to a different form of withholding tax, introduced in May 1983 and brought into effect in September 1983 to be levied on contract workers and subcontractors. This **prescribed payments system** (PPS but also referred to as the **black tax**) was designed to prevent cash payments from avoiding both payroll and personal income tax. Those employing builders, cleaning industries and any form of contract work should deduct part of the money paid for labour and services and forward that sum to the Tax Office.

wood duck   an unsuspecting counterparty in a trade who is likely to provide higher-than-expected profits for the alert professional operator.

working breakfast   similar to the working lunch but without the chardonnay, port, etc. Americans have been accused of inventing it. Working breakfasts have spread throughout the executive world as a concept to be embraced by all upwardly mobile business people who want to be taken seriously by both their peers and their superiors. Your schedule is just not full enough if you do NOT include a couple of working breakfasts in a week, particularly when out of town on a business trip. See **fringe benefits tax, Lunch, working lunch**.

working capital   what a business needs to carry out its day-to-day activities; essentially the excess of current assets over current liabilities, or put more simply, enough cash to be comfortable.

working capital ratio   see **current ratio**.

working lunch   another executive favourite, good for the restaurant trade. See **fringe benefits tax, Lunch, working breakfast**.

World Bank   the popular name for the International Bank for Reconstruction and Development, which was established at Bretton Woods in 1944, and opened its doors in 1946. The original objective was to help fund postwar reconstruction in Europe and foster steady and balanced growth in international trade. The bank now also lends to poor countries. Its headquarters are in Washington DC.

writ   a document issued by a court, usually applied to the document which begins a court action. There are, however, many forms of writ; the word means no more than a document signed by or on behalf of a court. See **writ of execution**.

write down   to reduce the recorded book value of an asset or liability to take into account a decline in its value, due for example to depreciation or a fall in its market value.

write off   to eliminate the recorded book value of an asset or liability. This would happen if a company or individual were to find it impossible to recover a debt. The amount would have to be 'written off' (deducted, recorded) as an expense or loss in the accounts.

writer (of options)   the seller of the options, the party who grants the purchaser of the option the right to buy or sell the underlying commodity at the agreed price.

writ of execution   a court direction to a court officer to ensure a judgment is carried out.

X

XB   *abbrev.* **ex-bonus.**

XBR   *abbrev.* **ex bonus and rights.**

XD   *abbrev.* **ex-dividend.**

XF   *abbrev.* **ex-offer.**

XI   *abbrev.* **ex-interest.**

XR   *abbrev.* **ex-rights.**

Y

Yankee Aussie   bonds denominated in $A, issued in the US bond market to US investors.

Yankee bonds   bonds denominated in $US, issued in the US by a foreign borrower.

Yankee Kiwi   bonds denominated in $NZ, issued in the US bond market, to US investors.

YCAN   *abbrev.* **yield curve adjustable note**.

yearling bonds   bonds issued with twelve months to maturity. The Australian government has, so far, resisted issuing bonds with such a short maturity, though there is support for such a short stock.

yield   the annual return on an investment expressed as a percentage. Yield differs from discount in its application to security purchases; yield is the actual rate of return expressed as a percentage per annum of the net outlay or net proceeds of an investment, not of its face value. See **discount, yield curve, yield to redemption**.

yield curve   a graph showing the relationship between the yield to maturity and the term to maturity of a group of similar securities. Yield curves come in several types:
- a **normal/positive/upward-sloping** yield curve which reflects a preference for higher interest rates for longer-term investments;
- a **downward/negative/inverse** yield curve which suggests high short rates; these are expected to stay high while longer-term rates are forecast to fall or stay low;
- a **flat/horizontal** yield curve (drawn as a flat line) which suggests little change is foreseen in rates and investors are indifferent about whether they put their money away for a short or long period;
- a **hump-backed** yield curve which indicates immediate liquid conditions, followed by temporary tightness, then a gradual decline in longer-term rates.

yield curve adjustable note   a form of floating-rate note that is fitted to the yield curve so that its return increases when interest rates move in a predetermined direction. In the 'bull' version the return would increase if rates fall and in the 'bear' version they would increase if rates rose. *Abbrev.*: **YCAN**. See **floating-rate note, yield curve**.

yield gap   a yield curve graph of the margin between bonds and equities, comparing the performance of the two over a given period.

yield to redemption   the actual rate of return on the security from its date of purchase till it matures, taking into account the interest payments and the investor's capital gain or loss.

yuppie   young urban professional; a trendy US expression, exported to Australia, to describe bright young persons, speeding up the career ladder, usually single, always ambitious.

Z

zaiteku Japanese term for what drives financial markets: the financial engineering and innovation behind new techniques such as futures, options and swaps which are used in various combinations to create the cheapest possible funding and to achieve the highest possible return on investments.

ZEBRAS *abbrev.* **zero coupon euro-sterling bearer or registered accruing securities.**

zero coupon bonds discounted bonds issued without a coupon. These bonds eliminate the income portion which normally derives from the coupon that is attached to a bond. The difference between the purchase price and the face value (which the holder receives on maturity of the bond) is the capital gain, and the return earned on the investment. The bonds offered the chance to defer tax until December 1984, when the tax treatment of these securities was changed, so that tax could not be deferred but had to be paid annually on interest accrued. Zero coupon bonds were issued in Australia under various names:

- **DIGGERS** (discounted investment government-guaranteed earnings return).
- **DINGOS** (discounted investment in negotiable government obligations).
- **DRAGONS** (discounted receipts of Australian government obligatory negotiable securities).

See **deep discount bonds, stripped bonds.**

zero coupon euro-sterling bearer or registered accruing securities. A member of the UK menagerie of securities, similar to **STAGS.** *Abbrev.*: **ZEBRAS.**

zero sum game Futures trading is an example of a zero sum game because for every purchase there is a sale, for every profit a loss. Zero sum games can be played in most fields. Basically they mean that any advantage gained by one side is matched by disadvantage to the other.